Stepping Out
of the Shadows

Stepping Out
of the Shadows

ALABAMA WOMEN,
1819–1990

Edited by
Mary Martha Thomas

THE UNIVERSITY OF ALABAMA PRESS
TUSCALOOSA AND LONDON

Copyright © 1995
The University of Alabama Press
Tuscaloosa, Alabama 35487-0380
All rights reserved
Manufactured in the United States of America

∞

The paper on which this book is printed meets the minimum requirements of American National Standard for Information Science–Permanence of Paper for Printed Library Materials, ANSI Z39.48-1984.

Library of Congress Cataloging-in-Publication Data

Stepping out of the shadows : Alabama women, 1819–1990 / edited by Mary Martha Thomas.
    p. cm.
    Collection of essays derived from a conference held in Birmingham, Mar. 1990, by the Alabama Women's History Forum.
    Includes bibliographical references (p.   ) and index.
    ISBN 0-8173-0756-7 (alk. paper)
    1. Women—Alabama—History. 2. Alabama—Social life and customs. I. Thomas, Mary Martha, 1927– .
HQ1438.A2S75 1995
305.4′09761—dc20   94-12230

British Library Cataloguing-in-Publication Data available

Contents

Stepping Out
of the Shadows

Introduction

MARY MARTHA THOMAS

Perhaps more than many other southerners, Alabamians have long been proud of and taken interest in the history of their state. Historians and lay scholars alike have investigated local and state events from the antebellum years in the early nineteenth century to the post–World War II period and the present day, which has resulted in the establishment of a substantial body of literature. But these writers have largely concerned themselves with traditional political and military history of white men. Little attention has been given to the women of the state. Since both black and white women have shared the constraints and the commitments of the state as a whole, the history of Alabama cannot be understood independent of its women's specific contributions.

To encourage Alabamians to appreciate the roles and contributions of women to the state's history, the Alabama Women's History Forum held a conference in Birmingham on March 30–31, 1990, focusing on the history of the women of the state. The essays in this volume are a result of that conference. Since the articles were limited to the papers presented, this volume does not pretend to offer a comprehensive narrative history of Alabama women. They do, however, demonstrate that the outlines of a general history are taking shape. More importantly, they challenge the view that Alabama history was exclusively a white male affair.

Women's history developed as a discipline from the convergence of an intellectual development (the rise of the new social history) and a social movement (the rebirth of feminism). Beginning in the 1950s and 1960s, some historians started to view history in a different light. Instead of studying only politics, wars, and diplomacy, scholars began to consider all of culture, not just some of its manifestations. These historians believed that diplomatic and political events were an expression of social institutions and cultural values; hence they viewed these social and cultural values as primary to politics and diplomacy. The new social history was most concerned with questions that related to private places—homes, hospitals, schools, clubs, churches, voluntary associations, ladies auxiliaries.

While all of these changes were taking place, a resurgent feminism stirred many historians to wonder about the lives and experiences of their mothers and grandmothers and all the women who had lived and died since the first settlement in North America. Others began to wonder about the women who were here when the Europeans arrived and about the African women who were brought here against their wills. Among the questions they were raising was the old one: why are women historically invisible? Some women and men took things into their own hands and began to train themselves as historians of women. The last twenty years has seen a burgeoning new field in research and scholarship.

Writing women's history is a difficult task because women have been less likely than men to create records. Many have lived and died and not left a trace. Evidence of the lives of many others survives only in parish records of birth, marriage, or death or in public documents such as tax rolls, probate and court records, and the manuscript census. In the nineteenth century, women, if they were literate, often wrote letters to keep the family communication going, or they kept diaries, which provide valuable sources of information. Slave women and antebellum free black women have been even less likely than white women to create records of their lives, but others have sometimes created one for them in a wide variety of slave narratives. Like white women, African-American women may often be traced in manuscript census records and legal documents.

When historians began to ask what the women were doing, the social reality of the past became much more complex. History is perceived differently by people in different parts of the social structure. The history of a white planter was different from that of his wife and certainly different from that of slave women on his plantation. Not only do women experience life differently from the way men do, but they also shape it differently. Women care about some things that men do not value highly. The part women play in families and child rearing perpetuates certain values. When women attain positions that enable them to affect political and social decisions, they often choose paths quite different from those approved by men.

The history of northern women is different from that of southern women, especially during the nineteenth century. The great majority of the scholarship in women's history deals with women of the urban North and East; the experience of rural southern women has yet to be fully told. Southern women's history has been slow to emerge as a recognized interest within southern history and American women's history. The aim of much of southern women's history has been to challenge the New England paradigm by stressing regional differences.

A major challenge of southern women's history has been to separate the myth of the idle lady from the reality of the experience of women. While white slave-owning women are usually thought of as frivolous "southern belles" or idle "southern ladies," African-American women are viewed as the strong loyal "mammies" who take care of southern families and mold the characters of white children as though they were their own. Yet the antebellum woman who is beginning to emerge from much research does not fit these stereotypes.

Anne Firor Scott in her pathbreaking book *The Southern Lady from Pedestal to Politics 1830–1930,*[1] published in 1970, was the first to attack this image. She shows that there was a wide gap between the image of the soft, submissive, perfect woman in the antebellum South and the actual woman whose life was shaped by harsh reality. Plantation wives did not have to work in the fields, as did the wives of small farmers, but they had to know how to spin, weave, sew, garden, care for the sick, and supervise all aspects of food preparation. Those who owned slaves had the additional responsibility of managing them in order that the plantation might function. Scott also believes that women were dissatisfied with their lot, were critical of the institution of slavery, and questioned their own subordination. Some women went so far as to suggest a parallel between their own situation and that of the slave.

Other authors have dealt with the experience of black women, notably Deborah Gray White in *Ar'n't I a Woman? Female Slaves in the Plantation South* and Jacqueline Jones in *Labor of Love, Labor of Sorrow: Black Women, Work and the Family, from Slavery to the Present.*[2] Living with the dual burdens of racism and sexism, slave women assumed roles within the family and community that contrasted sharply with traditional female roles in the larger American society. African-American women had to deal with being owned and having little control over their lives. They were constantly vulnerable to rape and domestic violence. White and black women shared a world of physical and emotional intimacy but one which contained mutual antagonism.

In 1988, Elizabeth Fox-Genovese challenged many of the current interpretations about both black and white women of the antebellum South in *Within the Plantation Household: Black and White Women of the Old South*.[3] She maintains that the lives of slave women and slave-owning women were closely connected, often fraught with violence, yet never linked in sisterhood. Class and race as well as gender shaped women's experiences and determined their identities. Because the lives of antebellum women were so different from those of northern women, Fox-Genovese believes it is impossible to understand southern women by applying models derived from northeastern sources. While white women may have expressed concerns about the institution of slavery, they were not abolitionists or feminists. Instead, Fox-Genovese contends, they were more apt to defend slavery and the patriarchal structure of the family than to dissent from them.

Fox-Genovese carries this argument further in her article in this volume, "Stewards of Their Culture: Southern Woman Novelists as Social Critics," with her analysis of southern women writers of domestic sentimental novels of the 1850s. She believes that southern authors of these novels criticized society from a conservative position and were in no way committed to women's equality. It is false, she maintains, to assume that women who were social critics inevitably favored an expanded democratization of society and politics. Since the rise of the women's rights movement was linked with the reform movements of the 1830s and 1840s, especially the abolition movement, scholars have looked for emerging abolitionists and feminists in the South of those years. However, Fox-Genovese maintains dissenting voices have been found only occasionally. But even those who might be critical usually only admitted the system required reform, not a complete overhaul.

These novelists were especially critical of Harriet Beecher Stowe, who in their eyes fostered revolutionary and socially disruptive beliefs that would undermine everything southerners held dear. These tensions erupted during the 1850s in outright literary war between northern and southern writers of domestic fiction. Using as examples the novels of two Alabama women, Caroline Lee Hentz and Augusta Jane Evans, as well as others, Fox-Genovese shows that these social critics see as their main purpose the defense of their people, institutions, and region.

The following essays, which deal with the history of a variety of black and white Alabama women, represent a first step in identifying the experience of women of the state. As these articles show, much work has been done, and an outline of women's role in Alabama is beginning to emerge.

Two of the essays, written by Ann Williams Boucher and Sarah Woolfolk Wiggins, are concerned with upper-class white women. Boucher in "The Plantation Mistress: A Perspective on Antebellum Alabama" examines the proximity of bondage and freedom in which wealthy Alabama women lived their lives. The author does not believe that the women of the state fit the stereotype of subversive, powerless southern women. She analyzes the juxtaposition of freedom and bondage in the lives of wealthy women with regard to their marriages, childbearing, motherhood, relations with kin, and property holding.

Using correspondence and public records, Boucher shows that in the choice of marriage partners, couples were influenced not only by family status but also by personal preferences. By comparing the childbearing of Alabama women with others, the author believes that women did have a choice about the number of children they bore. Alabama women did not turn over the primary care of their children to slaves but were directly involved in the care and education of their children. Despite the difficulties of travel, women were able to develop deep friendships with other women. Even in public matters, women's lives contained both bondage and freedom, as evidenced in the married women's property act. Boucher's analysis provides a meaningful perspective on antebellum society.

At first glance, Amelia Gayle Gorgas, the subject of Sarah Woolfolk Wiggins's biographical essay, would appear to be the quintessential southern lady of romantic fiction, but on closer examination, her life seems less than idyllic. Amelia Gayle (1826–1913) came from a prominent Mobile family, her father having been governor of the state. She married Josiah Gorgas in 1853, and eventually they had six children, one of whom was William Crawford Gorgas, the famous physician who eliminated yellow fever from Cuba and Panama. Josiah Gorgas served in the U.S. Army and later the Confederate army. After the Civil War, he was headmaster of the Junior Department at the University of the South for ten years, before being appointed president of the University of Alabama.

Sarah Woolfolk Wiggins's biography of Amelia includes her father, husband, and famous son, but Wiggins is primarily telling Amelia's story. Using a long series of letters between Amelia and Josiah, she paints the picture of a devoted wife and mother who was the focal point of her large family. But she was not a helpless female; she had to cope with relocating, living apart from her husband, managing finances, and eventually supporting her family after her husband's death in 1883. She took over his job as librarian of the University of Alabama, a position he had been given after he suffered a stroke. She held that position from 1883 until she retired in 1907, and today a campus library is named in her honor.

Both black and white women are the subject of two additional essays. Harriet E. Amos Doss investigated the history of African-American and white missionaries to former slaves during the Reconstruction period. White southerners had few resources and little inclination to engage in mission to blacks. As a result, white women working for the Freedmen's Bureau, the American Missionary Association, and the Women's Baptist Home Mission Society came to Alabama to educate the former slaves and establish Sunday schools. These missionaries prepared a host of black Alabamians to preach and teach church schools and public schools. They sought to uplift the black race by reaching out initially to its women and children. Their work was primarily that of nurturers and teachers, but they had broader influence.

Quoting extensively from the actual words of the missionaries, Doss shows the impact of the experience on both black and white women. White women fulfilled a desire to reach out and help others, but they found themselves ostracized by the local white community because of their work on behalf of blacks. However, all these women broadened the roles of women in church life by serving as agents of religion and social change.

Mary Martha Thomas wrote about black and white women during the era of progressivism, 1890–1920. As a result of the industrialization and urbanization of the New South, Birmingham developed a host of social and economic problems with which the city and the state were unprepared to deal. Both black and white women rose to the challenge by creating the Woman's Christian Temperance Union, the Alabama Federation of Women's Clubs, and the Alabama Federation of Colored Women, organizations that attacked a wide variety of issues of the day, such as the problem of poverty in an urban community, juvenile delinquency, prohibition, prison reform, the abolition of child labor, improved education, and eventually the right of women to vote.

As women became active in these reforms, they tended to break down the barriers between the public world of men and the private world of women. They changed the definition of the home by broadening it, allowing women to maintain that they were acting in the name of the home and family. Women's sphere visibly expanded as a result of the single-sex associations, which they used to penetrate public affairs. As a consequence of women's involvement in the temperance drive, the women's club movement, and the campaign for suffrage, women could no longer be characterized as passive and dependent. They were no longer bound by the ideology of the southern lady; women were ready, able, and willing to participate in public affairs.

African-American women were as equally active in reform activities and the suffrage movement as white women were. Adele Logan Alexander, in her essay "Adella Hunt Logan and the Tuskegee Woman's Club: Building a Foundation for Suffrage," contends that blacks worked in the suffrage drive from its inception in the 1840s through the passage of the Nineteenth Amendment. She shows how these women were barely tolerated by white suffrage leaders. Indeed, African Americans were often scorned or ignored, despite their awareness of the importance of the vote.

Alexander examines in detail the activities of the women of Tuskegee, especially Adella Hunt Logan, who was the author's grandmother. As the most vigorous proponent of women's suffrage, Logan presented programs to the woman's club, lectured to various other women's clubs in the Southeast, and wrote articles that were printed in *The Crisis* and the *Colored American*. When women did obtain the vote, black women of Tuskegee showed more interest in voting than did the white women.

By the early twentieth century, Alabama women had indeed become active in public affairs, as three other essays document. Martha H. Swain writes about the life of Loula Dunn, a pioneer in public welfare administration; Norma Taylor Mitchell recounts the life of Louise Branscomb, one of the first women doctors in Birmingham; and Joanne Varner Hawks chronicles the story of the women who were members of the Alabama state legislature.

Loula Dunn (1896–1977) was a representative of the second generation of women who went into social work, following such national leaders as Jane Addams, who had established Hull House in Chicago in 1889. Dunn joined the Alabama Child Welfare Department in 1923 as a caseworker. The department had been created in 1919 at the insistence of the Alabama Federation of Women's Clubs. The drive to gain support for the children of the state had been one of the progressive reforms that club women had sponsored.

Martha H. Swain skillfully traces the public life of Dunn from her childhood in Grove Hill to her role as a leading social welfare worker of the state and later the nation. Dunn served as director of the Department of Public Welfare from 1937–49, guiding the welfare of the state through the Second World War. Dealing with the wartime problems of migration and defense-impacted areas, Dunn also began to play a national and even an international role in public welfare. Her reputation increased until she was appointed executive director of the American Public Welfare Association, a position she held until she retired in 1964.

Unlike social work, medicine was definitely a male field, even the practice of obstetrics and gynecology. Louise Branscomb (1901–   ) was one of the first women doctors to establish a practice in Birmingham. Despite her medical degree from the prestigious Johns Hopkins University, Branscomb found it difficult to find acceptance in the medical community when she arrived in the city during the depression in 1931. Opportunities for female doctors had actually declined from the previous decade. Coming from a distinguished Alabama Methodist family did open a few doors, but most of the time, Branscomb struggled against an undertow of sexism and social and political conservatism that was stronger than she had expected.

Using diaries Branscomb kept from 1912 to 1920, as well as oral interviews, Norma Taylor Mitchell describes Branscomb's decision to study medicine, her struggle to find paying patients, the opposition she encountered dispensing information on birth control, and her eventual success with women patients who actually chose her because she *was* a woman. After her World War II service in North Africa, she gave up the obstetrical part of her practice in order to devote her time to her personal philanthropies, which she continues even today.

While medicine was a difficult field for a woman to enter, politics was even more of a challenge, as Joanne Varner Hawks makes clear in her essay on women in the Alabama legislature from 1922 to 1990. When women gained the right to vote in 1920 with the passage of the Nineteenth Amendment, they also assumed they could hold political office. Despite the fact that Alabama was one of the ten states that refused to ratify the amendment, voters in the state elected Hattie Hooker Wilkins to the legislature in 1922. Wilkins, who had been an active member of the Alabama Equal Suffrage Association, served only one term; it was nearly a decade before another woman was elected. Between 1922 and 1972, only five women served in the legislature; by 1990, the number had reached only twenty.

Hawks provides the reader with a comprehensive analysis of these twenty women, their race, marital status, occupation, dates of election, terms served, and stands taken on issues. Despite the small numbers, women have shown they have a right to be in the legislature. No longer does the press refer to them as "girls" or "comely young blonds." Nor do their colleagues elect them "Sweetheart of the House," as one representative was dubbed in the 1960s. Hawks concludes that the more recent women have both the knowledge and the confidence for using the political process. They have formed alliances with other women, local delegations, the black caucus, and other ad hoc groups. Small in number, Alabama's women legislators have nevertheless been a force to be reckoned with by focusing attention on issues an all-male legislature might have overlooked and by bringing to bear women's perspectives on measures under consideration.

In the last article of the collection, Sheryl Spradling Summe recounts the life of Juliette Hampton Morgan, a sensitive upper-class southern white woman who publicly supported black civil rights in Montgomery in the years following the Second World War. She did not march or take part in boycotts, but she wrote letters to the editor of the *Montgomery Advertiser* expressing her views. Her privileged position in Montgomery society gave her an opportunity to dissent, but it did not protect her from the hatred of other whites who disagreed with her position.

Morgan was reared to be a southern belle but never quite fit the role. After graduation from the University of Alabama, she taught high school for three years before becoming a reference librarian at the Montgomery Public Library, a position she held with only one brief interruption until 1957. As early as 1946, Morgan began speaking and writing of her support for racial justice, but it was during the bus boycott of 1955–56 that she became most vocal. She wrote letters to the newspapers expressing her views and attended meetings of the Council on Human Relations, where she found support from other liberals such as Clifford and Virginia Durr. Her actions offended the library board, which considered dismissing her from her job. This sensitive and frail women could not survive the rejection and condemnation of the white community, and her life ended tragically in 1957.

These essays have made it clear that Alabama women have a rich and varied history that is only beginning to be understood. Women have played an important role in the development of the state that has yet to be appreciated. Many questions remain to be answered. We need to know more about black and poor white women in the years before the Civil War. How did African-American and white women relate to each other during Reconstruction? What effect did the two world wars have on the roles of women? The activities of both black and white women during the civil rights movement of the 1950s and 1960s have yet to be told. Scholars need to ask about the experience of women in higher education. Another fertile field is the history of wage-earning women, both black and white. The list can go on and on; the sources in the libraries and archives of the state are numerous and only waiting to be explored by some future historian who will write a comprehensive history of the women of Alabama, showing the diversity of the female experience in the state.

1

Stewards of Their Culture
Southern Women Novelists as Social Critics

ELIZABETH FOX-GENOVESE

The temptation to view southern women as committed, if frequently secret, social critics has been strong but may rest on a misunderstanding. For the view of women—any women—as social critics too frequently rests on the assumption that women will, first and foremost, criticize their own social subordination. There is, in other words, a strong tendency to associate women as social critics with the emergence of feminism. This tendency especially derives from the pioneering work in women's history that linked the rise of feminism to women's associations for the moral reform of society, particularly to the rise of antislavery, which, it is argued, provided women with a powerful analogy for their own subordination.[1] It rests on the further and palpably false assumption that women, as social critics, inevitably favor an expanded democratization of society and politics.

One premise of this argument, at least, is compelling. Feminism as a social movement has, as its most vociferous critics have always insisted, tended to promote the leveling of hierarchies, beginning with that most resilient of all, the hierarchy of gender relations within the family. But the argument also rests upon a serious fallacy, namely the assumption that all women equate social criticism with feminism. It ignores, in other words, the evidence that many women, like many men, criticize society from a conservative position; it assumes that women's social criticism necessarily presupposes a commitment to women's equality—either with men or among themselves.

Today we are beginning to understand that women may criticize aspects of their society and may even support elements of feminism without embracing the sisterhood of all women across class and racial lines. But even those who recognize this much may balk at the recognition that some women actively oppose even the basic equality between women and men implied by mainstream bourgeois feminism, if they perceive it as threatening other social values that they cherish. We are loathe to see women actively championing what we now view as repressive regimes and, perhaps, are even more loathe to see them as complicit in their own subordination.[2]

The work of feminist scholars on women's culture, especially the tradition of sentimental or literary domesticity, has taught us to recognize the ways in which women manipulated the discourses available to them to criticize a variety of social relations and practices. Mary Kelly and Jane Tompkins have especially insisted upon the conflicts about authority and role that wracked women writers, and upon the ways in which they manipulated conventions of proper male and female roles to subvert prevailing discourses and relations of power.[3] Today domestic sentimental novels are no longer dismissed as a "sub-literary" genre unworthy of serious critical attention and are widely, if not universally, recognized as "powerful and important in their own right."[4] According to Tompkins, sentimental fiction may rank as "the most influential expression of the beliefs that animated" the widespread religious revival movement of the antebellum period. For, like the evangelical reformers themselves, "the sentimental novelists wrote to educate their readers in Christian perfection and to move the nation as a whole closer to the City of God."[5] The leading exponents of the sentimental tradition set themselves nothing less than a millennial mission to relocate the very center of power from the government, the courts of law, the factories, and the marketplace, to the kitchen.[6] Thus, even when overtly embracing their culturally prescribed roles as angels of the hearth, they sought to draw from their subordination a transformative social vision.

Antebellum southern women writers, whom many have viewed as participating in the sentimental domestic tradition, would have agreed with Tompkins's assessment of what their northern counterparts were about. But they did not approve. Roundly castigating northern literary domestics, above all Harriet Beecher Stowe, for their poorly disguised, revolutionary and socially disruptive intentions, they berated them for precisely those subversive tendencies for which modern critics praise them. Under the protective mantle of self-proclaimed womanly virtue, northern women were foisting a radical, leveling social vision upon an unsuspecting public. Claiming to realize the deepest evangelical implications of woman's domestic mission, they were, in fact, undermining it and everything else that respectable folks held dear.

Throughout the antebellum period, southern women novelists diverged from their northern counterparts, primarily by developing their own interpretation of domesticity, which always included an acceptance of slavery as an appropriate foundation for a worthy society. During what has been called the "feminine fifties," the tensions between northern and southern domesticity erupted in an outright literary war. In this war, southern women novelists united in their defense of their region, specifically its values and social system. But as the war unfolded, they also began to develop variations upon their common theme. And increasingly, in the common effort, Caroline Lee Hentz and Augusta Jane Evans, both of whom were living in Alabama, took the lead, thereby supplanting the traditionally genteel voice of Virginia women with the more modern and, if anything, more unambiguously proslavery voice of the Cotton Kingdom of the Old Southwest.

The political turmoil of the decade that opened with the Compromise of 1850 and closed with the election of Lincoln found its sharpest literary expression in the realm of domestic fiction. The appearance of *Uncle Tom's Cabin* in 1852, which crystallized southern women writers' opposition to the subversive tendencies of northeastern literary domesticity, provoked them to a succession of direct and indirect responses and, above all, prompted them to undertake a searching examination of their own social vision. Caroline Lee Hentz and Mary Eastman attacked directly, seconding in their fiction the anger and the social values that Louisa McCord had displayed in her polemical review. Caroline Gilman, Maria McIntosh, Mary Virginia Terhune, and Augusta Jane Evans avoided a frontal attack on Stowe but took her challenge no less seriously.[7] And Hentz and Evans, both of whom lived in Alabama, especially defended the experience and attitudes of the Deep South.

Uncle Tom's Cabin rent the veil of genteel domesticity that had shrouded the growing divergence of northern and southern domestic fiction. Its very success precluded polite dissembling by associating the dominant female literary voice with the cause of antislavery.[8] Doubt was no longer possible. At issue was not merely a struggle over competitive social systems, but a struggle over the very definition of womanhood. Domestic fiction, apparently the privileged locus of consensus and harmony, became a distinctly female battleground, although unlike Louisa McCord, the southern literary domestics did not plunge into unfeminine polemics. Ever mindful of their manners, ever respectful of the characteristic domestic idiom, they persisted in wrapping their message in the conventional package of woman's duty, religious uplift, and domestic values. But decorum and literary convention notwithstanding, they increasingly insisted that the North, led by its women, was proceeding rapidly to perdition—down the road of revolution.

If *Uncle Tom's Cabin* brought the issues into focus, it did not inaugurate them. By 1852, as Elizabeth Moss argues, southern literary domesticity, which she sees as extending from Caroline Lee Hentz's *Lovell's Folly* of 1833 to Mary Virginia Terhune's *Sunnybank* of 1866, had a respectable pedigree.[9] Caroline Gilman's pair of novels, *Recollections of a New England Housekeeper* (1834) and *Recollections of a Southern Matron* (1838), laid the true foundations of the genre, which owed as much to the emerging genre of plantation fiction as to northern literary domesticity.[10] From the start, the southern literary domestics, like their northern counterparts, believed themselves the embodiments of a mission. And, again like their northern counterparts, they believed that that mission above all concerned women's special role in the defense of fundamental religious and familial values.[11] But the similarities ended where they began, at the general levels of passion and rhetoric. For the southern women knew from the start that the values that they were defending depended upon the persistence of slavery as a social system. And well before the tide of northern antislavery began to crest, they perceived that the North was embarked on a course that threatened everything they cherished.

During the 1830s and the 1840s, southern literary domestics, like southern writers in general, primarily came from the elite of the more settled states, notably Virginia and South Carolina. They tended to represent southern values as the aristocratic values of the entire country, claiming that the South embodied the true legacy of the American Revolution. Thus they associated what they viewed as the more radical of northern values with the disruptions of accelerating capitalist development. Borrowing from late eighteenth- and early nineteenth-century classical republican rhetoric, notably its suspicions of commerce and celebration of rural virtue, Gilman sharply criticized the fashionable corruption of urban life, to which she attributed the dissolution of woman's virtuous character and sturdy independence. Superficially, that critique had much in common with many northern women writers' distrust of the corrosive and debilitating effects of fashion, but Gilman endowed the general trope with specific social referents. "What a blessed thing to childhood," she writes in *Recollections of a Southern Matron,* "is the fresh air and light of heaven! No manufactories, with their over-tasked inmates, to whom all but Sabbath sunshine is a stranger, arose on our plantation." Slaves enjoyed an infinitely superior fate to that of northern workers. "Long before the manufacturer's task in other regions is closed, our labourers were lolling on sunny banks, or trimming their gardens, or fondling their little ones, or busy in their houses, scarcely more liable to intrusion than the royal retirement of a Guelph or a Capet."[12]

There is no mistaking Gilman's intent. Slaves, who lead a healthier life than urban workers, enjoy the benefits of leisure, gardens, children, and private homes—explicitly identified as their castles. Membership in a plantation household, moreover, ensures their full exposure to the highest benefits of civilization. The influence of the plantation mistress's manners "was evident on the plantation, producing an air of courtesy even among the slaves," who held her in the deepest reverence and who were themselves capable of the most unswerving loyalty.[13] A planter's daughter, Gilman notes in passing, "fears none but white men."[14] She assuredly credits the beneficent influence of country life upon the character and bearing of women, whom cities can transform from healthy lasses into polished belles, who spend their time "calculating all night and dressing all day."[15] The country she celebrates is not rural life in general; it is the southern household within the confines of which slavery exercises a mutually beneficial influence on owners and owned. Enslavement affords slaves the benefits of religion, decent living conditions, and frequently an appreciation for refined taste unknown to northern workers. Most southern plantations, Gilman insists, "were regulated with almost military precision. No punishment was ever inflicted but by an authorized person, and if he overstepped the boundaries of mercy in his justice, he was expelled from his authority. From my infancy, I had never seen a gentleman forget the deportment of a gentleman to our slaves."[16]

Even as the responsibilities of slaveholding encourage the development of the highest gentlemanly conduct, so do they encourage the development of responsible womanhood. The plantation mistress does not preside over a limited household, but over a number of dependents who "would constitute a village." Obliged to listen to grievances, to nurse the sick, and to distribute "the half-yearly clothing," a planter's lady lives with the "arduous" responsibility of keeping "so many menials in order . . . and the *keys* of her establishment are a care of which a Northern housekeeper knows nothing, and include a very extensive class of duties."[17] To meet these responsibilities, "many fair, and even aristocratic girls, if we may use this phrase in our republican country," must develop the ability to measure supplies "with the accuracy and conscientiousness of a shopman," and matrons "who would ring a bell for their pocket-handkerchief to be brought to them, will act the part of a surgeon or physician with a promptitude and skill which would excite astonishment in a stranger."[18]

Thus Gilman, at the dawn of the southern domestic tradition, establishes slavery as the necessary foundation for the general discourse of virtuous womanhood upon which both northern and southern writers drew. Systematically appropriating the values of religion, duty, charity, and social responsibility for the particular condition of the slaveholding woman, she conjoins to them the more masculine values of a shopman's accuracy and a physician's skill. In training to assume the position of southern matron, her protagonist, tellingly named Cornelia, shares equally with her brothers the instruction of a tutor. Initially, her father worries that "the full cultivation of [her] mind in the branches studied by [her] brothers" would "lead her to consider herself more learned than her father." And why, the deeply religious tutor counters, "should she not . . . if humility be so wrought in her as to make her feel her own inferiority to the true standard of mind?" The father has no grounds to fear. "Intellectual women are the most modest inquirers after truth, and accomplished women often the most scrupulous observers of social duty."[19]

Slavery and sincere religion, which constitute the twin poles of an orderly society, provide a structure within which women should be free to cultivate their intelligence.[20] Gilman, like many of her successors, notably Augusta Evans Wilson, refused to deny women the full cultivation of their minds, provided that they cultivate them in the service of higher values. To be sure, she deplored women's self-aggrandizement, but, for her, fashion, not intellect or learning, constituted its premier sign. Fashion, which she associated with urban mobility and corruption, resembled free labor in corroding society and religion. Female intellect and learning, in contrast, could serve them and, pursued in the proper spirit, offered no challenge to established hierarchies, notably gender hierarchy. In Gilman's view, a primary commitment to slavery and religion permitted women the freedom of a responsible self-cultivation by ensuring that their accomplishments would enhance their contributions to their households and society rather than lead them into wanton individualism.

Gilman's contemporaries Caroline Lee Hentz and Maria McIntosh embroidered the same themes in their fiction of the 1830s and 1840s. Never complacent in their defense of southern society and values, they, like she, remained alert to the internal dangers that might threaten it. In *Recollections of a Southern Matron,* Gilman herself introduces what would emerge as one of southern literary domestics' favorite targets, the dissolute elite southern man. Lewis Barnwell, heir to the plantation adjacent to that of Cornelia Wilton's father, possesses all of the advantages of class and breeding but is marred by a deep-seated strand of self-indulgence. The reader first learns of this charmer's weakness when Cornelia discovers a young male slave whom he has inappropriately beaten. Slaves, Gilman insists, require "a strict superintending hand . . . to maintain that discipline, without which not even the social hearth can be preserved from strife." But "Lewis's was not the hand to chastise" the slave. And Cornelia, observing the young slave, "could not check the mental inquiry if one who could yield to his passions with an inferior, would not be an imperious companion with an equal."[21]

Events confirm Cornelia's fears. Lewis's unchecked passions lead him from the abuse of slaves into the tentacles of fashionable life—drinking and gambling—from which he lacks the character to extricate himself. The tragic death of the young woman who loves him unmistakably signals the infectious danger of his proclivities. Gilman, like other southern literary domestics, warns her readers that men's passions threaten the very fabric of the households and society that men should protect and order. The attack on men's capacity for irresponsibility echoes an older strand in women's fiction but acquires new meaning in the southern context.[22] For southern women writers, like their British predecessors and northern counterparts, a man's dissolution frequently testifies to his parents', normally his mother's, failures or absences and thus testifies to the importance of maternal guidance to the development of male character. And in this view, the women were overwhelmingly seconded by the articulate men of the South, especially the ministers and educators.

Southern literary domestics also normally attribute special importance to distinct attributes of manhood, notably the ability to command others responsibly, which is the necessary sign of the ability to command oneself. Frequently loathe to criticize an older generation of plantation masters, whom they are wont to associate directly with the legacy of the Revolution, they may fall back on the notion of an inherited strand of weakness to explain the failure of men to rise to the exigencies of household governance. For, however essential a mother's influence, male character requires appropriate male guidance.[23]

The dissolute young man, who recurs throughout southern domestic fiction, acquires special resonance as the distorted reflection of male strength. His vices invariably represent the pernicious excesses of necessary male virtues. In his characteristic incarnation, he succumbs to the lure of drink, gambling, fast horses, and unbridled temper. He thus offers a terrifying caricature of the qualities of command and daring that are essential to the man who must master other men. The unflinching will of the good master surfaces in the dissolute rake as the unbridled willfulness of the unsocialized child. Southern literary domestics' abiding preoccupation with male strength and its perversions reflects their abiding commitment to a distinct, socially grounded ideal of maleness, which they deem necessary to the survival of their most cherished institutions. The dissolute young man appears early in the southern domestic tradition and persists to the end as the sign of a continuing attempt to sustain a viable model of masculinity. From Lewis Barnwell in *Recollections of a Southern Matron* to Eugene (Rutland) Graham in *Beulah*, he manifests the same flaws and falls prey to the same temptations, but as the debate over slavery intensifies, his virtuous alter ego gradually changes. Increasingly, southern women writers focus their primary effort on the presentation of a compelling model of male strength.

Throughout the antebellum period, the dissolute young man figures as a primary object of southern women writers' social criticism. In so using him, they are superficially following a path similar to that followed by the northern literary domestics, but beneath the surface, they are elaborating a very different agenda. Whereas the northerners increasingly sought to make men more like women, to subject them to domestic standards, southerners sought to make them adhere more closely to traditional standards of manhood. In their hands, the weakness of the dissolute young man disconcertingly evokes effeminacy, merging with their image of undisciplined women. Their determined insistence upon the significance of sharp distinctions between male and female excellence testifies to their commitment to differentiating the values of slave society from what they perceive as the corruption of capitalist society. In this spirit, they invariably link male dissolution to the contagion of fashion as embodied in urban life. The line that northern women writers figuratively draw between the home and the world, southern women writers draw between the North and the South, although by the late 1850s, many are reluctantly acknowledging that northern corruption is extending its tentacles into southern cities.

Even when southern domestic writers most sharply castigate the failures of their own society, they link those failures to northern values and forms of behavior and even to direct northern influences. Where Harriet Beecher Stowe attributes southern vices to slavery, southern domestic writers attribute them to the erosion of slavery as a social system—or to northern intrusion into southern life. In the 1830s, Caroline Gilman could present slaveholding households under the governance of strong masters as the natural embodiment of the principles of the Revolution. Her novels thus echo an indigenous southern representation of slavery as a positive good. By the 1850s, southern domestic writers, like southern proslavery writers in general, are inescapably slipping into a more polemical, defensive tone in their attempts to answer the rising criticism of their values and institutions. The predilection to present themselves as the true heirs of the Revolution persists, but increasingly it is enlisted to combat a newly aggressive northern definition of freedom as the natural right of each individual and as the absolute antithesis of slavery.

Under the northern onslaught, southern literary domestics intensify their defense of their region and their concomitant outright attack on the North, but as the issues become more complex, they branch out into a variety of arguments. Caroline Lee Hentz, in *The Planter's Northern Bride,* takes on Stowe most directly. Reversing every one of Stowe's premises, Hentz depicts the North as the graveyard of young women. She opens with a heartrending portrayal of a young worker whose wages afford her aged mother's only support but who, suffering from tuberculosis, is being turned out into the snow by her heartless employer. To drive the point home, she has her heroine, Eulalia, come close to death because of her fatuous abolitionist father's refusal to allow her to marry the gallant southern planter whom she loves. The threat of her death chastens her father, who permits the marriage but does not forswear his destructive principles. Safely removed to the South, Eulalia thrives, learning more each day of the goodness and strength of her husband. But renewed threats to the felicity and stability of their lives surface, first, in the form of his first wife, a willful and undisciplined, if lusciously beautiful, orphan daughter of traveling musicians. They surface a second time when an abolitionist preacher, who insinuates himself into the confidence of the master in order to foment a revolt of his slaves, in effect offers the master his finest moment. The discovery of the plot to revolt leads Moreland, who customarily adopts a demeanor of loving compassion, to reveal the unflinching strength and iron will that undergird and inform his customary gentleness. Facing down his slaves, who cower under his gaze, he embodies the very essence of the right to command and incarnates the substance of righteous justice. He plays out, in short, the southern man's favorite role of the chivalric knight, at once personally gentle and yet ever ready to mete out stern justice in the name of social duty.

For Hentz, the core of the response to Stowe lay in the concept of slavery as a beneficent social system—as the best way of ordering a society in which some are necessarily unequal to others. Good women, she demonstrates, benefit from men's protective strength, while flawed women deservedly provoke their repudiation and wrath. Slaves, too, benefit from the protective structure of slavery. Never homogenizing her black characters into a single type, she nonetheless assumes that only fools could view them as the equals of whites. Allowing for considerable variation in personality, she assumes that slavery provides the best possible structure for them. Like Mary Eastman, who in *Aunt Phyllis's Cabin* also engaged the confrontation with Stowe, she offers a searing picture of the desperate plight of free blacks. Both Hentz and Eastman include discussions of slaves who succumb to the lure of abolitionists and attempt to trade their comfortable situations for the chimera of freedom. In both instances, the misguided slaves find themselves abandoned or even preyed upon by their purported saviors and rapidly come to regret the security they have so thoughtlessly jeopardized.

Unlike Hentz, who would tolerate no chink in the proslavery armor and no defensiveness in the proslavery tone, Eastman is even willing to acknowledge that slavery may have disadvantages, but she does so in a way that prompts her to greater racism without softening her attacks on northerners in general and abolitionists in particular. Northerners, she insists, maintained slavery so long as it suited their economic interests. And their slavery was altogether more draconian than anything known in the South, as one of her southern gentlemen pointedly reminds a northern acquaintance. Northerners too had slave laws, he insists, and pretty tight ones at that. "'A woman could be picked up and whipped, at the report of any body, on the naked body.'" Not so in the South. "'Why, sir, if we had such laws here, it would be whipping all the time, (provided so infamous a law could be carried into execution.)'" Northerners made the most of slavery while it suited their convenience, and now that it does not, they attempt to foist their "principles" on others. But do they consider the best interests of the slave? No. Their principles reduce to their pockets. If the abolitionists mean what they say, why do they not give the profits from their books "to purchase some of these poor wretches who are whipped to death, and starved to death, and given to the flies to eat up, and burned alive"?[24]

Southerners, who have been "left with the curse of slavery upon us (for it is in some respects a curse on the negro and the white man)," know enough to leave the ending of slavery to God.[25] They also know that it is impossible for slaves to enjoy freedom within the United States. Virginia's laws prohibit freed people from remaining in the state of their birth. Northern states exploit all free laborers, white or black, Irish or African, with a draconian cruelty unimaginable in the South. Eastman's southern gentleman, Mr. Chapman, has seen enough in England to last him a lifetime. "I saw some of your redeemed, regenerated, disenthralled people—I saw features on women's faces that haunted me afterward in my dreams. I saw children with shrivelled, attenuated limbs, and countenances that were old in misery and vice."[26] If the abolitionists had a shred of conscience, they would cease their irresponsible meddling, spend some of their wealth to purchase slaves, and send them to Liberia. But it is too much to expect them to behave according to reason. *Aunt Phyllis's Cabin,* Eastman states in her preface, is not intended as a history of slavery or abolition. "Slavery, authorized by God, permitted by Jesus Christ, sanctioned by the apostles, maintained by good men of all ages," she explains, in a rehearsal of familiar southern arguments, "is still existing in a portion of our country." And only "the Almighty Ruler of the universe" can determine "how long it will continue, or whether it will ever cease." Abolition, "born in fanaticism, nurtured in violence and disorder" also exists. "Turning aside the institutions and commands of God, treading under foot the love of country, despising the laws of nature and nation, it is dead to every feeling of patriotism and brotherly kindness; full of strife and pride, strewing the path of the slave with thorns and of the master with difficulties, accomplishing nothing good, forever creating disturbance."[27]

The abolitionists, in their fanaticism, are turning their backs on scripture and history. "Knowing that the people of the South still have the views of their revolutionary forefathers, we see plainly that many of the North have rejected the principles of theirs." The constitution, like scripture, recognized slaves as property. "Our country was then like one family—their souls had been tried and made pure by a united struggle—they loved as brothers who had suffered together. Would it were so at the present day."[28] Eastman's view of slavery as an unavoidable evil concedes the possibility of its historical disappearance but rejects the abolitionist claim that it must be acknowledged a sin. To follow that view would be to have the father no longer control the child, the master no longer control the apprentice. "Thus the foundations of society would be shaken, nay destroyed." Christ, she enjoins her readers, "would have us deal with others, not as they desire, but as the law of God demands: in the condition of life in which we have been placed, we must do what we conscientiously believe to be our duty to our fellow men." And Christ, she adds, "alludes to slavery, but does not forbid it."[29]

Eastman's position suggests that she, like her sister Virginian Mary Virginia Terhune, basically identifies with the southern Whig tradition. Proposing a qualified acceptance of historical development and cautiously endorsing some benefits of modernity, she entertains the possibility of slavery's eventual disappearance and thereby edges away from the extreme proslavery position of her South Carolinian contemporary Mrs. Henry Schoolcraft. In "The Black Gauntlet," Schoolcraft, explicitly arguing the proslavery case from the perspective of both masters and slaves, insists that the scriptural and historical cases for slavery are as one. History demonstrates that slavery "has been the efficient cause of civilization and refinement among nations."[30] For South Carolinians in particular, the "exemption from *manual* labor" afforded by slaves "is at the foundation of a class of elevation and refinement, which could not, under any other system, have been created," and which provides for the slaves with a care and instruction that far exceeded anything provided to northern workers.[31] Let the abolitionists look to "perfecting the morals of those poor, degraded pale-faces, that surround the doors of their own State," who suffer an oppression so intense "that negro slavery is far preferable."[32]

Writing in the midst of mounting sectional crisis, Schoolcraft, like Eastman and Hentz, is in part responding to the abolitionists, but more than the others, she is challenging frontally not merely the abolitionists' actions but also their worldview. South Carolinians, she approvingly avows, are "'old fogies'" who, unlike the abolitionists, do not believe "that *God* is a progressive being; but that throughout eternity *He* has been the same; perfect in wisdom, perfect in justice, perfect in love to all his creatures." From this perspective, she finds it impossible to credit "the new-light doctrine, 'That slavery is a sin.'"[33] Mrs. Stowe's vision of a world in which "all are born equal" is nothing but a millennial fantasy. Even Thomas Jefferson's celebrated words in the Declaration of Independence defy six thousand years of historical experience, not to mention scripture, and have caused nothing but mischief.[34]

For each of these writers, differences notwithstanding, women may appropriately take up their pens as social critics when the stakes are high. As social critics, they understand their primary responsibility to lie in the defense of their own people, institutions, and region, which, they staunchly insist, embody the highest social principles. And they all take as objects of their criticism, not the failings of slave society, but the failings of the North. Above all, they berate northerners, including northern women, for abandoning scripture, the foundation of true religion, and for espousing the destructive doctrines of individualism and equality, including abolition and women's rights. She who cares to see the consequences of such pernicious doctrines has only to look at the northern laboring poor and ponder the dissolution of family and social ties inherent in their condition. Among the ranks of those poor, she will find abundant examples of faithless men and women; drunken, violent, and improvident husbands; downtrodden, overworked, and fatally ill women; broken marriages; neglected children; and impoverished, despairing elderly people. Although few southern literary domestics explicitly label their project, they are, in effect, holding up the dregs of northern poverty as a harbinger of what the free market threatens to impose on the South and the world. A people that heedlessly repudiates the divine and natural order of hierarchical conditions is asking for what it will get. What can women expect of a world in which each is free to labor and think as she pleases? Household drudgery, brutal and faithless husbands, and wanton children—in sum, the destruction of precisely those domestic values that northern women writers believe they are extending into the public sphere.

In the measure that the southern domestics admit that the vices of free society are beginning to infect their own region, they tend to attribute them to northern intervention: the actual intervention of abolitionist agitators and the metaphorical intervention of northern ideas. During the fifties, those who accept the explicit struggle over slavery as the principal arena of combat are especially likely to focus their novels on the slavery question and thereby allow their opponents to define the terrain. Their social criticism, accordingly, more often than not focuses on slavery narrowly defined as the condition of workers, and they risk falling into the trap of juxtaposing material well-being against legal condition. In this context, freedom can appear as a mere ideological dream that counts for little against the assurance of adequate food and housing, reasonable working hours, and support in old age.

Augusta Jane Evans of Mobile, arguably the most passionate and assuredly the most learned of these female defenders of southern values, avoids the trap.[35] Her two antebellum novels, *Inez* of 1855 and *Beulah* of 1859, barely mention slavery and do not so much as acknowledge Stowe's existence. Yet in *Inez*, she turns the tables on Stowe by equating northern aggression with expansionist Catholicism and by casting her two young southern women protagonists as the defenders of true Protestant values.[36] In *Beulah*, Evans further adapts the classic domestic novel to her own purposes, attacking her northern counterparts on the high ground of woman's identity and purpose.[37]

Beulah contains none of the familiar pictures of degraded northern laborers or of happy, well-fed slaves. It does contain a healthy dose of social criticism, most of it directed against southerners whose misguided lives testify to the disarray into which their society is plunging. Eugene Graham dramatically evokes the pitfalls of southern manhood gone astray. His proclivities toward self-indulgence and material comfort lead him to marry his beautiful, wealthy, and irredeemably selfish cousin, and the disastrous marriage accelerates his own collapse into dissipation. Excessive drinking and gambling destroy the last vestiges of his youthful promise; uncontrollable horses almost destroy his life. His stepsister, Cornelia Graham, embodies the tragic decline of the ideal of republican motherhood that her name evokes. Pampered from childhood by irresponsible parents, she suffers from an incurable heart ailment. But the physical weakness of her heart pales beside the consuming cynicism of her spirit. Bereft of faith and all but bereft of meaningful human attachments, Cornelia dies in a spiritual desert, an index of the barren prospects of a people that has lost its spiritual moorings.

Both Eugene and Cornelia, amply seconded by an array of fashionable, materialist, and faithless characters, represent the pernicious penetration of northern values into the very heart of southern society. Evans spares nothing in her castigation of their failings. Materialism, empty fashionable religion, and narrow selfishness all provoke her to a devastating critique of a society gone awry. Beulah herself, however, embodies the greatest trial of southern society, for she falls prey to the siren call of learning and female independence. Most of the novel is taken up with extensive discussions of the reading and ambition that fuel her progress to the very brink of agnosticism. Bypassing the specific question of women's rights, Evans plunges into the maelstrom of faith and skepticism. Shifting from the manifestations of corruption to its source, she scathingly attacks the temptations of northern and European philosophy, denouncing the intellectual pretensions of the abolitionists as nothing less than the ambition to substitute the human mind for God. That she locates the struggle of faith against philosophy in the mind of a woman testifies above all to her conviction that to grant men the license of freethinking while holding women responsible for religion is sheer self-deception. Where man's mind roams, there will the intelligent woman's mind follow. Nothing is safe against the northern onslaught—nothing, that is, save the will of the southern people to save themselves.

Beulah's tragedy lies in her frozen heart, her inability to recognize and accept love. Her heart, Evans insists, is a woman's heart. But Evans never endorses the view that she has Beulah scornfully reject woman's nature as dependent and clinging. She simply insists that woman's nature, like man's, requires divine assistance in order to recognize the path of duty. To determine duty for the self alone is to assume the place of God Himself, to accept the pernicious Emersonian view that creature and creator are one. In this respect, Evans articulates a distinct southern view of identity as grounded in particular stations, a view that women must accept their natures and their proper social roles. But she is not endorsing the view that women depend on men for their salvation. Women, like men, must accept their guidance direct from God. Women, like men, are capable of rejecting true duty and forfeiting salvation.

Beulah has most commonly been read as a female *Bildungsroman* laced with a heavy measure of social criticism. But it may also be something more. Those who have emphasized the meaning of Beulah's name as "married woman" have slighted its meaning as a (married) land. They have thus ignored the possibility that Evans intended her novel to double as an allegory for the South as a whole. In my judgment, the novel is best read as such an allegory, with Beulah's struggles taken as sign of the struggles of the southern people. Certainly, well before the 1850s, the great southern divines were launching those appeals for self-reformation that would reach a crescendo during the dark years of the war. The virtues that they were urging upon their fellow southerners strongly resembled those that Evans urges upon her heroine, notably those of a deep and trusting faith that puts aside the graven images of materialism and, especially, unbridled individualism. The good of the self can only be found in the good of the whole, in hewing to the lines that God has laid down.

In many respects, the voices of the southern sentimentalists merge in a distinct regional voice, for each, in her own way, strove to defend what she took to be the superior values of her region. Thus regional loyalty to what many southerners were increasingly prepared to view as a separate society, if not a separate nation, tended to submerge differences by state in letters, just as it was coming to in politics. Yet within that regional convergence, Hentz and Evans, the two southern women writers who arguably ranked first among their peers during the decisive 1850s and who both came from Alabama, seem to have been developing a voice and vision that reflected the distinct experience of the Old Southwest. For both of their works, especially that of Evans, embody a commitment to the South that has been hewed out of the frontier and still bears some of its traces. In their novels, the reader finds no lingering deference to Virginia as the cradle of the Revolution but rather finds a forthright celebration of the new world of a modern slave society that southerners have wrought. No less significantly, they who most firmly insist upon the worth of the South's distinct social order also are most ready to generalize about social order and, above all, most ready—as their contemporary Henry Hughes of Mississippi was doing during the same decade—to defend southern slave society not as a legacy of the past, but as a model for the future.[38]

The war and emancipation destroyed the foundations of this view.[39] In the aftermath, disillusioned southern women writers did not abandon their commitments to the distinct values of their region, but they did confront the necessity to ground them in new institutions. Sadly, some, including Evans herself, increasingly turned to racism and sexism to justify what seem increasingly arbitrary restrictions. Others gradually groped toward a new critique of both. But that is another story.

Feminist scholarship, understandably concerned with recovering its legacy, has primarily focused on the ways in which women have struggled against the social relations and narrative traditions that have hedged them in. In this context, the northeastern women novelists of the nineteenth century offered an especially attractive perspective. Protesting the twin and related injustices of chattel slavery and the subordination (even "enslavement") of women, they fashioned a narrative to which women can now comfortably turn. Women such as Harriet Beecher Stowe and Susan Warner also criticized aspects of emerging industrialization and may thus be said to have harbored their own ambiguously articulated reservations about capitalism. But even in criticizing what they viewed as capitalism's excesses, the northeastern women critics remained generally committed to the core of the ideology of bourgeois individualism.[40]

The arguments for antislavery and woman's rights both rested squarely on individualist principles; both unquestionably assumed that the social relations of the capitalist North were essentially superior to those of the slaveholding South. To the extent that northeastern women criticized capitalist social relations—and they did—they sought to extend the sway of women's values and, in some instances, to retard capitalist development. Their southern counterparts were more likely to see the vices of capitalism as endemic to the system and, accordingly, to dismiss the possibilities for its reform. For southern women, the social relations of slavery, which, they admitted, themselves required reform, offered a superior model. Above all, the southern domestic novelists assumed that women found their highest calling as vigilant members of the communities into which they were born.

2

The Plantation Mistress
A Perspective on
Antebellum Alabama

ANN WILLIAMS BOUCHER

In January 1845, Henry Watson, a wealthy Greene County planter, wrote to his sister about his plans to marry Sophia Peck. In describing his fiancée, Watson provides a glimpse into the nature of women's lives in antebellum Alabama. Obviously proud of Sophia, Henry Watson described her first as a "girl of intelligence" but then rejected that portrayal, crossed through the words, and wrote "woman of intelligence."[1] His change of mind merits attention.

The view that Watson captured in the words "girl of intelligence" strikes a familiar chord. Many antebellum southern writers were given to descriptions of white women that emphasized their delicacy, weakness, and dependence—in a sense, their girlhood. Certainly among the most notable advocates of this view, George Fitzhugh, an antebellum defender of southern culture, wrote that, "in truth, woman, like children, has but one right and that is the right of protection. The right of protection involves the obligation to obey. A husband, a lord and master, whom she should love, honor, and obey, nature designed for every woman. If she is obedient she stands little danger of mistreatment."[2] This assessment of women as powerless and, in that powerlessness, as similar to children appeared in many popular novels and stories describing the antebellum South.

While departing from a strict comparison between the status of women and that of children, some more recent historical studies continue to view white plantation women as uniquely bereft of individual freedom and authority, over either themselves or those about them. In her 1982 study of the lives of plantation mistresses, Catherine Clinton emphasizes the burdened and confined character of their existences. In Clinton's treatment, the proper analogue for women's lives is not so much those of children as it is those of slaves. Surveying many aspects of women's lives, Clinton concludes that "they were merely prisoners in disguise. . . . However sheltered they were from the market economy and class oppression, plantation mistresses spent much of their lives under constraint and in isolation: fettered nonetheless."[3] Slavery "rendered tyranny just,"[4] and slaveholding men willingly exercised the same extraordinary control over their women that they did over their slaves.

From Clinton's perspective, there is comparability in the effects of slavery upon white and black women. Elizabeth Fox-Genovese in *Within the Plantation Household* (1988) vehemently disagrees, arguing that slavery produced very different experiences for white women than it did for black women. To Fox-Genovese, black women were not crippled by slavery in the same way white women were. Slavery gave status to white women and made their work lives much easier, but at a cost. Well-to-do southern white women could not accept the social and economic benefits of slavery and reject the power relationship that was at its core. They had to live in households "that contained within themselves much more basic economic production than was common in the North or in western Europe. Each of these households came under the direct authority of a single man, the master, who assumed accountability for its internal and external order." Many slave women opposed that authority, but it is Fox-Genovese's assessment that white women accepted the rule of husband and father as "legitimate and natural."[5] The acceptance cost them their individuality. While the differences in Clinton's and Fox-Genovese's studies are numerous, the two historians share a belief that southern white women lived an extreme version of the patriarchal family where their development as individuals was severely and uniquely circumscribed.

The ambiguity that marks Henry Watson's description of his fiancée is not entirely absent from these historical accounts, but it is given little importance. In the first thirty pages of her long study, Fox-Genovese introduces Sarah Gayle, another young Alabama woman who seems to share at least some characteristics with Sophia Peck. Gayle is an appealing and intelligent person, but in Fox-Genovese's assessment, these qualities "cannot be divorced from her willing complicity in a social system that permitted them to flourish through the enslavement of others. . . . Her experience and perceptions as a woman depended upon the social system in which she lived."[6] In short, slavery overwhelmingly determined the character of Sarah Gayle's life and that of other white women in the antebellum South.

Other historians propose a different understanding. This other view, which comports more favorably with that expressed much earlier by Henry Watson, has been spelled out in detail by Suzanne Lebsock in her study *The Free Women of Petersburg* and by Jane and William Pease in *Ladies, Women, and Wenches.* In an analysis quite different from Clinton's, which preceded it, and from Fox-Genovese's, which followed it, Lebsock argues that the general direction of change in white and free black women's lives in the Virginia town between 1784 and 1860 was unmistakable. "Women in Petersburg experienced increasing autonomy, autonomy in the sense of freedom from utter dependence on particular men."[7] Evidence of this is seen in women's choices about marriage and paid work and in the greatly enhanced ability of married women to hold property in separate estates. As traced by Lebsock, the causes and effects of this autonomy are complicated, involving things over which women had control and things over which their influence was greatly constrained.

In *Ladies, Women, and Wenches,* Jane and William Pease use this concept of choice and constraint to compare the experiences of women in antebellum Charleston and Boston. The regional differences emphasized in other studies exist in the Peases' analysis but are much less pronounced. In fact, Pease and Pease argue that well-to-do women in Charleston and Boston had more in common with each other than they did with poorer women in either city. While emphasizing the importance of class and race in women's lives, Pease and Pease conclude that choice and constraint had profoundly individual dimensions in both cities. "All knew that their choices were more limited than men's. All knew that the constraints surrounding them were not completely rigid. Most realized inherent contradictions in the rules governing womanly propriety. Some barely tested the possible alternatives. Others pressed the outer limits. None was altogether victim. None was altogether free."[8]

Neither Clinton and Fox-Genovese on the one hand nor Lebsock and Pease and Pease on the other describe southern white women as in absolute bondage, and certainly no one takes the position that they were completely autonomous. But Clinton and Fox-Genovese see white plantation women as fundamentally limited, either because they were victims of slavery or because they were so thoroughly implicated in the maintenance of the slave system. Lebsock and the Peases acknowledge the existence of limitations but also argue that freedoms existed. The white women of their studies are less dependent on male authority, are more practiced in making choices, and have significant measures of personal autonomy. In both their limitations and their freedoms, southern white women in their studies have more in common with other white women of antebellum America than do southern women in Clinton and Fox-Genovese's accounts.

Given these different interpretive positions, one of the purposes of the analysis that follows is to assess the value of one position over another in understanding the experiences of one group of southern white women, those who were members of Alabama's wealthiest slaveholding families in the late antebellum period. These women, among whom was Sophia Peck Watson, were the wives and daughters of slaveholders owning one hundred or more slaves in 1860. A small number of the women were themselves among this elite group of slaveholders.[9] This consideration uses the ownership of slaves to locate these women in time and place but finds that slaveholding was not as important a determinant of their lives as Clinton and Fox-Genovese have argued. Reflecting rather than refuting Henry Watson's mixed view of his fiancée, this essay will argue that wealthy Alabama slaveholding women experienced limitations and freedoms, and that both are important. Their experience is appropriately described by the conceptual frameworks of Lebsock and Pease and Pease—frameworks that envision the experience of southern white women as a continuum in which bondage and freedom exist in some proximity. This essay will examine that proximity in four major areas: their marriages and their reproductive experiences; their roles as mothers; their friendships, especially with women kin; and their property holding. From these experiences, conclusions are drawn on the character of these women's lives and the perspective that these provide on antebellum Alabama.

Living in many parts of the state but concentrated in the agriculturally rich Black Belt, these women conducted their lives within families, and families became the most important arena for both their freedom and their bondage. Daughters were expected to marry and, with their husbands, establish separate households and families. None of the historians cited earlier argues that slaveholding parents controlled their children's choice of mates or arranged marriages, and there is no evidence to suggest that wealthy Alabama planters did this either. Had families exerted strict control over marriage, women might have been expected to marry in strict sibling order. But in fact, evidence of such rigid parental control is not present in the plantation families in any larger measure than in other well-to-do families for which information is available.[10] The finding does not mean that parents lacked influence over their children's choices of mates, and historians have attempted to define this influence.

Emphasizing the authority of southern fathers over their daughters, Catherine Clinton cites three major differences between marriages in plantation families and those in New England. Southern fathers more rigorously screened out suitors who were not of an acceptable economic standing, were more insistent on daughters' marrying their cousins and thus strengthening family ties, and were more vigorous in prompting daughters to marry when they were younger and thus more malleable.[11] Reflecting Clinton to some extent, Fox-Genovese emphasizes the importance of class as the primary determinant of a suitable spouse. To her, class established an "invisible barrier" to marriage into the plantation elite for those outside. Some breached the wall, but Fox-Genovese implies that this was rare.[12]

The experience of Alabama's wealthiest families confirms some of these arguments, but emphatically not all of them. During the later antebellum period, marriages with near kin were not a prominent characteristic of experience. Certainly such marriages occurred, but not in large number and not nearly to the extent that they did in the years after the Civil War.[13] While differing from Clinton's observations on kin marriages, the experience of wealthy Alabama women comes closer to supporting her findings on age at marriage and the significance of wealth to marriage formation. But in both matters, there are differences that make the Alabama experience one in which individual freedom and familial limitations existed.

Early marriage for women and large age differences between husbands and wives have traditionally been seen as evidence of the unusually powerful influence of fathers over daughters and the particularly unequal character of southern marriages. But the experience of wealthy Alabama planter families does not fit easily into their mold. The 1860 census "snapshot," supported by other genealogical records, presents an interesting picture of change in women's ages at first marriages and the age differences between husbands and wives that resulted. Some of the planters are older, having married in the early nineteenth century; others are much younger, having married in the years around midcentury. In the marriages formed earlier in the century, women married on average just before their nineteenth birthdays and were nearly seven years younger than their husbands. In the marriages formed around midcentury, which included marriages of some planters' children, women married on average at twenty-one and were five years younger than their husbands. Age at marriage for men stayed the same in both groups.

From these data, a trend in ages at marriage and differences in ages of husbands and wives at first marriage can be developed. Clinton's study focuses on women who married in the later eighteenth century and were eight years younger than their husbands.[14] This difference had dropped to five years for those marrying in Alabama at midcentury. Even though these southern husbands and wives were still separated by more years than was the normal expectation in New England, the declining age disparity prompts new considerations. While the larger age gap of the older generation is taken to suggest the possibility of a particularly unequal power relationship, the change in the younger generation may be interpreted as a step toward moderating this difference in marriage.

The question of the influence of wealth and class in marriages among Alabama's wealthiest planter families can, along one dimension, be answered fairly simply. It was rare for marriages to be formed out of economic motives alone. Courtships were reported to be romantic affairs, focused on developing bonds of affection. Henry Watson's courtship illustrates this. He realized that it was time to think seriously about marriage, but in 1843, he was not sanguine about his opportunities. A marriage with the daughter of a business associate, the wealthy planter John Irwin, was a possibility, but Watson was not interested. His outlook on marriage changed when he became acquainted with Sophia Peck. In January 1845, he asked Sophia to marry him. When he had her consent, he asked her father for his permission.[15]

Watson's correspondence shows, however, that marriage, while an individual matter, had economic and familial dimensions. He wrote his sister that he considered himself rich enough to marry. He also thought about the family into which he was marrying. One of Sophia's uncles was particularly irksome to Watson, but in Henry's estimation, most of her kin were people of honor and integrity.[16]

Marriages in Alabama plantation families were influenced significantly by family status and class consideration, but wealth alone was not of sufficient importance to exclude a person from the circles of potential spouses. William McAlpine, who became one of Alabama's richest planters, came to Greene County from Georgia. When he married Nancy Watson, William owned six slaves. Nancy's father, also a Greene County planter, owned seventy-one slaves. In 1850, Amelia Glover married James Luske Alcorn. Her family was extremely wealthy; Alcorn was a man of ability but, at the time, not of wealth.[17]

These examples show one side of the equation, but there is another. Sons and daughters of wealthy planter families also married people whose family wealth was similar to their own.[18] Both patterns were important in the dynamic environment of the new state. The marriage patterns suggest that young men and women's individual considerations and personal preferences were important. Family status and class were also, but these did not strip away individual choice in this important decision.

Once women were within the bonds of marriage, as both Catherine Clinton and Elizabeth Fox-Genovese describe, their positions were powerless and subservient. To Clinton, planters thought of their wives as they thought of their land, as possessions.[19] Fox-Genovese allows that the relationships between husbands and wives could appear affectionate, but that their essential character was a sharp denial of women's autonomy. Husbands controlled the plantations, which combined production and reproduction. Women were subjects of male authority and lived by a set of gender conventions designed to express the social standing of husbands and fathers rather than to define meaningful roles and relationships for women within the family.[20] These are strong claims that can be agreed to in part, but not in total.

The relationships between husbands and wives in wealthy Alabama planter families are difficult to summarize, expressing, as one might expect, a wide range of emotional content. Family letters show evidence of deep affection and of quarrelsomeness and disagreement. Court records show that a few women who were treated brutally sought legal remedy for their husbands' abusive behaviors.[21] Because of the difficulty of assessing written exchanges between husbands and wives, other ways are used to see into women's status within marriage. One of the most important of these is to examine patterns of childbearing. From this perspective, high fertility is associated with lower evaluation of women's position in the marriage and the family.

Historians have described frequent pregnancies as the normal experience of well-to-do white southern women. Anne Firor Scott recounts the lives of Mary Pratt Edmonston of North Carolina and Mrs. Andrew McCollum of Louisiana, whose experiences indeed indicate unrestrained fertility. Mrs. Edmonston bore eleven children over a period of twenty-one years, and Mrs. McCollum had ten children over fifteen years.[22]

Catherine Clinton argues that the patriarchy exacted the "frequent birth of heirs as a kind of tribute from planter wives," and that children were seen as physical evidences of the planters' power.[23] When linked with descriptions of women's character as docile and subservient and with their marriages as extreme examples of male dominance, high fertility substantiates women's powerlessness in marriage. Such descriptions also place southern white women at odds with a national trend in the nineteenth century of declining white marital fertility, a trend historians have connected with higher status for women within the family.

The women of this study bore larger numbers of children than was the usual experience of white women in the United States in 1860, but completed fertility on the scale of Mrs. Edmonston's or Mrs. McCollum's was not the average experience. When examined by age cohort, it is evident that wealthy Alabama women's experience was at least consistent with the national trend of fertility decline in the nineteenth century. Completed fertility for those Alabama women born between 1780 and 1799 was 5.86 children, compared to 5.6 for those born between 1800 and 1819, and 5.0 children for those women born between 1820 and 1839.[24]

For Alabama women, fertility depended to a significant extent on age at first marriage and therefore on the length of time a woman was sexually active and at risk to become pregnant. For a group of eighty-six wealthy women for whom age at marriage and completed fertility are known, average completed fertility was 5.7 children. Despite the fact that most of the women studied (62 percent of the eighty-six) married at a younger age than was the national average, they had less than one child more than the national white fertility rate for 1860 (5.21).[25]

An age-specific birth ratio shows interesting similarities and differences between the childbearing experiences of wealthy planters' wives and those of other Alabama women. For this analysis, the wives of wealthy planters and other women were combined into three age groups: those who were fifteen to twenty-four years of age; those twenty-five to thirty-four; and those thirty-five to forty-four, as recorded on the census. Because of their better overall health, the wealthy women had higher fertility between the ages of fifteen and twenty-four than women in any other group. Between twenty-five and thirty-four years of age, the differences disappear, with all women examined experiencing their highest fertility between these ages.

In the final stage of childbearing, an unexpected divergence occurs between the experience of wealthy women and that of other women.

Between the ages of thirty-five and forty-four, the fertility of the wealthy women is the lowest of any group observed. For example, the age-specific birth ratio of wealthy women in this age category is 1.43, compared to 2.18 for women in two Dallas County precincts in 1860, and to 2.29 for women in Coffee County, an Alabama wiregrass county, in 1880. A contrary pattern could reasonably have been expected. Wealthy women were healthier, had better diets and lighter workloads than other women, and could be assumed to be physically more capable of successful child-bearing later in life than other groups. That their fertility is lower than other women who were much less advantaged suggests the possibility that wealthy women consciously restrained their childbearing in the late stage of their reproductive lives.

Taken as a whole, the fertility of wealthy Alabama plantation women presents a complex picture of constraint and choice. These women had many children, and their lives were shaped substantially by their re-productive experiences. Yet comparison of their fertility to that of others argues that wealthy women, especially those in the last stages of their reproductive lives, may have made choices. Elizabeth Fox-Genovese argues that the control of women's sexuality, the limitation of choice, was a major focus of antebellum gender conventions.[26] Yet the experience of Alabama women suggests that they may have been exerting some control over themselves, rather than bowing to conventions. Did they refuse their husbands sexual access; did they, like other American women, come to some agreements with their husbands to restrain their fertility? Whatever the explanation that may be given, their childbearing patterns do not comport with a view of southern marriage as an institution that system-atically stripped away women's individuality in ways that were extreme and unique.

Concern with marriage and reproduction leads into the related ques-tion of maternal roles as a part of women's experience. Slavery, it has been believed, gave southern motherhood a particular character. In this view, maternal roles of white plantation women were primarily man-agerial, with many day-to-day responsibilities delegated to slaves. It has been thought that plantation mistresses delegated so extensively that they regularly gave up to slaves one of the most intimate of the maternal roles, infant breast feeding.[27] The belief that well-to-do white women willingly relinquished this responsibility contributes to the view that they handed over many other duties of child care and rearing to slaves. Expressing a version of this assessment, Fox-Genovese generalizes that motherhood had a significant theoretical place in the South's view of women, but that slavery rendered motherhood of much less actual daily importance in that region than in other places.[28]

The correspondence of wealthy Alabama women raises questions about this assessment. Several wealthy women record their experiences breast feeding their own children. Jessie Walton Webb wrote her husband, James Webb, that she had weaned their son Jim, who was a year or slightly older at the time. Sophia Watson nursed her first child, Frederick, for at least a year and a half and another child for nearly two years.[29] Drawing on the larger context provided in Sally McMillen's excellent study *Motherhood in the Old South*, it appears that these women are examples of the many well-to-do southern women who chose to breast feed their own children rather than rely on a slave wet nurse.[30]

If plantation women held on to this intimate task of child care, perhaps they also retained others to an extent greater than has been generally assumed. The letters of wealthy Alabama women certainly suggest this. Women were quite familiar with the development of their children, comparing one child's walking and teething to the timing of these developments in older children. These mothers were knowledgeable concerning their children's day-to-day activities, recording in letters what the children were involved in, which games they played, and how they progressed with their lessons.

Mothers both cared for sick children and directed slave nurses. Amelia Walton Glover offered to care for her sister Louisa Creswell's sick children while she went on a long-awaited trip to Mobile, but Amelia wrote her mother that Louisa would probably decide to cancel the trip and remain at home to care for the children herself.[31] Sophia Watson nursed her oldest daughter, Julia, during a very severe illness, and Jessie Walton Webb cared for her children, writing her mother, "It seems to me I can stand no more—for I have had a very sick child constantly since I got well."[32]

While they could delegate some child-care tasks to slaves, several wealthy women record assuming full responsibility for the education of younger children. In the 1830s, when Sarah Lide Fountain moved to Dallas County, she was very concerned about the education available to her children and so taught them at home until a school was established. Both Jessie Webb and Aurelia Fitzpatrick wrote of either instructing the children or having a young woman relative teach them at home. In 1858, Henry Watson wrote that neither of his oldest children, a girl nine and a boy seven, had ever attended a school. His wife had taught them at home.[33]

Margaret Calhoun, wife of Andrew Calhoun of South Carolina and Alabama, was very involved in the decision to send her son away to school in Philadelphia. Aurelia Fitzpatrick wrote her son that she hoped he would study "with earnestness and get a *good education.* You know how I have tried to impress upon you the importance of being a well-educated man." With similar expectations, Mary Louisa Hall wrote her daughter at school in Pass Christian, Mississippi, "I shall hope to have an intelligent and pleasant companion not a mere machine to move only when set in motion, or a doll to be dressed but, a sensible, refined, and reasonable woman."[34]

This summary of some areas of maternal responsibility is not a denial that slaves were involved in the care of white children. Certainly the labor of slaves was important, and women directed that labor, but the maternal roles of wealthy Alabama women went beyond the managerial. The correspondence of wealthy women indicates that they both carefully supervised and had direct involvement in the care and education of their children. Slave labor lightened the workloads of wealthy women, but motherhood was an occupation of substance and significance for them.

The responsibilities of wife and mother, which have been discussed thus far, have been seen by some as sources of loneliness and isolation for southern women. Catherine Clinton maintains that the plantation mistress was alone, "an island," without a sense of community comparable to that enjoyed by the slaves who moved around her.[35] This atomization is, to Clinton, a key element in the success of the patriarchy in controlling women. Elizabeth Fox-Genovese sees the world differently. To her, southern women were not isolated but were enmeshed in the slave system. They engaged in a very stylized form of visiting, designed not to meet human needs for friendship but to reinforce the rigid boundaries of class in antebellum southern society. Women had friendships of a sort, ones that were determined by slavery and the hierarchical systems necessary to support it.[36] Although different, both arguments portray southern women as bereft of friendships that they and others deem important and in which they acted relatively autonomously.

It is no doubt true that the responsibilities of household, husband, and children limited women's opportunities for friendships. Difficulties of travel could set women apart from friends and kin. Class divisions set well-to-do women apart from poor neighbors. These constraints were significant, but they coexisted with deep friendships. The case of three sisters in Greene County illustrates this point. The daughters of the planter Justina Walton, Jessie Webb and her sisters Amelia Glover and

Louisa Creswell, depended on each other for long-term support and for friendship. When Jessie was to be married, Amelia and Louisa helped her in gathering things for her new home. Later when Jessie learned that Louisa was ill, she was ready to come home to help her sister. As the mistresses of plantations, the three women exchanged household goods and discussed the health of children and slaves.[37] They lived relatively close to each other and enjoyed a lively face-to-face relationship, as well as exchanges through letters.

Mary Louisa Hall and her sister Sarah Anderson Crenshaw did not live near each other and had to depend more on letters to keep their friendship alive. They began their correspondence shortly after each had married and begun having children. Their exchanges suggest that transportation difficulties and sparse settlement left both women in need of companionship, and because of that, they engaged in a long, though irregular, correspondence. Each would occasionally write complaining bitterly because of the long absence of letters from the other, then go on to share family news and talk of children. They were good friends. As Sarah wrote, "Oh Sister Louisa if you knew how lonesome I am Walter has to be away so much you would pity me. . . . Oh that is a great deal to have one kind female friend, Just one."[38] However flawed by factors of plantation life—distances, difficulties of travel, and demand of many children—the sisters filled in important ways the need Sarah Crenshaw expressed so touchingly.

Mary Louisa Hall and Sarah Crenshaw's friendship both proves and disproves the view of southern women as isolated and alone. Clearly, features of plantation life made their friendship difficult, but it existed and appears to have been important to each woman. Their friendship and that of Amelia Glover, Louisa Creswell, and Jessie Webb point toward a different view of the experience of southern women. Their experiences combined love and loneliness, isolation from and bonds with other women and their communities. It is possible to interpret the imperfect but deep friendships that emerge in the women's correspondence as sources of an enhanced sense of themselves as individuals. These women were clearly not uniquely bereft of friendships and support but were people whose relationships with others expressed the limitations and choices, freedoms and constraints that characterized other parts of the experiences.

This continuum of experience is present in the final concern of this essay, in the property holding of well-to-do Alabama women. These women lived through a period of substantial change in the practice of women's property holding. Elizabeth Fox-Genovese minimizes these changes, maintaining that the South was throughout the antebellum period "especially intransigent" in its opposition to women's property rights.[39] This position contrasts with that taken by Suzanne Lebsock in *The Free Women of Petersburg.*

Lebsock argues that women in Petersburg between the 1780s and 1860, and especially after 1830, gained greater autonomy over their own lives, and that their ability to hold property was a significant measure of this improved status. To Lebsock, two trends are very important. The first was that toward the establishment of separate estates for women, and the second was the increased willingness of well-to-do husbands to place greater responsibility for the management of property in the hands of their widows.[40]

Well-to-do men in Petersburg during the years 1781 to 1830 were quite reluctant to give their wives control over substantial wealth. They rarely named their wives as executors of their estates and favored placing restrictions on their wives' inheritances. Lebsock sees change in these practices after 1830. In this later period, wealthy Petersburg men show a significantly higher evaluation of their wives' abilities to manage property by naming them more frequently as executors and by giving their wives estates in fee simple more often.[41] Lebsock believes that these were advances in women's status and independence, but that these changes did not spring from deep public commitments to equality.[42] Much the same case can be made for Alabama.

In antebellum Alabama, married women's legal rights were limited. Before the late 1840s, individual wives could overcome some limits by petitioning the state legislature for the right to hold property as a *femme sole,* an unmarried woman, but the right of all married women to hold property was not guaranteed. However, in 1848, Alabama became the second state in the Union to pass a married woman's property act enabling married women to hold a separate estate of real and/or personal property coming to her before or after marriage. In further elaboration of the law, the Alabama Code of 1852 provided that a husband be given the legal trusteeship of the wife's estate, particularly if it included slaves who were to be part of the plantation labor force. A husband was not compelled to detail the usage of her property, but if he proved a poor manager, the wife could sue for his removal and have her property restored to her sole control.[43] A few women took advantage of this protection.

The development of such limited legal guarantees on property holding contributed nevertheless to changes in the treatment of Alabama women in inheritance. Catherine Clinton observed the earlier pattern in which southern fathers treated sons and daughters differently in inheritance. Sons would receive land, but because of the insecurity of women's property holding, daughters would receive only slaves.[44] This was not the case in late antebellum Alabama, where wealthy planters treated their sons and daughters alike in deeding or willing property.

In passing property to their wives, planters acted in ways generally similar to those described by Lebsock in the post-1830 period. Of the approximately ninety located wills written by members of wealthy Alabama families, thirty-five were wills written by husbands leaving property in either fee simple or fee tail to their wives. Of these thirty-five, fifteen were like that written by Napoleon Lesuieur of Marengo County. He left all of his real and personal property to his wife, Penelope, but directed that his property was to be divided among their three children when she died.[45] However, twenty of the wills were like that of James Calhoun, who devised an estate in fee simple to his wife. By her own will, Susan Calhoun passed her estate in land and money to her children, with her daughter Sallie receiving the largest part.[46] John McRea of Marengo County left his entire estate to his wife, Josephine, to dispose of as she saw fit. In his will he expressed his confidence in her "judgment and prudence" to handle their property wisely. Josephine McRea directed the affairs of her large family and was one of the few women listed among Alabama's wealthiest planters in 1860.[47] In Petersburg and in Alabama, the percentage of wealthy men leaving some or all of their property to their wives in fee simple was virtually equal, at 56 to 57 percent. While both John McRae and James Calhoun named their wives as sole executors, just slightly fewer Alabamians did this than was the case in Petersburg. Just over 50 percent did in Petersburg, but in Alabama the percentage was 48.5, indicating quite similar types of behavior.

The married woman's act was not revolutionary. It capped a long-standing practice of married women's seeking individual legislative acts to ensure them of the right to act as *femme sole*. Women continued after its passage to turn their property over to their husbands for management. Many men supported the woman's act because it promoted economic security and class consolidation, not because it was a means of enhancing the individual rights of women. But the act had important ramifications. In the 1861 Convention of the People of Alabama, the secession convention, Mr. Henderson, a delegate from Macon County, decried the act, saying, "I have no doubt, that one of the most prolific causes of Divorce in this State is the practical operation of what is known as the Woman's

Law. As originally enacted, I do not doubt, it was intended to protect her rights. But results have shown, that what was intended for her protection, has proven to be the reverse. It creates, by law, two separate interests in the same family, where God designed there should be but one."[48]

Mr. Henderson's criticism parallels Henry Watson's earlier change of mind. In both statements, the shadow of bondage is present but so are hints of a more complex reality. This essay has explored this complexity by examining experiences of wealthy Alabama women in marriage and childbearing, in motherhood, in relations with women friends, and in property holding. In each area, there is evidence of choice and constraint, of freedom and bondage.

These experiences make it difficult to fit the perspective of Alabama's wealthiest women into historical interpretations of southern society as rigidly structured and of the position of planters' wives as fundamentally limited by their involvement in slavery. The experiences of Alabama's wealthiest women does provide a meaningful perspective on antebellum society as one fraught with differences and tensions. Antebellum Alabama was a frontier state with a rapidly expanding economy and a society given to change, not stability. It was also a slave society. As the historian J. Mills Thornton has explained eloquently, Alabama was a state deeply involved in both freedom and slavery.[49] The perspective of women in the state's wealthiest families enhances rather than contradicts this understanding of the state's antebellum past.

3

White and Black Female Missionaries to Former Slaves during Reconstruction

HARRIET E. AMOS DOSS

Reconstruction sparked a host of changes other than the political and economic ones that scholars have studied so often. Both educational and religious opportunities opened to former slaves during the postwar era, and women of both races helped to open the doors to change. Yet female missionaries to former slaves have received relatively little mention in general studies of Reconstruction, women's history, and religious history.[1] Females made up three-quarters of the northern teachers to freed blacks. Hundreds of black and thousands of white women left the North first for the occupied war zones and later for isolated rural areas in the postwar South. They found a new focal point for sharing their evangelical missionary spirit as they educated people recently liberated from bondage.[2] Scores of women entered Alabama as teacher-missionaries during Reconstruction. Most remained only a few years, yet during that time, they fostered educational and religious development not only of local blacks but also of themselves.

Much of the story examined here comes from letters and reports that missionaries filed with federal and charitable organizations, especially the American Missionary Association, Women's Baptist Home Mission Society, and the Woman's American Baptist Home Mission Society. Some of the missionaries were native Alabamians or southerners; others came from outside the region to engage in the process of religious Reconstruction. They came from a variety of Protestant backgrounds. Like other American Protestant women involved in missions during the late nineteenth century, they felt Christian responsibility to reach the unconverted. They took special interest in the social problems of women and children. Espousing the Victorian view of women, American Protestants believed that female Christians exercised tremendous moral and religious influence.[3] As they ministered to former slaves in Alabama, missionaries shared the goals of leading them to salvation and church membership along with "uplifting" the black race.

The challenges of missionary work appealed to women who wanted vocational opportunities besides teaching. Many restless, ambitious, and pious women from small towns and farms across American found release from their confined circumstances as they entered the frontiers of educational missions. Like many of the leaders of their national or local sponsoring missionary societies, they believed in the views of the era about white racial and cultural superiority. On the field, missionaries developed their own talents and leadership skills, sometimes pragmatically performing some of the functions once reserved for male missionaries or clergymen.[4]

Since white southerners had few resources or inclinations to engage in missions to blacks at the end of the Civil War, white and black missionaries from the North took a leading role. In the 1870s, white southern Baptist, Methodist, and Presbyterian women established foreign mission societies, but they did relatively little for home missions. In the 1880s, they increased their efforts in domestic missions, including aid to freed blacks in their plans.[5]

In the immediate postwar period throughout Alabama, as elsewhere in the South, former slaves sought to organize schools so that they might secure an education for themselves and their children.[6] When student demand exceeded local resources, sponsors of schools pleaded for aid from the North. In 1865, black residents of Talladega sponsored a school that quickly outgrew space in a private home and later temporary quarters. Sponsors decided that they needed a teacher with better qualifications than those of a local young freedman who had been doing his best to teach a large enrollment. After they sought aid from the federal Bureau of Refugees, Freedmen, and Abandoned Lands (Freedmen's Bureau), the Cleveland Freedmen's Aid Commission sent Cynthia M. Hopson of Hudson, Ohio, to take over instruction of the school in 1866. Talladega's whites shunned her, forcing her to board with an elderly black couple. By the fall of 1866, Hopson had two assistants, one of whom was Carrie Phelps, an experienced teacher from Rockport, Ohio.[7] From these cooperative efforts by local blacks and northern white philanthropists evolved Talladega College in 1867. Blacks in Marion organized Lincoln School, for which they eventually secured missionary teachers from the North. Throughout Alabama, female missionaries substantially furthered efforts to educate ex-slaves.

Simultaneously with efforts by local blacks to establish their own schools came ventures by the Freedmen's Bureau and a host of denominational and nondenominational mission organizations. A number of women found employment in schools sponsored by the nondenominational American Missionary Association (AMA), which expanded its educational work after the Civil War as the Freedmen's Bureau was preparing to disband. The AMA was organized as an amalgam of antislavery missionary groups. In the 1850s, it provided financial support for antislavery missionaries in the Northwest and in the slave states of Missouri, North Carolina, and Kentucky. And it sent preachers, teachers, and clothing to runaway slaves who had settled in Canada. During the Civil War, the AMA sponsored missionaries who traveled to areas of the South opened to them by the Union army. As the war brought emancipation, the AMA viewed its responsibility as shifting from temporary relief and antislavery propaganda to permanent transformation, reconstruction, and redemption. Education became essential in the process of change if social emancipation were to follow legal emancipation. In ministering to former slaves, the AMA, motivated by religion and patriotism, aimed to achieve full citizenship for blacks. Officials of the AMA viewed themselves as Christian abolitionists who shouldered the responsibility for liberating former slaves from their bonds, including those of ignorance, superstition, and sin. Realizing that the majority of white Americans, northerners and southerners alike, did not believe in the equality of blacks, AMA agents nevertheless thought that Christian education would result in blacks' achieving meritorious status for advances in knowledge, temperance, and morals. Thus the AMA maintained educational, religious, and political goals. Agents believed that they could help to create a literate, temperate, and godly society by religious education as they headed to the South with their schoolbooks, the Bible, and their belief in the New England Way. Missionary teachers, regardless of their race or institutional or denominational affiliation, agreed on their goal of providing freedmen with the qualities expected of civilized citizens, those virtues admired in mid-nineteenth-century America and taught in most schools and pulpits, namely "industry, frugality, honesty, sobriety, marital fidelity, self-reliance, self-control, godliness, and love of country."[8]

Shortly after the war, AMA agents entered Alabama. They organized normal schools in Mobile, Montgomery, Marion, Athens, and Talladega.

They also founded a number of Congregational churches. Their missionaries came from a variety of places in the North. For instance, women teachers at the freedmen's Trinity School in Athens came from Methodist Episcopal churches in Mosherville and Ann Arbor, Michigan. Female teachers at the AMA's Emerson Institute in Mobile came from New York, Iowa, Illinois, Michigan, and Ohio.[9]

In their academic assignments, missionary teachers faced large classes of eager pupils with limited resources. According to the principal of the AMA's Emerson Institute in Mobile, each teacher had twice as many students as she should. At Trinity School in Athens, where Mary F. Wells served as superintendent, classes for each of the two teachers included fifty pupils. Classes in the Normal School at Talladega also had fifty students, while classes in the primary school there had forty pupils. Schools in Eufaula, Union Springs, and elsewhere maintained large classes. In addition to day schools for children, teachers often taught night schools for adults.[10]

Low salaries created challenges and hardships for missionary teachers. Pay varied depending on the sponsoring charitable organization and the gender of the teacher. Women received lower wages than men, as they did in other employment throughout the nation. The AMA compensated its female teachers in the late 1860s with salaries of fifteen dollars per month plus room and board during the school year. They did not always receive their salaries on schedule or in the full amounts, because the AMA operated with a deficit from 1866 to 1878 (it kept schools open by understaffing, underpaying teachers, and borrowing). Some women could not afford to continue long as teachers under these circumstances. Mary McAssey resigned from the faculty of Talladega College in 1876 since she could not repay her college loan of $700 from her annual salary of $120.[11]

Those women who persisted as teachers in schools for former slaves managed to adapt creatively to their circumstances. Josephine Pierce, a native of Tallmadge, Ohio, shielded herself from the cold floors of her dormitory room at Talladega College by tying a string to a square of carpet and dragging it from her bed to her washstand to her writing table. "It is a new sensation in Alabama," she announced with good humor, "to hop out of bed in the morning, and the feet touch a carpet."[12]

Teachers often appeared more concerned with their students' spiritual growth than their academic progress. Women often taught Sunday school classes that furthered the work of evangelism in such places as Tuscaloosa, Eufaula, Oswachee, Athens, Mobile, and Selma. One teacher from the North came to Alabama to work among southern blacks because, as she wrote, "I have ever felt a missionary spirit & strong desire to be useful to others." In Athens, a missionary wife was "actively engaged in the religious work" as she taught singing in the school and rehearsed the church choir.[13] Lucy Brown, whose husband, Henry, served as the AMA's first superintendent of Talladega College, held cottage prayer meetings and helped to teach older adults to read the Bible. She praised Phoebe Beebe, a teacher from Tifton, Michigan, as "not only a faithful teacher, but a devout and zealous missionary, carrying the gospel into the homes of the people with an interest that will ever crown her name with living memories."[14]

These missionaries helped to prepare a host of black Alabamians to preach and to teach Sunday schools. Emma C. Dejarnette, a black student from Talladega College, taught Sunday school in Childersburg, where lessons were preceded by singing, praying, and scripture reading.[15]

In many localities, women missionaries led their own separate meetings for prayer or sewing classes. In Mobile, female Congregationalists conducted their own prayer meetings. In Selma on Sunday afternoons, women and girls held meetings that were "a source of very great profit and interest" at a time when the church lacked a minister. Every Saturday afternoon in Marion, the daughter of the AMA missionary taught a very popular sewing class in which the female pupils learned a variety of fancy work that they used to adorn their homes. These same skills also could be used to earn a living. Other female missionaries conducted prayer meetings for women.[16]

In 1878, black Baptists of Alabama founded their own college or theological seminary in Selma, a town with a large black population. Adopted by the American Baptist Home Mission Society (ABHMS) in 1880, Selma University, as it was eventually called, received financial aid from northern Baptists toward its operating expenses and construction programs. At great sacrifice, Alabama's black Baptists matched sums contributed by the ABHMS for the erection of specific buildings.

Like other denominationally affiliated schools, Selma University promoted revivals and mission activities. As teacher Libbie M. Seeley noted, "Our pupils are always interested in religious matters, but during the past month we have had a revival of God's grace in the hearts of professing Christians and a manifestation of His convicting and converting power over sinners."[17] Organizations at the school fostered missions. Upon enrollment, every Christian student became an active member of the ABHMS, and every unconverted student became an associate member. A number of students conducted mission Sunday schools in Selma and its environs and raised money for their own mission society and special collections for other causes.[18]

Selma University attracted aid from the Women's Baptist Home Mission Society (WBHMS), which was formed in 1877 in Chicago to conduct evangelism among former slaves and other needy people in America. On an exploratory trip through the South in 1878, WBHMS missionary Joanna Patterson Moore found a warm welcome from the Reverend Harry Woodsmall, president of Selma University. In 1881, she and another missionary from the society launched their work in that community.[19]

Like other missionary teachers sent by the WBHMS, Moore was considered a faculty member at her school, with particular responsibility for the departments of biblical and industrial education for women. Her work entailed teaching women daily classes about the Bible and Sunday school teaching; providing daily instruction in domestic arts and industries, physiology, and hygiene, including nursing of the sick; and teaching practical missionary work on the field for pupils as time permitted.[20]

Some of her curriculum resembled that at a new type of educational institution, the missionary training school. Women who wished to prepare themselves formally to become missionaries or religious workers could enroll in the Woman's Baptist Missionary Training School in Chicago, founded in 1881 by the Woman's American Baptist Home Mission Society. There in its early years literate women could study a practical curriculum, taking courses for one to two years in the Bible, religious pedagogy, history of missions, and practical mission work in the local area. In addition to the official curriculum, student missionaries also cultivated piety by attending frequent prayer meetings and having visits and letters from missionaries.[21] Formal instruction in Selma may not have been on the same educational level as that in Chicago, but the concept of the two programs remained similar.

Solid preparation at Selma University enabled three black "Bible women," Charlotte Thompson, Ella Jackson, and Charlotte Jenkins, to continue the mission work begun by Joanna Moore when the sponsoring board could not find a missionary to place in Selma. These black Alabamians displayed fervent dedication to their calling. Charlotte Thompson recalled that two white female missionaries came to her house and prayed with her and her mother as she was seeking God's will for her decision in life. Soon she began helping Moore in her mission work.

Selma University, founded in 1878 by the Colored Baptist Convention of Alabama. Later it received financial support from the American Baptist Home Mission Society. (Photograph courtesy of the American Baptist Historical Society, Valley Forge, Pennsylvania. Used with permission)

Another of Moore's "helpers," Ella Jackson, noted, "I believe it is the work that the Lord has chosen me to do. I have long wanted the opportunity that I now have to work for Jesus. I believe the Lord opened the way by sending Sister Moore to teach us."[22] After Moore relocated to another mission field, her former "helpers" carried on the work. During one year, Charlotte Thompson reported establishing three Sunday schools, two sewing schools, and one Band of Hope for children; holding women's meetings each week; and visiting the women of Selma as time permitted. The executive board of the WBHMS praised Thompson, noting, "She has labored faithfully not only to carry help to her people, but to arouse in them a spirit which will lead them to do good to others as they have opportunity."[23]

Missionary organizations sought to employ their most outstanding black students such as Charlotte Thompson. When she graduated from the Normal Department of Selma University in 1885, she studied for one month in Morgan City, Louisiana, where Joanna Moore had been transferred to teach a training class. Then the WBHMS appointed her to assist

Joanna Patterson Moore, missionary to former slaves from the Women's Baptist Home Mission Society. (Photograph courtesy of the American Baptist Historical Society. Used with permission)

Moore in her general work in Louisiana just as she had previously assisted her in Selma. In response to an earnest plea from the president of Selma University, Charlotte Thompson was appointed by the ABHMS as a missionary teacher at her old school in Selma in October 1886. She took particular joy in the conversion of a number of her pupils, noting that she was receiving blessings in her own spiritual life. For the 1887–88 year, in addition to her regular teaching at Selma University, she reported making 309 religious visits, conducting ninety-nine meetings for women and children, and distributing many items of clothing and Sunday school literature. She played a part in the conversion of about thirty people. "I am greatly encouraged in seeing so many fruits," she wrote, "and hope the Lord will send more laborers into his vineyard." On behalf of Selma University, she addressed the Alabama Colored Baptist Convention in

1887, when delegates voted financial support that sustained the school in her hometown. She continued her service at Selma University to 1889.[24]

Besides working through black educational institutions, white missionaries of the WBHMS also assisted black churches in their educational and evangelical efforts. Two of the WBHMS missionaries agreed to help W. L. Walker, the black superintendent of the East Selma Baptist Church Sunday school. Not only did the women get the Sunday school to flourish, but they also established a sewing school and Bible class that met two evenings a week. One of these female missionaries in Selma, M. R. McAroy, noted that the pupils sewed for one hour before studying their scripture lessons. During one session, a twelve-year-old girl said, " 'Pray for me; I want to be a Christian.' " When an adult woman became a Christian and was baptized, McAroy observed, "my heart swells with gratitude to God for this ransomed one."[25]

McAroy and her associate, Ella Cassidy, proudly reported that several women were converted after attending their sewing schools and mothers' meetings. They maintained that their work could not be overestimated, for "by it Christian homes are strengthened, and the impure and vile are brought to a saving knowledge of Christ. A love for home and children is awakened, and the more intelligent and educated are taught to work for their race." These white women missionaries sought to uplift the black race by working to reach its women. As Cassidy and McAroy contended, "In no other way can they be more effectually helped out of degradation than by this house to house teaching, where alone with the mothers and daughters we sit down, and from the Bible teach them purity of heart and life."[26]

As rewarding as their work was, it also was quite strenuous. Cassidy became so exhausted that she had to leave Selma for a period of rest in the North. According to the *Baptist Pioneer* published in Selma, "She [had] gladdened the homes of many who had never received a visit from a white Christian, and who felt that none cared for them." After Cassidy's departure, McAroy received help from some girls in the school and women members of the church.[27] The WBHMS maintained its work in Selma with other white women coming to take the places of those whose health had failed them.

Northern Baptist women also supported another mission organization to reach southern blacks. The Woman's American Baptist Home Mission Society (WABHMS), which was organized in 1877 in Boston, worked to raise support for missionaries to conduct "the evangelization of the Women among the freed people, the Indians, the heathen immigrants, and the new settlements of the West. . . ." The members of the society claimed that intelligent Christian women had to go among blacks, "become acquainted with them in their homes, exhibiting in themselves examples of true womanhood, and thus awaken in the minds of their colored sisters a desire for a higher and better life." These black women "were the prospective wives and mothers of millions of future voters." According to the society, "this is emphatically woman's work; she *alone* can do it."[28] The WABHMS sent Mattie A. Roach, who was described as "a very intelligent, well-educated young colored woman of Nashville," to work among fellow blacks in Alabama. Soon "she had established four Sunday schools and had under her instruction five colored ministers and one deacon."[29]

While finding husbands may not have ranked high among female missionaries' priorities, some did exactly that. Mattie Roach had begun mission work in Alabama in 1879 and by 1882 had married a black minister named Charles Octavius Booth. They had eight children, four of whom died while young. Mattie Roach Booth opened a school for women in her husband's parish in Selma. One of her younger pupils told a seventy-five-year-old student who tottered in with her primer that she was too old to attend school. The older woman replied, " 'I know my time is almost out here, but I would like to learn just to spell the word God, then I shall be satisfied.' " "There is something touchingly sorrowful in teaching these mothers," Booth observed.[30]

During the time her husband served in leadership positions in the Alabama Colored Baptist Convention, Booth also held leadership roles in the denomination and in reform organizations. She presented a paper on foreign missions to the Alabama Colored Baptist Convention in 1884. As president of the Alabama Woman's Christian Temperance Union, she addressed the twentieth session of the Alabama Colored Baptist Convention in 1887. The Booths continued their service in Alabama long past Reconstruction. In 1910, both taught at the Agricultural and Mechanical College in Huntsville.[31]

While Mattie Roach created a happy marriage with C. O. Booth, other female missionaries who thought that they had found a mate from their male co-workers were not always so fortunate. Blatant betrothal deception was practiced by Edward P. Lord, an AMA missionary who was concurrently engaged to marry six different AMA teachers. Wedding dates for each woman ranged from two months to two years in the future. Three teachers at Emerson Institute in Mobile, where Lord served as principal in the early 1870s, discovered in the course of a conversation that each of them was engaged to Lord. Their engagements had occurred between 1874 and 1876. After further investigation, the women found that he had made two more engagements in 1875 and 1876. By 1878, two years after Lord had begun serving as principal of Talladega College, missionaries learned that he had found a sixth fiancée at his new post.[32] To say the least, Lord's deceit undermined faculty relationships at two educational institutions.

While white and black women perhaps viewed their places in Christian work primarily as that of nurturers and teachers, they actually had broader influence. As evangelists, the missionaries of the WBHMS traveled "from house to house with Jesus by our side, the Bible in our hands and the old story of Jesus and his love on our lips. . . ." Besides making home visits, they also established sewing schools and children's meetings. "Our first lesson is Jesus," Joanna P. Moore reported, "and that dear name is the power that reforms and makes beautiful the children we find in our visits." Missionaries also taught the children "to keep their clothes, their homes, and their persons neat and clean, and to be kind and helpful to their parents."[33] As they reached women and children and, through them, men, the female missionaries in many ways served as preachers. They did not carry that title, but widely read denominational publications referred to them in language that was usually reserved for preachers. For instance, in publishing a letter from Joanna Moore in Selma, the *Baptist Home Mission Monthly* noted that she was delivering "one of her characteristic sermons."[34]

Educational and evangelistic work among former slaves brought their own satisfactions to northern white missionaries, but southern whites shunned them for their choice of mission. In towns that had schools for blacks staffed by northern teachers, local whites frequently felt bitterness toward the missionaries. Some Alabamians ridiculed the northern women teachers as "slab-sided old maids." The *Eutaw Whig and Observer* claimed that a number of "Radical women" came south ostensibly to teach in black schools but were "we have no doubt in search of negro husbands."[35] Social ostracism prevented the missionaries from associating with local whites. They often refused even to speak to the newcomers. One missionary observed in 1867, after four months of residence in Tuscaloosa, that "there are not half a dozen white people who speak to me in the place, aside from the [AMA] teachers."[36] Mary F. Wells, a teacher at Trinity School in Athens, went to Boston on vacation to "see and converse with cultivated men and women—*be recognized* by Christians of my own race—feel that I am no longer a leper."[37]

Social ostracism discouraged missionaries, but violence and arson endangered their lives. During Reconstruction, black religious or educational gatherings became particular targets of white repression. White missionaries who worked with blacks also suffered from attacks by southern whites. Sometimes they could not even count on protection from federal soldiers, for all of them did not sympathize with the principles of the Freedmen's Bureau. On a Sunday afternoon in July 1866, when a black Baptist congregation in Huntsville assembled at a spring for a baptizing ceremony, five drunken soldiers disrupted the occasion, which was witnessed by a large number of whites and blacks. The soldiers' commanding officer had announced quite openly "that he did not come . . . to support the Bureau and he was not going to do it." A Freedmen's Bureau agent admitted, "The Bureau to fulfill its mission must have a Military back-bone—As it is now I am powerless."[38] Even when troops did try to protect black residents, they could not be in every place they were needed. In Greenville in 1868, "disguised white men burned a freedmen's school-house, and the residence of the poor widow lady because she taught the freedmen."[39] Arsonists frequently torched black churches and schools. Within a few weeks in 1866, arsonists in Mobile burned three black church buildings and a black school supported by the AMA.[40] Fires that usually occurred when the buildings were fairly empty may not have caused much loss of life, but they served to intimidate religious workers and teachers. Some feared for their lives. Others worried about the wisdom of rebuilding charred ruins. For still others the attacks only strengthened their resolve to continue their service as missionaries.

Even in adversity, teachers of ex-slaves manifested sincere interest in their calling. An AMA female missionary, J. E. Biegle, opened a school for blacks in Oswachee in May 1869. At that time, she "felt there was considerable feeling against the school" and herself, but nineteen months later, she thought the animosity was "about dead." A former Confederate colonel who was one of the most influential men in the neighborhood where she taught called on her. As she remembered, he "informed me that it was generally acceded by all that I was doing a good work & the school would prove a blessing & not a curse as was feared when first opened." He said that whites wanted her to stay in the area as long as she could. He even asked her to teach on his plantation of a thousand acres.

"An effort has been made," Biegle reported, "to have me teach a White school, but I felt my duty was with the colored people, therefore declined."[41] Another AMA teacher who keenly felt an obligation to southern blacks was Maria Waterbury, who pleaded from Mobile for the cause of the AMA school there. She observed that teachers in the free public schools were southerners whom local blacks hated, saying that they did not treat their children well. Public schools under the Democratic school board, Waterbury noted, were "so conducted that they are demoralizing to those in attendance."[42]

Racial prejudices and preferences, although not frequently addressed, complicated the tenure of missionaries. While southern blacks clearly appreciated white missionaries from the North, they often preferred blacks, whether from the North or South. In the early years of Reconstruction, few qualified black teachers were available. Local blacks sought northern aid in employing well-qualified white teachers. On behalf of blacks in Marion who supported the Lincoln School, James F. Childs praised the AMA teachers Mary C. Day and Helen M. Leonard as "considered among all the colored people the most enterprising and successful teachers . . . than ever was in this place before."[43] In numerous other places in Alabama, local blacks developed a genuine attachment to their northern teachers. Talladega College, Selma University, and a host of grammar and secondary schools continued into the 1870s to employ a proportionately large contingent of white missionaries from the North. However, Alabama blacks still longed for teachers of their own race. After noting the racial composition of several schools in Alabama in 1878, a Methodist minister wrote the *Christian Recorder,* the paper of the northern-based African Methodist Episcopal Church, "We trust the day is not far distant when we can demand colored teachers for our colored schools."[44]

Southern black women indeed found that northern mission organizations opened the profession of teaching to them. Black women found some teaching positions in schools in Alabama aided by the AMA, the ABHMS, and the African Methodist Episcopal Church, which in 1889 founded Payne School in Birmingham as its first school in the state. In each school, male administrators, according to custom prevalent in late nineteenth-century America, paid women less than men and paid black women less than white women. Southern black women teachers were dedicated to work among blacks, but they were also frustrated by the lack of employment opportunities outside the black community.[45]

These white and black women missionaries to former slaves in Alabama during Reconstruction not only established classes and organizations for the education and salvation of blacks, but they also broadened the leadership roles of women in educational and religious activities. At a time when many southerners were not very receptive of women's speaking in public places, they led a variety of religious meetings, usually for women and children. They visited in homes as part of their evangelistic crusade, and they provided academic instruction to children and adults, sometimes even ministers and deacons.

White northerners may have acted in some respects paternalistically toward southern blacks, but they often were the first whites to take special interest in their welfare. They helped freedmen and freedwomen to develop talents that some eventually used as educators or church workers. They led the way toward preparing black teachers for public schools in the state. White missionaries who persisted in their service in Alabama withstood discouragement, exhaustion, social ostracism, and even threats or violence from southern whites. Convinced of their calling, they weathered obstacles to their own comfort and security. Their efforts and those of their black coworkers broadened the roles and responsibilities of women in church and charitable activities. Together they also participated in the movement to uplift the black race.

4

Amelia Gayle Gorgas
A Victorian Mother

SARAH WOOLFOLK WIGGINS

"Love is the principle of existence and its only end." On this belief Amelia Gayle Gorgas based her life, wrote her son William Crawford. She "liberally showered" love upon everyone around her, first on family and friends and then on those associated with her public career.[1] The key to her success in both realms was that she felt unselfish, loving "sympathy for everyone with whom she came in contact, and roused the same feeling in them."[2]

Amelia's lifetime, 1826–1913, spanned the Victorian era, when the role of women and the functions of the family changed dramatically. Now production moved out of the home, and the family was no longer an "enterprise or the world in microcosm." Instead, the family became a refuge from the world. Husbands went out to work in the world, and wives stayed home to cherish the children and prepare them for the difficulties of adulthood and to create for the husband a sanctuary in which to recuperate from the stress of work. These two realms of labor and activity represented two spheres—"man's world" and "woman's place." The arrangement's success hinged on the woman's willingness to sacrifice her personal preferences to the well-being of others. Amelia epitomized the selfless keeper of the home sphere in the Gorgas family.[3]

Amelia came from "Old Guard" Mobile. Her paternal and maternal ancestors included distinguished Revolutionary War veterans. Her father, John Gayle, was an Alabama governor, congressman, and judge; her mother, Sarah Haynsworth Gayle, a great beauty, descended from an equally distinguished South Carolina family.[4]

Amelia possessed an outgoing personality that was apparent at an early age. Amelia's mother recorded in her journal an occasion when she returned after a brief absence, and Amelia "seemed wild" with joy as she "flew over the path" and threw herself into her mother's arms "with every demonstration of delight." When Amelia was eight, her mother's assessments were mixed. "Constant care is requisite to manage her," said Sarah Gayle. "She is very affectionate and warm hearted," "very frank," "not at all indolent," but "easily led into temptation."[5]

As the third of six children, Amelia attended classes with local teachers in Greensboro and Tuscaloosa.[6] After Sarah Gayle died in 1835, when Amelia was eight, the children were scattered to live with relatives or friends. Amelia lived for two years in Tuscaloosa with her mother's close friend Mrs. Alva Woods, wife of the president of the University of Alabama. During this period, Mrs. Woods functioned as Amelia's mother and teacher, until Judge Gayle remarried in 1837 and reunited his family in Mobile. In 1841, when Amelia's older sister Sarah returned home from school in New York, Amelia left to attend Columbia Female Institute in Columbia, Tennessee. A year later she returned to Mobile. When Sarah married in 1842, Amelia became the oldest daughter at home; she now assumed responsibilities of assisting with the family's young children—half-brothers and a half-sister and nieces and nephews. Amelia continued her role as the caregiver for the family's children for the next ten years, a practice that ultimately led to her romance with and marriage to Josiah Gorgas.[7]

Amelia met Josiah, a career U.S. Army officer from Pennsylvania, while he was stationed at the Mount Vernon Arsenal near Mobile in 1853. He always insisted that since he had overheard Amelia's reading daily to children on the veranda next door to the arsenal, he fell in love with her voice before they met. A few months later, when Amelia was twenty-eight, they were married, and between 1854 and 1864, the couple had six children.[8] If there was ever a love match, that couple was Amelia and Josiah, for theirs was an affectionate and companionate marriage. Their romance and devotion never dimmed throughout their thirty-year marriage, and their letters during long separations reflect the heat of their passion.

For the next three decades, Josiah's career shaped the perimeters of Amelia's private world. Her husband's rootless military career before 1861 assigned the family to arsenals in Maine, South Carolina, and Pennsylvania before he resigned his commission to become Confederate chief of ordnance. The family lived in Richmond during the Civil War. In

1865, Josiah fled with the Confederate government, and Amelia and her sister Maria Bayne refugeed with their children to Maryland, where Amelia remained for a year. The Gorgas family reunited at Brierfield, Alabama, where Josiah opened an ironworks, which proved to be a financial disaster.[9]

In 1868, when Josiah accepted the position as headmaster of the Junior Department at the University of the South and moved to Sewanee, Tennessee, Amelia and their five youngest children remained at Brierfield for over a year. The arrangement permitted Josiah time to construct a home at Sewanee and Amelia time to salvage what she could of their financial investment at Brierfield. When the family was finally reunited at Sewanee, they had lost what money they had possessed at the end of the Civil War. Unfortunately, the Sewanee experience provided only a temporary postwar livelihood. Soon Josiah was reduced to borrowing money from their children's nurse. After ten years at Sewanee, mounting difficulties with the school's trustees forced Josiah to seek a new job. He was then sixty and in fragile health.[10]

Unexpectedly, the trustees of the University of Alabama elected Josiah president of that institution in July 1878, and he immediately resigned from Sewanee. Again, he left Amelia and some of the children behind for a few months until arrangements could be made for the family's move. The family was hardly settled in Tuscaloosa when Josiah suffered a severe stroke in February 1879. He never fully recovered. When he resigned as university president in July 1879, the trustees appointed him university librarian, a post Amelia and their daughters could ghost for him, and gave the family a residence on campus. Amelia's panic that they would have to leave the university with no money and nowhere to go now subsided.[11]

As Josiah's health fluctuated and then steadily worsened, Amelia increasingly assumed duties as university librarian. When he died in May 1883, Amelia became librarian in name as well as fact. For the next two decades, while university presidents came and went, Amelia continued as librarian until her retirement at the age of eighty in 1907. The university then rented to her the house that had been her home since 1879 and that by now was so thoroughly identified with the Gorgas family.[12]

Until Josiah's health collapsed, Amelia's mothering confined itself to the private world of her large family and friends. Then, thrust into the public sphere as University of Alabama librarian, she expanded her mothering to what became her new extended family, the university boys. There she lived publicly as she had lived privately at home. The image of

Amelia that emerges as a Victorian mother is that of a woman who believed that it was her duty to promote the happiness of others selflessly and to meet their needs cheerfully.

Amelia was no siren of a southern belle. No one, not even Josiah, ever referred to her as a beauty or even as pretty. Five years after the couple married, Josiah wrote what he termed a "verbal daguerreotype" of his wife that focused more on her personality than on her looks. Amelia was "just five feet two and one-half inches high" with a

> very taper waist, and a very pretty foot and ancle. . . . Her complexion is brunette—which infers dark hair and eyes—and these latter are large and *prononces;* from which you may conclude, . . . that she has the organ of language largely developed, and knows how to use her mother tongue. Her mouth is large and good-natured, and does only one thing better than talking. . . . She greets her friends with a smile, and is never ill-tempered with a somewhat impatient husband. . . . She is hospitable . . . and is never happier, than when her table is well supplied with guests. . . . She is industrious by nature, and supervises her household affairs personally. She is kind and considerate towards her servants, and studies how she can give them a new pleasure. If it may be called a fault, she has that of being too indulgent to her domestics.[13]

Here was Josiah madly in love, and his best compliment to Amelia's physical appearance was to praise her small waist and pretty feet.

In a family where antebellum portraits and postwar photographs abound, no portraits or pictures of Amelia before she was almost eighty have been located.[14] Amelia may have deliberately avoided photographers or portrait painters, conscious that she was no beauty. Once when she informed Josiah of her arrangements for daguerrotypes of the children to be made and delivered to him in Charleston, she advised him that her picture was not to be included: "my homely phiz I cannot consent to give you." On another occasion, Amelia sadly noted the resemblance between herself and one of her daughters: "Poor little Minnie they say inherits my appearance as well as name."[15] Existing photographs taken in the early 1900s show a tiny, birdlike woman dressed in a black dress that swept the ground. White ruching circled her neck and trimmed the cap that she wore to cover thin white hair piled upon her head. Huge ears peeked through her hair, and she looks for all the world like Minnie Mouse in a black dress and glasses.

Throughout Amelia's childbearing years, one or more nursemaids resided in her household. One remained twenty-five years. In 1857, while the Gorgas family lived at Kennebec Arsenal in Maine, a young Irish girl, Anne Kavanaugh, joined the family. Anne had come to America to marry her sweetheart, only to find that he had been killed before she arrived. A priest sent the young girl to the Gorgas household, where she helped Amelia with housekeeping and nursing the children. Anne so endeared herself to the family that she remained with them for the rest of her life, leaving only once for a few months in 1858. She became the children's beloved Nana, whom all considered to be a family member, not an inferior household servant.[16]

Despite the presence of live-in servants, Amelia lavished time and care upon her "babies." For Amelia, as for other southern parents, her earthly treasure was her children.[17] Her correspondence with her absent husband in 1858 glowed with accounts of her interaction with their children. One Sunday morning, she reported taking the children outside after breakfast for them to play in the warm sunshine. "I dare say," she wrote, "the pious church people thought me a heathen but my babies are my first duty." A week later, she wrote to her husband while one child "perched on the window at my side." Again she had sent the nurse to church while she "played muse to our three babies." Time to write to her beloved husband was difficult to find. "The children claim their usual morning so I must be short & sweet."[18]

Amelia heard their prayers, took them driving, or sat with them while they played. Proudly she described their activities to Josiah when he was away from the family. Willie, the eldest child, played at the "back door all morning wheeling stones, making hills of dirt for his flag staff & doing just as he pleases," and a few days later, both of the older children were "wheeling stones" while the youngest child encouraged them. Soon she reported Willie happily "sailing two little boats made of pea shells." On the Fourth of July, the children awakened her at 5 A.M. to join them in celebration. When the baby's nightly teething pain made her restless, Amelia sat up comforting the toddler. In Maine, when a friend suggested to Amelia that she send the children to a farmer's wife "that they may be benefitted" while Amelia was "relieved of all care," Amelia dismissed the idea as "well meant insanity."[19] Her personal involvement in the care and amusement of her children continued throughout their childhood and refutes the notion that southern mothers abandoned their offspring to the hands of servants.[20]

Amelia's personality made her the focal point of her large family. They made the Gorgas household their headquarters and moved in for varying periods of time. When Josiah described their home at Brierfield, Amelia jokingly predicted that they would "be obliged" to construct "a log cabin in the yard . . . for our numerous visitors."[21]

A year later at Brierfield on the brink of bankruptcy in 1867, Josiah noted in his journal one instance of what occurred at his home regularly: Amelia's brother-in-law and his family had been there "for six weeks." Then Josiah calmly counted the number of Amelia's family members within his household. "Let me see," he wrote in his journal, "how many *whites* in the house, 9 of us," plus Amelia's brother mentally broken by the war, her half-sister, one niece, another sister with her husband and five of their children, "making 19." Then he remembered that Amelia's stepmother would soon arrive with one more of Amelia's nephews, one of Amelia's half-brothers, and a nurse, "making 23, besides servants," he wrote. A month later, he observed that the total had shrunk, as the family then included only "8 grown white people, and 10 children with 4 colored Servants." Two more children were expected with Amelia's stepmother again the following week. "Besides," he added, "we expect some visitors soon! Mamma seems to think the more the merrier."[22] Obviously, Josiah did not consider Amelia's family "visitors."

At Sewanee on another occasion, Josiah noted that in addition to his own family of a wife, six children, and a nurse, his household then included Amelia's stepmother, her daughter with baby and nurse, and one of Amelia's sisters with her husband and four of their children. The Gorgas family correspondence and Josiah's journal reflect that after the Civil War wherever the Gorgases lived, there was rarely a time when at least one of her siblings and family was not living with Josiah and Amelia.[23]

"Home" to Amelia's family was wherever Amelia was, and they came home to her to give birth and to die. There Amelia's sister Sarah spent her last years of declining health and ultimately died with Amelia nearby.[24] Two of Amelia's four grandchildren and at least one of her great-grandchildren were born there, with the mothers-to-be traveling hundreds of miles to be with Amelia. The Gorgas house always remained as a refuge in the minds of family members. Even after Amelia's death, the family's daughters came to the house to have their children. In 1919, William Crawford, the eldest son, wrote to his sister Jessie: "One more born in the old house but Mother not there. I know that she is interested and sympathizes. No space & time could limit her human sympathy."[25]

Amelia's ease with people made her a natural comforter to the ill. The health of family members improved with visits to Amelia, and Amelia welcomed them. "It is such a joy to me," she wrote her son, "to be able to have the different members of the family visit me and to have a nice old house in which to accommodate them. I would be almost willing to give my services to the Univ for the house alone." Even during these years, as Amelia lived in a private world out of the public spotlight, hers was an extended family, peopled with her stepmother, siblings, in-laws, nieces, and nephews.[26]

When Amelia's siblings and their families were not living with the Gorgases, Amelia, her sisters, and her stepmother freely exchanged children. Between 1849 and 1854, the children of Amelia's older sister became Amelia's responsibility for several lengthy periods while Sarah traveled with her husband in vain efforts to improve his health. The dying husband described Amelia as "a second mother to our children." During the Civil War, the Gorgases' eldest child, William Crawford, spent the summer of 1862 with Amelia's sister Mary in Winnsboro, South Carolina.[27] In 1867, Amelia's daughter Jessie spent part of the summer with Amelia's sister Sarah in Eutaw, Alabama, and in September 1867, Amelia's sister Maria took Willie and Amelia's half-sister, Helen, to New Orleans to stay until mid-1868.[28] In 1872, Maria left her six children with Amelia at Sewanee for the summer, and in 1875, Willie lived with the Bayne family in New Orleans for a year. In 1877, Amelia's daughter Mamie wintered with one aunt in New Orleans and then in 1880 divided her time for five months between aunts in Mobile and New Orleans. After Amelia's son Richard graduated from college, he moved in with the Baynes in New Orleans while he read law with his uncle.[29]

The separations of Amelia from Josiah in Maine, Richmond, Brierfield, and Sewanee for periods ranging from months to a year left Amelia to cope on her own. During each separation, Amelia managed very well, although she often consulted Josiah by mail. Once the family was reunited, however, she again deferred to his leadership without attempting any womanly wiles to shape his decisions. Amelia's abilities to cope always surprised Josiah.[30] When she and her pregnant sister Maria fled from Richmond to Maryland at the war's end in 1865, Josiah remarked to their older sister how "strange" it was for the two women to be "running about with a dozen children."[31]

Their choice of refuge was not by chance and demonstrated the importance of what southerners call "connexions." Fleeing the captured Confederate capital, the Gayle sisters took refuge with the father of the Yale roommate of Thomas L. Bayne, Maria's husband. After a brief stay in Baltimore, they moved to the country home of their protector in Cambridge, Maryland, where Amelia remained for a year. Amelia regularly wrote to assuage Josiah's fears about her well-being and that of the children. "Do not feel the least anxiety concerning us. We are well and comfortable with many kind friends able and more than willing to assist if I require it."[32] She urged Josiah to write to her regularly from Alabama, for, she said, "I can be very strong if I know of your well being, but weak as a baby if ignorant of you."[33]

During the year-long separation in Maryland, Amelia managed financial matters for herself and her children. When she accounted to Josiah of her management, he judged her "statement of finances" as "quite satisfactory" and a "great credit" to her "learning in that branch." Three years later, when Josiah left Amelia and the children at Brierfield while he went ahead to Sewanee, he instructed her on how to sign his name and confidently left her to manage their business affairs, which entailed salvaging what she could from an ironworks teetering on bankruptcy. "You will have to be a business woman," he wrote her.[34] When Josiah found Sewanee had no money to build a house for the new headmaster, Amelia was not too proud to propose that they take in boarders to make ends meet, although she admitted that she did "not *hanker* after them."[35] Later, when Josiah was absent from Sewanee in 1876 on a fund-raising trip, he seemed to trust Amelia's judgment more on matters of money than on those related to the management of animals. While his advice was brief about financial matters, he instructed her in great detail on buying a sow, killing hogs, and nursing a sick cow.[36]

These absences provided Amelia with unwitting preparation for the time when Josiah's physical collapse made her the family's provider. After Josiah's stroke, Amelia wrote to Willie that if Josiah did not improve, he would resign, and they would sustain themselves by "taking boarders or opening a school." "I will not flinch when the time comes," she said.[37] During the next four years, as Josiah's health alternately improved and then worsened, Amelia assumed entire responsibility for management of the family's finances. Years later, one of her daughters remembered Amelia as the one upon whom the entire family leaned. "She seemed to know better than any one else just what to do & did it all with so much ease. We did not quite appreciate her wonderful qualities, just accepted everything as a matter of course."[38] Clearly, Amelia possessed a sixth sense of when to lead and when to follow, when to assume control and cope with necessity and when to defer to her husband's management of their affairs.

Amelia's personality, which made her household the center of the Gorgas family, manifested itself beyond the family circle. Amelia might be no great beauty, but she still cut a wide swath in social circles throughout her life. As a young girl in Mobile, when her father was supporting his own family plus those of his sister and his brother, Amelia had little money for clothes, but she "cheerfully" made do. "One year her principal party material was a quantity of gauze ribbon she had picked up at a great bargain. She used this to trim and retrim her dresses and always looked well," recalled her half-sister. "Another year she really had no nice visiting dress, but this did not make her give up society. She ran in to see her friends informally. . . . No dinner party was complete in Mobile without her presence . . . she was much sought after." When she declined an invitation to one masquerade ball, her brother-in-law begged her to go with him, went out, and bought her a domino costume. Completely disguised, she had a "royal time. People followed her around the ball-room, she said so many bright, pertinent things, and finally slipped out without disclosing her identity."[39]

In 1855, a year and a half after Josiah and Amelia married, Josiah found that his reception from strangers warmed when they discovered his relationship to Amelia. In Pensacola, Florida, to attend to repairs at Fort Barrancas, he called upon a friend only to find the friend absent from home. He recounted the incident to Amelia: the "'aunty' who 'came at our call,' finding that I was from Mount Vernon, asked how 'Miss Amelia' was & was quite delighted when she found it was of that lady's husband [that] she was inquiring."[40]

When Amelia visited Mobile in 1870 for the first time since her move to Maine fourteen years earlier, she found herself "a belle" among her old friends. Her appearance at church announced her arrival to her friends, and a "regular reception" followed. So many "visitors arrived in quick succession that a neighbor came over to see what the matter was." One friend thought that Amelia could be elected to Congress because her popularity was "as great among the colored aristocracy as the white folks." The warm reception in Mobile continued for days. Amelia wrote Josiah, "Such a triumphal visit never before was made"; she had been "handsomely entertained every day" since she arrived and would be out all of the following week if she remained in town."[41]

After Mobile, Amelia traveled to New Orleans, where she was equally a triumph socially. She hastily wrote Josiah before breakfast, since she would "not have a half hour again" that day, given her schedule of engagements. Life in New Orleans was a "delightful whirl," where dinner parties and lunches followed callers to the point that she was almost overwhelmed. "How shall I bear all these honors and kindnesses," she asked Josiah.[42] Her husband took quiet pleasure in her social success, commenting, "What a belle you are (& deserve to be)."[43]

Friends sought out Amelia, and she rewarded them with her undivided attention. She was the ultimate good listener, even when the speaker was a bore. On one occasion, she wrote apologetically to her eldest son that her usual letter had to be brief because an elderly friend had been "holding forth on the 'War' steadily for nearly two hours." She had reproached herself for recently neglecting this gentleman, and on this occasion she "rather encouraged his long talk by showing him in . . . the Records of the Rebellion how strong his battery was at the surrender. It does the good & brave Col. so much good," she wrote, "to have an attentive listener as I can easily assume to be on occasion." Knowing that her friend was "entirely alone now," she planned to invite him often to Sunday dinner, as had been their custom before the family "learned the 'war stories' verbatim & could keep awake to listen."[44] Amelia understood that loneliness had no age limit, and her sympathy with people of all ages drew them to her, the sympathetic and "attentive listener."

Distance and time might separate friends from Amelia, but strong ties remained. In January 1878, while Amelia's nineteen-year-old daughter Minnie wintered with relatives in New Orleans, the girl glowingly reported her warm reception there. She felt like thanking her mother everywhere she went: "I am always meeting friends of hers who are so kind to me on her account."[45] Still later, when the adult children of a former business associate of Josiah were to visit Tuscaloosa, the father made elaborate arrangements for them to call on Amelia, saying, "I particularly want them both to see you." Twenty years had passed since the father had left Alabama to become an illustrious chemistry professor at the University of Virginia, but to him Amelia's magnetism had not diminished. Another twenty years later, this distinguished friend wrote to one of Amelia's daughters, directing her, "Pray give your mother my best love—at my age the phrase may be pardoned, and it speaks the truth."[46]

Amelia was also sensitive to the needs of servants, and they returned her sympathy. Josiah once commented in his journal about Amelia's inclination to "spoil" servants by "indulgence."[47] After Josiah's death, condolences comforted a grieving Amelia. A particularly moving letter came from Mary Anne Gayle, once a slave in the Gayle household. Amelia had taught Mary Anne to read and write and had partly supported her for a period after the Civil War. "Dear Miss Amelia," she wrote, "your sorrows has so deeply touched my heart." Glad that Amelia was surrounded with "good and kind friends," Mary Anne still wished that she could come personally to be of comfort. Her letter closed with an invitation: "Miss Amelia do come down [to Mobile] and stay too or three weeks I think you will gain strength from it."[48]

The sacrifices of other people on her behalf deeply touched Amelia. When Josiah was stationed in Charleston, she was troubled to sense that he was "not entirely contented" with his new post. "I know dear Jesse," she wrote, "that you are there solely for my sake & that you would not have applied for it but for me so I really feel responsible for your contentment & happiness. What will I not do for you darling in compensation for so many sacrifices."[49]

Yet Amelia was oblivious to any sacrifices on her part. Not until they were adults did Amelia's children realize how pervasive her unselfishness had been in their lives. William Crawford repeatedly commented upon this quality. Her "most remarkable characteristic was the entire absence on her part of any idea that she was undergoing any particular self sacrifice."[50] To her oldest son, no one had accomplished as much as had his beloved mother, if accomplishments were "measured by effort for others and negation of self. . . . No one ever toiled & sacrificed in this life with as little consciousness that they were sacrificing." Many are "willing to make sacrifice," but they "want to get credit." He expected that when he explained to "the omniscient Judge" that he had worked to follow his mother's footsteps, the reply would be that his "motive was in great part worldly reward & the acclamation of your fellow man. . . . Mother strove from love of her fellow man, and was not influenced by desire of acclamation." William Crawford believed Amelia's children should take her "example & work more for love of man & less for reward."[51]

When Amelia's oldest daughter sought William Crawford's help in an effort to memorialize Amelia, he patiently explained the futility of such attempts in the face of fleeting immortality. Amelia's father, Governor John Gayle, had been a prominent man in his day, he explained, but after his immediate descendants died, the governor would be as "completely forgotten as other equally prominent men of his day." William Crawford expected no more for Amelia. What was left of their mother in this world was the "knowledge of her sweet personality which all who knew her have and the love which we therefore gave her. All that will be perpetuated will be this love," which would be a "source of pleasure & happiness to Mother & ourselves through all eternity."[52]

William Crawford thought that Amelia would say that she had lived a happy and pleasant life. She did "her duty and live[d] a most useful life doing a woman's work in this world."[53] Amelia's life demonstrated that opportunity had "little to do with happiness. We all have opportunity every day. When we get up every morning the days work is before us. If we do that to the best of our ability we have accomplished just as much as the greatest of men. Mother acted all through life as if she appreciated this," doing "each days duties efficiently and cheerfully." He saw much unhappiness caused "by men sitting with folded hand & bemoaning" lost opportunities. The past was gone, but the duties for tomorrow were as "clear as if we had not failed yesterday. . . . If Mother did not formulate such a philosophy," he added, "she certainly lived it."[54]

Josiah's decision to open an ironworks in the Alabama wilderness represented one of the great sacrifices in Amelia's life. Josiah had been aware from the early days of their marriage of Amelia's preference for city life. In 1854 he wrote her, "I dislike the country nearly as much as you do."[55] After the war, Josiah changed his mind, but Amelia did not: "I know you abhor the country, & yet with our limited means city life would be simply *absurd*." "You like the city, I the country. We shall have to compromise by getting a country home where we can live during the summer, & I must examine some vocation which will take me to the city in winter. . . ." Josiah confided to his journal that he was "almost afraid to bring her" to Brierfield, "so desolate" did the place look.[56] Amelia freely confessed her preferences: "I *hanker* after the city though *upon my honor* I am perfectly willing to live in the country if you prefer."[57]

Indeed, she was "willing to go to the *woods*" if Josiah's "interest or happiness" could be promoted, and they "could *only be together*." The "want of churches, schools, society" did not "intimidate" her.[58] Amelia detested the isolation of living in the country; yet, with grace and no complaint, she went to Brierfield. There is no evidence or even a hint in Josiah's journal or in the voluminous Gorgas correspondence that Amelia ever consciously or unconsciously resented Josiah's decision to go to Brierfield, where, Josiah said, all their high hopes "burned to ashes in my mouth." Amelia never questioned her husband's prerogative to decide where the family should live. "As to our future," she wrote, "I know you will decide for the best. I am willing to do any thing, go any where you think best."[59]

The other ultimate test of Amelia's generosity and sacrifice came when her eldest son, Willie, whom she called her "chief jewel," "her dearest child," and her "first-born darling,"[60] confessed his love for a Cincinnati lady, Marie Doughty. The reaction of Amelia, a die-hard Confederate widow, was swift as she confronted head-on the issue of her beloved son marrying a northern girl in the 1880s. She invited Marie to Tuscalooa for a visit and wrote her son, "I want you to marry the woman you love & who loves you setting aside all preferences of the family. Your wife will be my daughter & I shall love her as such."[61] When Marie arrived in Tuscaloosa, she had held her ardent suitor at bay for over two years. However, in "one second," Amelia's "gracious manner" captured the girl's heart. Marie always insisted that she "fell in love" with Amelia before she did with William Crawford. "That Mrs. Gorgas could so entirely forget self in her desire to further the happiness of her son in love with a young Northern girl . . . showed as perhaps nothing else the strength of her beautiful and unselfish character."[62]

After Marie and William Crawford were married, Amelia treated Marie as she had promised, as her daughter, not as a rival for her son's affection. The relationship between the women was such that when Marie was to have a child, she came to Amelia, while William Crawford was stationed hundreds of miles away at Pensacola. Years later, Amelia wrote her daughter-in-law, "my son's wife is a dear daughter to me & makes her husband happy & what more could a Mother ask." Amelia never stinted on praise for Marie's contributions to William Crawford's successful career "I well know dear Marie, how much you have added to the success & popularity, socially, of my dear 'Boy' & what a comfort & support you are in every way to him."[63] Amelia's letters to Marie always closed with "Fondly your mother," or "Devotedly your mother."

In later years, the adoring son remembered his mother as one capable of living in the highest places in life. Yet the Civil War had dashed such possibilities. "She would certainly have made a most brilliant lady of the White House" or adorned any other position. "But she always seemed to be perfectly content wherever she was. I doubt if the lack of the life she loved caused her any particular unhappiness." She was "entirely unconscious of unusual ability or that she had any complaint against fortune."[64] "The lovable part of her character was that she never had to 'cast her heart.' When she made sacrifices she was so entirely occupied with the good [that] she did others that she did not feel her own pain." She never seemed to feel that she was "making a sacrifice in her every day life, or that her children were not appreciative, as we very often were not."[65] Through these years, Amelia had created a haven for Josiah and a wondrous home life that forever glowed in the memories of her children.

By the early 1880s, Amelia's children were adults, and adversity made her university librarian. Now her mothering extended to lonely schoolboys, as she emerged from a private world into the public spotlight. At the university, she became, in the words of the *Crimson-White,* the student newspaper, the "College Mother" to the boys who "loved her and recognized her home as their own." It was "not that she did such big things or that she accomplished any remarkable reforms. . . . Her greatness lay in her ability to do the little things . . . that require great thoughtfulness—a mother's heart, not only big enough to hold close her own children, but also the children of other mothers."[66]

The *Crimson-White* described Amelia in the same terms as did her children, focusing upon "above all her sympathy." The yearbook dedication in 1896 commended her "Motherly counsel" and "words of encouragement." When alumni returned to the campus, "We must see Mrs. Gorgas" was often heard, as "men of all classes, father and son, went together" to visit Amelia.[67] They were interested in her because she had been interested in them at a crucial time in their lives, and although advanced in age, she "understood the very young."[68]

For her part, Amelia was in her element, as she loved the university boys. Her excellent health she attributed to the "quiet country life & the pleasant occupation" her position afforded her. "Such constant association with young people of necessity keeps me cheerful & hopeful," she wrote to her eldest son. She particularly watched among the students for relatives of old friends. For example, when Amelia learned that an old friend's grandson was to enroll at the university, she excitedly wrote Willie that she intended to "take a great interest in the boy."[69] A daily visitor to the library in the early 1880s was the son of another old friend. "I think he is a real Mother's boy," said Amelia, "& likes to come in just for a minute's chat with me."[70]

In the early 1900s, William Crawford discovered the extent of her influence when he thanked Congressman John Hollis Bankhead, Sr., for aid on a government matter. Bankhead replied that what W.C. could do in return was "to tell your mother that I helped all I could—that I did my very best as some return for her kindness to my boy when he was at the University." When William Crawford thanked Senator Edmund Pettus, the senator replied that he had aided him for "your mother." A grandnephew then at the university had written to the senator about Amelia's kindnesses to him.[71]

Relatives of prominent Alabamians were not the only university students to receive Amelia's loving attention. One alumnus, who became a distinguished University of Georgia professor, asserted that if he accomplished anything in life, Amelia deserved "no small part of the credit. My life," he said, "in this world and in the world to come has been lovingly influenced by her."[72]

As Amelia prepared to retire in 1907, university alumni presented her with a loving cup to express their affection. The occasion elicited an outpouring of congratulations from alumni, who agreed with the sentiments of the president of the alumni association: that her "influence and good deeds" would live and flourish "long after the youngest of us have passed away."[73]

When Amelia received a pension from the Carnegie Foundation in 1907, she selflessly gave the credit to her famous son. She proudly wrote William Crawford that a "gentleman" told her that he thought she had received the pension "because I was your Mother, which doubles its value to me."[74] Former University of Alabama students rejoiced with her over her good fortune. "What a company of 'your boys' from every county and every corner of the state . . . are radiant with this very same feeling!" wrote one. "Nothing could . . . so honor the state . . . [as] recognition of the inestimable services of one of her noblest and best women. I would be one of a multitude who retain ever vividly the most delightful memory of the goodness, the queenly womanliness, of dear Mrs. Gorgas & the University."[75] Another graduate wished Amelia a long life "to enjoy this honor as well as the love of all the old University boys throughout the state."[76]

During her lifetime, the university recognized Amelia's particular contributions to campus life by permitting her and her family to remain after her retirement in the house that had been her home for so many years. University president George H. Denny wrote Amelia that her presence on campus was "a great favor to us." Denny, a man not especially known for his charity, insisted that the university pay her utility bills: "I am sure you will allow me to have my way concerning this. We are perpetually *your* debtor to a degree that cannot be measured in terms of dollars and cents."[77]

Condolence letters after Amelia's death described her impact on her extended family of university students. "I do not believe," wrote one alumnus, "any other person in Alabama, living or dead, male or female, has ever done as much for the young manhood of Alabama." During her years at the university, he continued, "at least ten thousand" young men "from every section of the state have known her and loved her, have placed her as a standard of excellence of tender, noble, womanhood. . . . One of the greatest privileges of being a student at the University was to know that consecrated splendid woman."[78]

Amelia Gayle Gorgas with her son Dr. William Crawford Gorgas on the steps of
the Gorgas home, Tuscaloosa, 1910. (Courtesy of the Hoole Special Collections
Library, The University of Alabama, Tuscaloosa)

Another wrote that the friendship of few people had touched his life so
deeply as had that of Amelia. He thought her "in many ways the most
remarkable person" he had ever known, and "surely no woman has ever
been the . . . inspiring friend of such a great body of young people as has
she." Her friendship had been an influence on his life that could not be
measured. A prominent Alabama attorney summarized the contributions
of Amelia's life: "In fullest measure has she left the world better for
having lived in it." After her death, William Crawford finally admitted
that his mother probably had accomplished more "real good in life by
her influence over the boys in Tuscaloosa than she could have accomplished in a more exalted position."[79]

A few years later, university alumni launched a campaign to raise
money for a new university library to be named in her honor. The Amelia
Gayle Gorgas Library remains as the only academic building on the
University of Alabama campus to so honor a woman.

If Amelia appears to be a candidate for sainthood, that image is what
emerges from the family manuscripts that span 1820 to 1955. The image
is too strong to be dismissed as merely the pattern of idealized motherhood of the late nineteenth and early twentieth century. Tens of thou-

sands of letters, the journals of her husband and two sisters, the memoirs of a nephew and a brother-in-law, and a book by her daughter-in-law depict family frictions and the very different personalities of the four Gayle sisters. Maria, the family beauty who enjoyed considerable wealth, was demanding and difficult to live with. The two widowed sisters coped poorly with life on their own and, after the deaths of their husbands, leaned heavily on family members for support, Sarah on her stepmother and Mary on Amelia and Josiah. After Maria Bayne died, leaving six children, Mary stiffened her resolve, moved into the Bayne household, and became a surrogate mother to Maria's children. Mary and Bayne never married. Amelia gave freely, to her family and friends and ultimately to her extended family of university students, her unqualified affection and approval; neither had to be earned. Approval was never a weapon of power in Amelia's hands. Amelia always welcomed the extended visits of members of her family. They were never a burden. Her behavior reflects that she understood the rule in the southern code that a hostess always entertains guests as if advance preparations for them were made without any effort by the hostess.

The only unflattering quality of Amelia that emerges from the voluminous existing sources is a touch of snobbery. This quality may be seen as Amelia described a postwar overture from an officer whom the family had known in Maine. Amelia reminded Josiah that when the officer had married, the couple had the "impudence" to invite the Gorgases. In 1865, the officer and his wife, living in Richmond, sent word through friends to Amelia that they "wished very much" for her to pay a call. Amelia's reaction was, "How vulgar & indelicate these people are."[80]

Amelia was always the source of moral and physical support for her family, nursing fragile health or bruised egos. If Amelia succumbed to or indulged in self-pity, unhappiness, resentment, or depression over her responsibilities, the Gorgas manuscripts, written from a variety of viewpoints over a long time span, do not reflect such feelings.

Nor does evidence exist to suggest that Amelia or the University of Alabama considered her to be a professional woman as university librarian. Her responsibilities were to catalog and shelve books and to check them out to students. The circulation book for the school year 1901–1902 survives, listing the books checked out of the library and the students' names, all written in Amelia's hand.[81] Who selected and purchased the books is unclear. Two other women followed Amelia as university librarian, and the post did not acquire professional status until the appointment of a professionally trained librarian (a man) in 1944.

Over and over again, family, friends, and students commented upon the loving sympathy that Amelia extended to them. To both her own family in her private world and to her extended family in her public world, Amelia represented a sympathetic listener and a mother who cherished her children and created a haven for those around her. It is her strength and the power of her personality that have made the Gorgas name familiar in Alabama. Tucked on the back of the cross that marks Amelia's grave in Evergreen Cemetery in Tuscaloosa and barely visible above the grass are words describing the impact of Amelia's life: "She sowed sympathy and reaped friendship, she planted kindness and gathered love." If there was a creed in her life, whether in public or in private, it was as her son William Crawford phrased it: "Love is the principle of existence and its only end."

5

White and Black Alabama Women during the Progressive Era, 1890–1920

MARY MARTHA THOMAS

During the decade of the 1890s, the women of Alabama created a large number of clubs and organizations that took them out of the home and provided them with a role in the public sphere. These women began to erase the line between the public and private world as they tried to ameliorate the problems posed by rapid industrialization. Julia S. Tutwiler was involved in every reform in the state, from improving education for women, to prohibition, the abolition of child labor, and prison reform. Martha L. Spencer, as president of the Alabama Woman's Christian Temperance Union, asked who was responsible for addressing the problems of poverty in an urban industrial community, while Elizabeth Johnston Evans Johnston of the Alabama Federation of Women's Clubs undertook to eradicate juvenile delinquency and to improve the treatment of juvenile offenders. Margaret Murray Washington worked in the black community to improve homes and schools in order to bring about the advancement of all African Americans. Pattie Ruffner Jacobs created the Alabama Equal Suffrage Association to fight for the right of women to vote so that these other problems would be resolved. These middle-class white and black women, working through their various organizations, sought validation for their members as homemakers and mothers and demanded a hearing in the political arena for issues that affected them and their families.[1]

The New Woman of the Progressive period was a product of the vast changes under way in American society as a result of increased industrialization and urbanization. The separate-spheres ideology that had been dominant during the nineteenth century was breaking down. According to this belief, women were restricted to the private sphere of the home and hearth, whereas men's sphere was the public world of business and politics. But by the 1890s, under the impact of social and economic changes, the division between the respective public and private worlds of men and women was beginning to disappear. The main result for middle-class white and black women was a dramatic expansion of opportunities to take their women's domestic concerns and values into the public arena. Female progressives directed their attention toward humanitarian and social reform—concern for child labor, long hours and low pay in factories, and unhealthy conditions in city neighborhoods. Women became a major element in the progressive reform coalition, creating organizations that confronted a wide range of social issues.

These middle-class women had many organizations with which to influence public policy. Beginning with the temperance societies, then followed by the women's club movement, women strove to fuse politics with their domestic ideals. Such an ideology also helped the creation and development of suffrage associations, which followed later. It was because of the efforts of women that governments increasingly took responsibility for improving the social welfare of citizens. Women's sphere was visibly expanded as a result of these single-sex associations, which were used by women to penetrate public affairs. Women moved from the domestic sphere into the public sphere, changing both in the process.

Southern women followed this pattern, although they were almost a decade behind their more emancipated eastern and western sisters. Women in the South first left home to work in the Woman's Christian Temperance Union (WCTU) in the 1880s. The main goal of these unions was temperance education, but the women soon broadened their agenda to include social issues of their day. The temperance societies were the first organizations to put southern women into the mainstream of American life. In the 1890s, southern women joined literary societies that had been formed for cultural purposes. They educated their middle-class members while providing an avenue to public affairs. By the turn of the century, club women had moved from self-improvement to concern with local and state issues and were engaged in a wide range of progressive reforms that brought them into the public arena. A major item on the Progressive agenda was woman's suffrage. During the 1890s, southern women organized suffrage associations and began to demand the right to vote, which was considered a far more radical proposal than any put forth by other women's organizations. The work of Progressive women was proof that women could be leaders and innovators in society. As a result of these new experiences, traditional gender roles were eroded. At all economic levels, women were breaking out of the confines of the home and entering the public arena.[2]

The first large women's organization created in Alabama by white middle-class women was the WCTU, which held its first state convention in Tuscaloosa in 1884. At that time, there were only six local unions in the state, the first having been established at Gadsden in 1882.[3] The WCTU grew rapidly, until a year later, it had twenty-four auxiliaries with a membership of 550. The greatest growth occurred after the turn of the century, when statewide prohibition became the major political issue of the day. By 1903, the WCTU began the publication of a newspaper, the *Alabama White Ribbon,* which provided a regular medium of communication between the unions and ensured more systemic work. In 1904, thirty-four auxiliaries reported a membership of 619; this number dramatically increased until by 1915, when statewide prohibition was adopted, over one hundred unions boasted a total membership of nearly 1,200.[4]

Women flocked to the WCTU for a variety of reasons. To begin with, temperance was viewed as a woman's issue because drink presented a threat to the home. The saloon was a male institution that was seen by women as a pervasive influence on their lives. A drunken husband could easily be a wife beater, a child abuser, or an irresponsible provider for his family. Temperance was also congenial with the dominant sexual ideology, the doctrine of the two spheres. Men functioned in the world of politics and commerce; women presided over the spiritual and physical maintenance of home and family. Women, as the protectors of the home and nurturers of children, had a compelling duty to save these trusts from external threats. Another reason was the presence of an existing network through which women could function in the temperance cause: the missionary societies and the churches of the several Protestant denominations provided already functioning female networks that could easily be converted into WCTU chapters.[5]

The Alabama WCTU embarked on an ambitious program as early as the first convention in 1884. The major thrust of the work was educational. The union aimed to teach the detrimental effects of alcohol and the principles of temperance to the Sunday schools, the public schools, and the general public. They encouraged the observation of Temperance Day, distributed literature, held medal and essay contests, signed temperance pledges, and attended rallies and speeches. They proposed that the churches use unfermented wine at communion services. They opposed the use of alcohol as a medicine and sought to educate the public to the dangers of patent medicines. They also tried to educate the public concerning the dangers of tobacco, opium, and other narcotics. By 1915, the WCTU had broadened its work to include opposition to child labor, establishment of industrial training programs for both boys and girls, and creation of juvenile courts. Members visited the inmates in jails and prisons, bringing them the temperance gospel and working for better conditions and treatment. They worked to secure the employment of police women and for the establishment of a women's reformatory. Their Traveler's Aid workers offered protection to migrating women and children. They established homes where friendless women and children could find refuge, and they tried to rescue "fallen" women. They carried their temperance message to black people, foreign-born people, railroad employees, and lumbermen. They encouraged members to wear their white ribbons, the badge of the WCTU, and to "Agitate! Educate! Organize!" These activities made the WCTU the major reform organization in the state. In 1900, Mary T. Jefferies of Birmingham, who was state president, observed, "The W.C.T.U. is favorably looked upon by the thinking people of the state, its influence being often solicited for movements which are for the betterment of conditions."[6]

Prison work attracted the energies of the most prominent woman leader of the state, Julia S. Tutwiler. During most of the thirty-two years she was a member of the WCTU, she was the superintendent of the Prison and Jail Department. Tutwiler was well known primarily as an educator, but she was involved in every reform in the state during her long life. Born in Tuscaloosa in 1845, she was the daughter of Henry Tutwiler, who was an early leader in education in Alabama. Julia was tutored by her father as a child, then attended Vassar briefly, studied in Germany and France, and took courses at Washington and Lee University. She taught first at Tuscaloosa Female College and then at Green Springs School, which her father had established. In 1881, she was made principal of the Livingston Female Academy, which shortly became the Alabama Normal College. Tutwiler was made president, a position she held until her retirement in 1910. She died in 1916. She worked for prohibition in Livingston even before the Alabama WCTU was organized; she worked for prison reform; she supported the drive to abolish child labor; and she was active in the early suffrage drive.[7]

Julia S. Tutwiler was primarily an educator serving as president of Alabama Normal College in Livingston, but she also worked for prison reform, the abolition of child labor, and woman suffrage. (Photograph courtesy of the Birmingham Public Library, Department of Archives and Manuscripts)

In the course of her many years with the WCTU Prison and Jail Department, Julia Tutwiler brought about many needed changes in the Alabama prison system. Alabama, like other southern states, used the convict lease system during this time. In 1893, Tutwiler described this system as "one that combines all the evils of slavery with none of its ameliorating features." [8] She was not successful in abolishing the system, but she worked to make life more tolerable for the inmates. She proposed the establishment of night schools for convicts and eventually pressured the legislature to provide funding in 1887. It was solely through Tutwiler's efforts that the legislature passed a bill in 1880 to provide heat for the jails of the state and to subject them to frequent sanitary inspection. She encouraged the state to provide separate facilities for women prisoners, which later became a reality. [9]

In addition to Tutwiler, another important woman leader who was farsighted enough to try to deal with a major problem of the day was Martha L. Spencer. Who is responsible for relieving the problems of poverty in an urban industrial community? Spencer posed this question to the Birmingham City Council in 1905. She had come to the conclusion that "the men of our city and State are indifferent to this question of the care of the dependent and defective and most of them seem to consider all efforts of this class a kind of woman's 'fad,' instead of an important social obligation." [10] She believed that care of the poor was an important obligation of the state, but if it failed to act, then private organizations would have to provide the necessary services. This Spencer and the WCTU did.

In 1892, the WCTU established the Mercy Home in Birmingham, a place of refuge for friendless children and women of all ages from the city and surrounding areas. Through its doors came victims of tuberculosis who had no families, women who worked and could not care for their children, children whose parents were in the hospital, pregnant girls, transients waiting transportation from the city, orphans, and delinquents. Spencer stated in her annual report for 1894 that "the sick, the helpless and hopeless, the semi-invalid and the aged, all appeal to us, and to each we endeavor to reach out a helping hand." The home began with an annual budget of just under $700. In 1893, it admitted fifty-nine persons and had an average of thirteen people in residence. By 1920, it had a budget of nearly $18,000 and had an average of seventy-five residents during the year. Margaret C. Ramsey, the longtime matron, managed the home with the help of two or three assistants. The adult residents were expected to assist in the work and to care for the children.[11]

Black women supported the temperance movement as well as white women and usually for the same reasons. African Americans desired to protect their homes and families from drunken, abusive husbands who deprived their families of necessities by wasting money in the saloons. They created a "colored state union" as early as 1886 at a convention in Selma. At that time, three unions listed a total membership of 285, which by the next year had increased to six unions with 324 members. They created only four departments through which to carry out their work, but in 1887, they contributed to the National WCTU $32.40, which was more than the white unions gave. The president, Mrs. C. C. Boothe, wrote that "we are with you in the battle against alcohol and I long to see the day when the colored mother, as well as the white mother, can shake hands and rejoice over glorious victories won for temperance." Helen M. Andrews, who worked with the students of Talladega College, said that temperance is the "only hope of the colored people" and that students need to learn the effects of alcohol and to let it alone.[12]

Despite this hopeful beginning, the Alabama No. 2 unions (as the black unions were called by the white women) did not thrive. By 1890, they had ceased to send in reports, and neither the national nor the state WCTU knew where to get information. In 1896, the national superintendent for Work among Colored People, Lucy Thurman, attempted to organize black Alabama women again. She met with success in Montgomery and especially in Tuskegee, where she found "an army of men and women numbering 1000" who wanted to sow the seeds of "temperance and purity." Encouraged by this situation, later that year Frances Willard (president of the National WCTU) and Frances A. Griffin of Wetumpka (who worked for the National WCTU at this time but later led the Alabama Suffrage Association) visited Tuskegee and were impressed with the leadership ability of Margaret Murray Washington, wife of Booker T. Washington. Willard and Griffin spoke at the meetings of Mothers' Clubs, which had been organized by Margaret Washington to teach African-American women the practical aspects of maintaining a home and family. They realized that Washington was the one to lead the temperance movement in Alabama among black women.[13]

Despite Washington's interest in temperance, she decided to use her energy and resources to organize the Alabama Federation of Colored

Margaret Murray Washington, founder of the Tuskegee Woman's Club, the Tuskegee Mothers' Clubs, and the Alabama Federation of Colored Women's Clubs. (Photo courtesy of Tuskegee University Archives)

Women's Clubs, which she accomplished in 1899. Thurman said of Washington: "She is full of zeal for the work, but is a woman with many cares." In 1900, the women of the Federation adopted a resolution at their annual convention, recommending the work of the WCTU and advising their members to start branch organizations in cities where temperance work had been neglected. Temperance work among black women then was carried on largely by the women's clubs. Separate unions for black women were few in number and limited in their activities. In 1903, Alabama No. 2 union experienced a revival led by Mrs. J. R. England of Birmingham, but it did not turn out to be long lasting. Since there were relatively few middle-class black women to provide leadership for organizations, they had to spread their abilities and energies over a wide variety of projects. Black women chose to concentrate their efforts on their women's clubs, in which they literally tried to "Do Everything."[14]

The largest organization in the state was the Alabama Federation of Women's Clubs (AFWC), which white women created in 1895. It was formed from literary clubs of Birmingham, Montgomery, Selma, Tuscaloosa, and Decatur, with an initial membership of 130 women. The federation shortly affiliated with the General Federation of Women's Clubs, which had been established only five years earlier. By 1915, the AFWC had grown to 153 clubs with an estimated membership of 4,250.[15] The typical women's clubs began by holding weekly meetings for lectures, discussions, and book reports. By the turn of the century, however, the thrust of the clubs had shifted to civic affairs, which shortly made the federation a powerful factor in the educational, civic, and social life of the state.

The first women who embraced the club movement did so with a certain amount of fear and trepidation as they moved out of accustomed domestic roles. A major concern was addressed in 1897 by Mrs. George M. Cruikshank of the AFWC in a paper entitled "Is Club Life at Variance with Home Life?" Cruikshank thought the topic would be of interest to men as well as women, because men doubted that women could unite in club work without shirking their home duties. Her answer to the question was that if women regulated their affairs properly, there should be no conflict between the two.[16] At first women were fearful of speaking out in public. Clara Berry Wyker said, "Do you remember, how afraid we all were of the sound of our own voices and how hard and often we had to swallow to keep that sound going." In 1906, a young delegate remarked that she did not know that women could speak out at a convention like men. She found it all very interesting and hoped she could come again.[17]

When, in the early 1900s, women turned their interests to civic and community issues, they were concerned with child labor and worked for its elimination. They sought to improve the educational system by making school attendance compulsory, by attacking illiteracy, by placing women on school boards, and by introducing kindergartens, manual training, and domestic science into the school system. They worked to secure a women's dormitory at the University of Alabama and to provide scholarships for women. They were instrumental in establishing industrial reform schools for both boys and girls.[18] They wanted to transform the state by creating a new understanding of what responsible government should provide.

Yet these club women were fearful of being identified with the objectionable "new woman." They did not see themselves as "advanced" or as supporters of "woman's rights." Even the term "club woman" was subject to wide differences of interpretations. They preferred to think of a club woman as "a home-maker in the broadest sense, her labors not confined to brightening merely her own fireside circle, but reaching State-wide, to countless homes where wretchedness and poverty sit side by side with ignorance and crime. It is here the Alabama club woman realizes her highest and noblest work."[19] Club women were playing a wider role, but they continued to do so in the name of the home and family.

One of the many social problems the women's clubs tackled was juvenile delinquency and the treatment of juvenile offenders. As mothers concerned with children and the family, they worked toward changing children's environments to improve the conditions under which they lived. Under the leadership of Elizabeth Johnston Evans Johnston, the club women persuaded the state in 1899 to establish an industrial school for boys at East Lake just outside Birmingham. Elizabeth Johnston, born in Greensboro, North Carolina, in 1851 and educated at Charlotte Female College, had moved to Birmingham in 1887 with her husband, Robert Douglas Johnston, and eight children. Both she and her husband became active in civic and philanthropic affairs in the city. She taught Sunday school for ten years in the prison camp located at the Pratt coal mine outside of Birmingham. She was appalled that boys, some as young as fourteen years old, were committed to prison for minor offenses and were housed with hardened criminals, especially in the day of Alabama's convict lease system. She decided she would establish a home for the training of boys in an environment that was conducive to good citizenship. Eventually the legislature appropriated money for the project, and the governor appointed a board of directors composed of members of the AFWC. Johnston served as president of the board from its inception until her death in 1934.[20]

As important as a Boys' Training School was to the AFWC, education had been a prior concern. Interest in the education of children came naturally to these club women, who saw themselves primarily as mothers. Their efforts were directed toward improvement of the public schools of the state by providing better-trained teachers; establishing qualifications for the county superintendents; attacking illiteracy; supporting laws to allow local taxation; placing women on school boards; securing a dormitory for women at the University of Alabama; introducing kindergartens, manual training and domestic science into the public school system; sponsoring libraries; and providing scholarships to help educate worthy and ambitious women.[21]

African Americans formed women's clubs at about the same time, organizing the first one in Montgomery in 1890. It was followed quickly by other groups, the most important and active of which was the Tuskegee Woman's Club, established in 1895. These clubs joined together in 1899 to create the Alabama Federation of Colored Women's Clubs, which affiliated with the newly organized National Association of Colored Women.[22] By 1904, there were twenty-six black women's clubs in Eufaula, Greensboro, Mt. Meigs, Birmingham, Montgomery, Selma, Mobile, and Normal. The black women's club movement had a distinctive mission, the moral education of the race; through the club movement, women intended to uplift all African Americans and took as their motto "Lifting as We Climb."[23]

Black women of Alabama followed their own agenda. The Tuskegee Woman's Club, under the leadership of Margaret Murray Washington, established a settlement school and cottage where mothers and children could take cooking and sewing classes. They held Mothers' Meetings to create among the women an interest in self-improvement and child development. They created a Reform School for black boys at Mt. Meigs and a home for delinquent black girls. Washington was instrumental in establishing the National Association of Colored Women in 1896 and later served as president of both this organization and the Alabama State Federation of Colored Women's Clubs.[24] In this way, black women demonstrated that they had the motivation and skills to contribute to the improvement of conditions in the black community.

The Tuskegee Woman's Club was an exclusive organization composed entirely of women connected directly as teachers or indirectly as wives of teachers with Tuskegee Institute. In March 1895, thirteen women attended the first meeting of the club, which was designed to improve its members intellectually, morally, and spiritually. Margaret Washington recalled in 1899 that "I said nothing of my plan to Mr. Washington or to anybody else beforehand, because I was uncertain as to how the experiment would turn out, and I thought if I failed I should not want anybody to know it." [25] Meetings were held twice monthly on the Tuskegee campus, and new teachers were encouraged to join. When the club celebrated its twenty-fifth anniversary in 1920, it had 130 members. The work was done through departments, some of the most important of which were temperance, night schools, community work, prison work, suffrage, Sunday schools, and mother's clubs. [26]

One of the most successful projects the Tuskegee Woman's Club undertook was the sponsoring of Mothers' Meetings or Mothers' Clubs. The idea for the Mothers' Meetings grew out of an experience of Margaret Murray Washington at the first Tuskegee Negro Conference in 1892. Booker T. Washington had called this conference to provide opportunities for blacks to discuss their problems and to seek solutions, and nearly five hundred people attended. While Booker Washington was trying to give the farmers new ideas, new hopes, and new aspirations, Margaret Washington realized that once again women were being ignored. It was assumed that women had no place worth mentioning in important concerns of life outside the household. Indeed, women themselves did not realize that they had any interest in the practical affairs that were being discussed by their husbands and sons. The thought came to Margaret Washington that the place to begin her work was with the women of Tuskegee and the surrounding area. When she realized that women came into the town on Saturdays seeking to vary the monotony of their hard and cheerless lives, she became determined to locate these women and utilize the time they spent in town to some good purpose. [27]

These clubs were aimed primarily at women who came to town once a week and learned their lessons in manners, dress, and morals from what they saw on the street. The purpose of these meetings was to create an interest among rural women for self-improvement, the betterment of their homes, and the development of their children. In this project the educated women of Tuskegee reached out to rural women who were less motivated to effect changes in their lives. Washington believed that teachers from Tuskegee Institute should spearhead the organizational process because they possessed the necessary skills. The idea spread quickly, and by 1920, hundreds of women throughout Macon County had attended the meetings. At most meetings, an average of fifty to seventy-five women were present.

The black women's club movement was led by middle-class women, as was the club movement of white women. But unlike white women, the members of the black women's clubs were often working women, tenant farm wives, or poor women. Thus, while the African-American women's clubs were equally concerned with education, self-improvement, and community improvement, they always placed a strong emphasis on race pride, on the defense of the black community and home, and on race advancement.[28]

The same factors that made possible the creation of the WCTU in the 1880s and the women's clubs in the 1890s also aided in the establishment of the first suffrage associations in the state. In 1892, women organized the Alabama Equal Suffrage Association with two chapters, one at New Decatur near Huntsville and the other at Verbena near Montgomery. Since large numbers of women had been drawn into club work and temperance work, these suffrage associations profited from a coattails effect. However, the suffrage drive presented problems that other reforms did not. Suffrage was seen as far more radical than temperance, child labor, or education. For these reasons, the first suffrage associations were weak organizations that lasted only about a decade. Alabama women flocked to the women's clubs and the temperance unions, but the suffrage cause had fewer supporters, at least in the 1890s.

The WCTU and the women's clubs were interested in reforms that correlated with their roles as wives and mothers. They saw their activities as an extension of the home and the private sphere. They in no way challenged the defined gender roles that separated the male sphere of the public world and the female sphere of the private world. They posed no threat to the patriarchal family. But suffrage was seen in a different light, because it called into question all the traditional activities of women. The suffrage movement demanded for women admission to citizenship and the public sphere of men. It demanded a kind of power and a connection with the social order that was not based on the institution of the family and women's subordination within it. By demanding a permanent, public role for all women, suffragists began to demolish the absolute, sexually defined barrier separating the public and private worlds. In the traditional or patriarchal family, a woman had been expected to subordinate her individual interests to those of her family; thus a husband could quite properly represent his wife at the polls, because a woman's interests were no different from those of her husband. But as voters, women could participate directly in society as individuals, not indirectly through their subordinate position as wives and mothers.[29]

During the decade of the 1890s, the suffrage campaign moved into the South. But the strategy behind the first stage of the campaign was not to argue for women's rights; rather, the suffrage leaders hoped to take advantage of the growing political movement to guarantee white supremacy. As in all issues in the South, race played a critical role in determining the strategy and even the timing of the southern suffrage movement.[30]

At this time, all southern states sought ways to disfranchise black men who had been granted the vote during the Reconstruction period. In addition to the usual devices of the poll tax and literacy tests, states considered the tactic of granting the vote to women; since there were more white women in the South than black men and women combined, the enfranchisement of women would greatly increase the white majority in the electorate and thus ensure white supremacy. Suddenly white suffrage leaders in the National American Woman Suffrage Association (NAWSA) saw an opportunity they did not even know existed. NAWSA organized a "Southern Committee" to establish suffrage organizations in the southern states. They even hoped that the South would actually lead the nation in the adoption of woman suffrage.[31]

At the 1901 constitutional convention of Alabama, which was called specifically to disfranchise black voters, the delegates briefly considered granting women the right to vote. Frances Griffin, the president of the Alabama Equal Suffrage Association (AESA), was actually allowed to speak to the convention on the subject. At first the convention decided to allow married women who owned property to vote upon tax and bond issues, but delegates changed their minds the next day and defeated the measure. The convention delegates had traditional ideas about women and women's role; they believed that a woman was the "Queen of the Household" and that if she departed from this role, the high standards of southern civilization would be jeopardized. After this defeat, the suffrage organizations fell into decline and virtually ceased to exist for nearly a decade.[32]

The second stage of the suffrage movement in Alabama began in 1910, when women of Selma created the Selma Suffrage Association, which was shortly followed by the Equal Suffrage League of Birmingham in 1911. These first two suffrage organizations can be traced directly to women's interest in two progressive reforms, prohibition and child labor.

Women were convinced that they could not attack these evils unless they had the right to vote. The two suffrage groups joined together in 1912 to re-create the AESA, which then affiliated with the NAWSA. Associations in Huntsville, Montgomery, and Mobile and in sixty to seventy small towns quickly followed, and state conventions were held every year from 1913 to 1919.[33]

At first members of the state WCTU did not support the demand for suffrage, despite the endorsement by the National WCTU as early as 1881. Indeed, the Alabama unions found this aspect of the national program to be an obstacle to organizing the state. The state corresponding secretary wrote in 1890: "You can not realize how that phase of W.C.T.U. meets us at every turn. It is the point of opposition when we solicit members or assistance."[34] At the 1885 state convention, a newspaper editor suggested to the delegates that women should demand the ballot and with it they could destroy whiskey. "If a thunderbolt had fallen it would not have created a greater sensation. The ladies at first grew indignant and uttered protestations." When they grew calmer, they adopted a resolution thanking the editor for his suggestion but maintained they were not ready to take such a drastic step.[35] However, by 1914, the WCTU did not find suffrage so shocking and voted to support the drive.

The AFWC had a brief discussion of suffrage in 1896 at the first convention, but the consideration of such a radical issue was barely acknowledged. By 1906, the president, Mabel Hutton Goode, stated that the federation had been asked to support an amendment to the state constitution enfranchising women. The convention voted at that time to table the motion. Ten years later, in 1916, the legislative chairman commented: "We women may not choose our lawmakers and may not ourselves attain that honor, but there is no power on earth that can prevent our telling them what we want and making things lively and interesting until we get it."[36] At last club women were beginning to understand political power. The AFWC, however, did not endorse the suffrage amendment until 1918.

African-American women also supported the demand for the vote. There is no evidence that they created suffrage associations in Alabama, but they did work for suffrage through their various women's clubs. Indeed, black women had a more consistent attitude toward the vote than did white women. By the 1890s, blacks tended to support a political philosophy of universal suffrage, while white women advocated a limited, educated suffrage.

The leading African-American suffragist was Adella Hunt Logan of the Tuskegee Woman's Club, who supported suffrage as early as the turn of the century. Logan soon became interested in the suffrage drive and worked for women's right to vote for nearly two decades. She was a life member of NAWSA as early as 1901. As a charter member and officer of the Tuskegee's Woman's Club, she participated in many of their activities, but her major work was on behalf of suffrage. She led spirited monthly discussions at club meetings and established a large personal library on the subject, which she opened to all who were interested. She worked regionally and nationally within the National Association of Colored Women to educate her associates about suffrage. She helped establish a Department of Suffrage within the organization and headed it for several years.[37]

Logan wrote that if "White American women, with all their natural advantages, need the ballot, . . . How much more do black Americans, male and female, need the strong defense of a vote to help secure their right to life, liberty and the pursuit of happiness?" She believed women especially needed the suffrage to demand that African-American children receive their share of public school funds. By 1912, Logan felt that more black women were becoming interested in politics and active in civic affairs. Under the influence of Progressivism, African-American women along with white women were beginning to realize that in order to be good housekeepers, they must be able to vote on such issues as pure food, sanitary and safe buildings, adequate school facilities, reform schools, and juvenile courts.[38]

With the creation of formal suffrage organizations in Alabama, Pattie Ruffner Jacobs of Birmingham emerged as the driving force behind the movement in the state. She served as president of the AESA from its inception until the ratification of the Nineteenth Amendment, with the exception of a short period when she was chair of the legislative committee. She made her debut at the 1913 NAWSA meeting, where she received recognition as the apostle of the "New South." During the crucial campaigns of 1915 and 1919, she was the association's chief strategist, and after 1915, she served as an officer in the National Association and worked closely with Carrie Chapman Catt.[39]

It was during the suffrage campaigns that the leaders and members of the various suffrage organizations had an opportunity to play their most public roles. Much of their efforts in early years had been spent in educating the public on the issue of suffrage. They made speeches, distributed literature, conducted essay contests, ran "suffrage schools," and held meetings. They became part of the suffrage network of speakers. Anna Howard Shaw, Jane Addams, and Charlotte Perkins Gilman visited the state and attracted large crowds. Kate and Jean Gordon of Louisiana, Belle Kearney of Mississippi, and Laura Clay of Kentucky were also frequent lecturers.[40]

In addition to supporting suffrage, the state association favored a number of other issues that were vital to women, such as equal pay for equal work, raising the age of consent to twenty-one (it was then twelve), abolition of child labor, an eight-hour day and minimum wage for women, mother's compensation, mothers as coguardians with fathers, and support for labor unions. The AESA reached out to working women in Birmingham by establishing a tea room at suffrage headquarters, where working women could come for lunch and buy tea for a penny a cup.[41]

The Alabama women conducted two major campaigns, one in 1915 to persuade the legislature to adopt an amendment to the state constitution enfranchising women, and the other in 1919 to convince the legislature to ratify the Nineteenth Amendment. Neither was successful, but in the process, the women learned how to organize the state county by county, to collect information on legislators, to conduct lobbying campaigns, and to work with a hostile press.[42]

Despite the defeat in the Alabama legislature, the women of the state celebrated the ratification of the Nineteenth Amendment on September 4, 1920, with a Victory Parade in Birmingham, which was viewed by over fifty thousand spectators. The emphasis now was on getting the women to register and vote. Citizenship schools were held in Birmingham and Selma instructing women in the basic concepts of government, and women also served in the general election as officers in the precincts. Even women who had opposed ratification urged their members to vote, so that by the time of the November election, nearly 124,000 women had registered.[43]

The AESA disbanded in April 1920 and was succeeded by the League of Women Voters. Women who had worked in the suffrage drive were in demand by the Democratic party: Pattie Ruffner Jacobs was appointed to the Woman's Advisory Committee of the Democratic National Committee; Amelia Worthington Fisk was the first women member of the state Democratic Executive Committee; and in 1922, Hattie Hooker Wilkins became the first women to be elected to the Alabama legislature.[44]

During this period, Alabama women learned the art of politics, perfecting the technique of lobbying their legislators and filling the gallery

Pattie Ruffner Jacobs, co-organizer and first president of the AESA, auditor of NAWSA, and opponent of child labor and the convict lease system. (Photo courtesy of the Birmingham Public Library, Department of Archives and Manuscripts)

with advocates for the various measures they were supporting. At first women were hesitant to push their programs and would not dare to testify before a legislative committee. For example, in 1899, when Elizabeth Johnston Evans Johnston wanted the state to provide money for a boy's industrial school, she had no idea how to approach the legislature; the only action she took was to speak privately with the governor. And in 1901, when club women adopted as their goal the improvement of the schools, they only wrote letters or sent petitions to the legislators, efforts that were either lost or ignored. But by 1915, women had become bolder and had screwed up their courage to deal with the legislators directly. During this session, women of the WCTU were on hand to lobby for prohibition, the Alabama Child Labor Committee and the AFWC were supporting a stronger child labor law, club women were also supporting substantial improvements in the educational system, and the AESA was pushing for an amendment to the state constitution to allow women to vote. Women from one group or another were in the capitol in Montgomery lobbying for their favorite causes and filling the halls and gallery. At first male legislators did not know how to respond to women who were so aggressive about their causes and who engaged in activities thought unsuitable for a lady, but the men, too, learned to cope with the new influence in state politics.

The white women reformers and suffrage leaders came largely from Birmingham, because it was there that the social dislocations that accompanied industrialization existed. Birmingham, as a city of the New South, with its iron and steel industry, its railroads, and its rapidly expanding population, experienced the problems of urban poverty and social injustice more acutely than other less industrialized areas did. Black women reformers were centered largely in Tuskegee, where most educated middle-class black women lived and worked at Booker T. Washington's newly established institute. It was from here that black women spearheaded the drive to uplift their race. Despite the similarity of interests of black and white women, these two groups never worked together but were always segregated, with each tackling the problems of its own race. Even by the 1920s, when women of both races began to work together in interracial committees in other states, there is little evidence that such cooperation took place in Alabama. The typical woman reformer, either black or white, was a married woman with children, not a single woman like Jane Addams, who personified the movement on the national level. These women usually did not confine their activities to just one reform but, instead, worked in a variety of areas. The same women who were members of the WCTU were also active in the women's clubs and sometimes in the suffrage drive as well. Black women tended to have only one organization, their women's club, which tackled reform programs in all areas.

Between the 1890s and the 1920s, the status of Alabama women in society changed dramatically. They first moved from the home to the WCTU and literary organizations at which time they became what can best be described as Domestic Feminists. These were women who employed the traits of the lady to justify their departure from home. They ended their confinement, took the ideology of the home with them, and began to influence the public realm. In short, they redefined the ideal lady and created the women's club movement.[45]

By the turn of the century, Alabama women moved from the study of literature to concern with a wide range of progressive reforms. They tackled a vast list of civic projects such as child labor, public health, industrial problems, prison reform, and educational reforms. They had enlarged their sphere and moved to a second stage of Domestic Feminism that can be defined as Municipal Housekeeping. But they still described their activities in terms of home and family. Women insisted that the good work they did outside the home would eventually improve domestic life. Club women had now attained public power and were even expected to use it.[46]

At the same time that club women began to occupy a larger public role, women who advocated suffrage also began to organize. Suffrage had never been a primary objective of club women. Such overt political participation was incompatible with their more cautious approach to obtaining influence through the invocation of women's traditional domestic qualities. But with the creation of the AESA in 1912, women began to agitate for the vote by lecturing and writing, by organizing political districts, and by lobbying state legislators. These women can be described as Public Feminists.[47]

In demanding the vote, as Ellen DuBois has pointed out, the Public Feminists were demanding political power and a connection to the social order that was not based on the institution of the family or women's subordination within it. These women were demanding to enter the public sphere as citizens and voters, where they would participate directly in society as individuals, not indirectly through their subordinate positions as wives and mothers. This view of women clashed with the traditional ideology of the women's role. For this reason, club women were originally opposed to the suffrage drive.[48]

However, by the early twentieth century, suffrage leaders shifted their arguments. They ceased to stress their view of women as atomistic individuals and instead stressed the role of women as wives and mothers. With this approach, club women became convinced that suffrage could do no more harm to the family and home life than club work did. The paths of the club women and the suffragists then united in 1914, when the Alabama WCTU endorsed suffrage and, more importantly, in 1918, when the AFWC voted to support the movement. The traditions of Domestic and Public Feminism then merged in the fight for suffrage.

By the end of the Progressive period in 1920, Alabama women had undergone significant changes in roles, life-styles, values, and expectations. The dividing line between the public and private worlds was disappearing. Women could now participate in the public world in large numbers. As a consequence of their involvement in the temperance drive, the women's club movement, and the campaign for woman suffrage, women could no longer be characterized as passive and dependent. They had gone forth from the home to deal with the issues of the day. Women's sphere had expanded; no longer bound by the ideology of the "southern lady," women were ready, able, and willing to participate in public affairs. Middle-class Alabama women had left the nineteenth century and were ready to step into the modern era.

6

Adella Hunt Logan and the Tuskegee Woman's Club
Building a Foundation for Suffrage

ADELE LOGAN ALEXANDER

"Government of the people, for the people, and by the people is but partially realized so long as woman has no vote," an African-American teacher from Alabama wrote in 1905. A few years later, this same woman, Adella Hunt Logan, further argued that "more and more colored women . . . are convinced . . . that their efforts would be more telling if women had the vote." These pronouncements are revealing and surprising only because not enough is yet understood about the southerners, both black and white, who involved themselves in the struggle for women's equal rights.[1]

The year 1848, more than half a century before Logan ever wrote about the importance of votes for women, may not have been the very first time that a group of American women had gathered together to raise and discuss concerns over their political impotence, but the widely reported conference that convened that year in Seneca Falls, New York, certainly was the first occasion on which they had spoken out in concert and made their voices so clearly heard. From that time until the woman's suffrage movement culminated in the passage and subsequent ratification of the Nineteenth Amendment to the United States Constitution in 1920, a number of African-American women and men wanted to, and indeed did, become part of that effort for at least three fundamental reasons. First, they believed deeply in the underlying tenets and promised inclusiveness of American democracy. Second, since black women often were victimized by both racism and sexism, many African Americans became convinced that acquiring the vote to gain at least some measure of political power was an essential step in helping to alleviate that two-pronged assault. And third, they considered universal suffrage a critical issue and an integral part of America's wide-ranging and ongoing moral and social reform efforts.[2]

In the middle decades of the nineteenth century, the great majority of black men, as well as all women, were denied the ballot in the South, where most African Americans were enslaved, and also in much of the North, where both law and practice treated them as second-class citizens. Nonetheless, several black men and one woman attended the 1848 Seneca Falls convention, where participants articulated and disseminated their demands concerning equal rights for women. In addition, throughout the country in this same period, a small but vocal number of African Americans expressed their support for woman's suffrage. Most of them were clustered in the politically "radical" northern urban centers, especially around Boston and Philadelphia, where men and women in several generations of some well-established and well-known African-American families were outspoken in their support of the issue. Like many whites who advocated woman's suffrage during the antebellum years, these black activists often had a primary interest in abolition, supplemented by a strong belief in equal political rights for all. Men such as the abolitionist and journalist Frederick Douglass formed coalitions with white reformers, but a number of black women, including the lecturer Maria Stewart and the vigorous and forthright former slave Sojourner Truth, involved themselves as well.[3]

In the years following the Civil War, a major schism emerged within the ranks of suffragists over the content of the proposed Fifteenth Amendment. Many white female reformers who had actively supported the abolition of slavery became outraged when politicians proposed a national voting rights amendment that included black men, who were only recently freed from slavery, yet excluded all women. The argument that it was "the Negro's hour" prevailed but created a rift within the woman's suffrage movement that would not be healed for more than twenty years. Political expediency and recognition of the importance of obtaining the ballot for the race convinced many black suffrage proponents to put aside the gender issue temporarily. During the 1870s and 1880s Frederick Douglass, a longtime colleague and supporter of Susan B. Anthony, among others, attempted to bring about a reconciliation between the two feuding factions, but to no avail.[4]

In the wake of this schism, most blacks who actively supported woman's suffrage allied themselves with the American Woman's Suffrage

Association, which took the position that it could advocate voting rights for black male Americans even while acknowledging that women had been unfairly slighted by the Fifteenth Amendment. On the other hand, outspoken members of the National Woman's Suffrage Association, including Anthony and Elizabeth Cady Stanton, sometimes vented their spleen through barely veiled racial epithets against African Americans, whom they viewed as ungrateful turncoats who had welcomed their support in the abolitionist movement but then abandoned women in their own hour of political need. Even during the decades that the rift lasted, however, many blacks remained active and vocal proponents of the issue of women's rights. They especially recognized and despaired over African-American women's lack of political power and continued to address the importance of universal suffrage, arguing that voters—black or white, female or male—made better reformers and better citizens generally, and that the progress and political empowerment of the race in its entirety required women's involvement.[5]

In 1890, the two feuding suffrage factions reconciled many of their differences and merged into the more inclusive and politically powerful National American Woman's Suffrage Association (NAWSA). During this same period, southern state legislatures adopted many Jim Crow provisions that, among other antidemocratic and racist results, increasingly stripped black men of their recently granted voting rights. The white women's club movement, which in most instances routinely denied membership to black women, both individually and organizationally, also expanded exponentially during these years. At least partially in response to their exclusion from the predominantly white General Federation of Women's Clubs, reform-minded African-American women around the country established their own clubs, and then, in 1896, a number of these local chapters came together to form the National Association of Colored Women (NACW), an alliance that would serve as their umbrella organization for many years.[6]

By the early twentieth century, a number of African-American women had become increasingly informed about and involved in suffrage matters through these clubs. They acknowledged an intensified need for the vote to help them retain at least a few basic political, civil, and economic rights, as awareness of and sensitivity to both black and female disfranchisement heightened, and as overt and legally sanctioned racial discrimination became entrenched throughout the South. A new generation of black women—among them, Atlanta University's Lugenia Burns Hope, the YWCA's Addie Waits Hunton, the crusading Chicago journalist Ida B. Wells-Barnett, and the indomitable educator and lecturer Mary Church Terrell from Washington, D.C.—became identified with the issue of votes for women. Within the black community, a number of women's reform organizations of all sorts (temperance unions, sororities, and church and educational groups, for example) included suffrage as one of many issues they supported. African Americans who, prior to this period, had mostly advocated woman's suffrage through verbal argument alone moved toward more organized means of participation.[7]

These black suffrage advocates, however, must have wondered about the beliefs, motivations, and support of some of their so-called allies in the movement when noted white spokeswomen such as Kentucky's Laura Clay and Mississippi's Belle Kearney developed and projected a racist philosophy for enfranchisement, which was designed to seek the vote for white women in order to counterbalance what they saw as the negative influences of black male suffrage, especially in the southern states. Kearney, in particular, argued on a number of occasions that the South was "compelled to look to its Anglo-Saxon women as the medium through which to retain the supremacy of the white race over the African." In the African-American community, on the other hand, *The Crisis,* the magazine of the National Association for the Advancement of Colored People (NAACP), for instance, recognized the commonality of African-Americans' and women's political disempowerment in a pithy yet lighthearted couplet, written in dialect, which read: "When it come ter de question er de female vote, / Der ladies an' der cullud folk is in de same boat."[8]

In spite of these obviously valid comparisons, many white women were reluctant to acknowledge any political solidarity with African Americans, especially after 1900, when they actively began to seek support for suffrage in the South. Early in 1913, for example, the combined forces of the woman's suffrage movement began organizing an ambitious parade for the nation's capital in hopes of influencing national legislators to pass the proposed voting rights amendment. For reasons of both political expediency and personal bias, some whites argued that black suffragists should be excluded altogether from that Washington march. "A few white women," reported NAWSA's *Woman's Journal,* "said they would not march at all if any colored women did." Failing that total exclusion, others urged African-American women to segregate themselves into a distinct assemblage at the end of the parade, and several groups, in fact, did march separately. Some state delegations, however, were more welcoming than others, and a few black women demonstrated their support for woman's suffrage by walking right alongside their white colleagues.[9] In this and in other instances, they were determined not to be shut out of suffrage activities. During these years leading up to 1920, several states, primarily in the West, also permitted women to participate in at least some elections, and, wherever they could do so, black women began to register and vote in substantial numbers.[10]

From the 1850s through 1920, there is no doubt that black women were widely discriminated against in their attempts to work for and to acquire the vote. In that same time frame, many outspoken anti-suffragists argued that, regardless of race, all women should be content to remain their husband's "helpmates," that they really did not either want or need the ballot, and that the "dirty" business of politics would corrupt their morals. Because of their race, however, black women encountered the additional argument that only the "educated elite" should vote, a position that was espoused by both white men and women, including a number of suffrage advocates. Many suffragists who embraced those beliefs considered black people—who always had far fewer opportunities to acquire an education—to be ignorant and otherwise unworthy of having and exercising the franchise. In addition, some white suffragists continued to blame African Americans for the failure to include women in the Fifteenth Amendment, and a substantial number doggedly discouraged any participation at all by black activist reformers within the ranks of their movement.

In the South especially, much of this rejection was grounded in intransigent racist traditions, the legacy of slavery, the backlash that followed Reconstruction, and also the purported "immorality" of all African Americans, both male and female. This characterization especially infuriated some of the more privileged and educated African-American women, who knew that these degrading assumptions not only fueled efforts to deny them the vote but also perpetuated their sexual vulnerability in a wide range of circumstances. Pragmatically, many white southerners also feared that in states where black people represented a sizable percentage of the population, large numbers of black women would rush to the polls once they had acquired the vote. Northerners, of course, harbored their own racial prejudices as they attempted to exclude African Americans from many suffrage activities and endeavors, but they also were extremely aware of southern segregationist customs and "sensitivities." Leaders of the movement argued that a national strategy for ratification of a voting rights amendment needed support from white politicians in at least a few southern states, and they feared that including black women within their ranks would wave a red flag at legislators from those states, thereby ensuring their opposition to the proposed amendment. At best, women of color enjoyed only intermittent and reluctant support from whites in the national suffrage organizations. Sometimes African Americans were tolerated; more often they were scorned, ignored, and even repulsed.[11]

Several consistent themes, therefore, characterized and directed the involvement of African Americans in the woman's suffrage movement. Black men and women, working individually and through organizations, participated in the movement from its inception through passage of the Nineteenth Amendment in 1920. At the same time, and in spite of the prejudice they frequently encountered from white suffragists, opposition to woman's suffrage was only minimal within the black community, and African-American leaders showed far greater unanimity concerning the importance of votes for women than did white leaders. In those few circumstances where they acquired the right to vote—as they did in a limited number of states and local jurisdictions and on certain specific referenda from around 1880 until 1920—black women went to the polls in substantial numbers. And then finally, the struggle to pass a constitutional amendment that would give all women the right to vote became a national effort, requiring the cooperation and support of white southerners who, by and large, not only were hostile to woman's suffrage in general but also adamantly opposed an empowered black electorate. This development, too, both influenced and circumscribed the involvement of African Americans in the struggle for universal suffrage.

The activities of one group of African-American women who worked for suffrage in Alabama's Black Belt can be placed within this overall context. The noted historian Rayford Logan characterized the late nineteenth and early twentieth century as the "nadir" for Negro Americans, and yet, even during those difficult years, these particular women were diligently trying to educate young people about the importance of their civic responsibilities.[12] They also were developing strategies to shape public opinion and reaching out beyond their home base of Tuskegee Institute to influence a larger circle of African Americans. In addition, they were beginning to build a solid community foundation that would support the democratic concept of votes for women, a concept that many Americans—especially southerners—considered a dangerously radical proposition.

In 1895, a number of faculty women and wives of Tuskegee Institute's officials met and formed the Tuskegee Woman's Club, an organization devoted to various aspects of community uplift, and then the very next year, their club became a charter chapter in the NACW. Among their other efforts, members of the Tuskegee group soon began to educate themselves in preparation for acquiring the vote, even though many people around the country and especially within the state remained convinced that the enfranchisement of women was only a remote possibility.[13]

Jim Crow laws enacted by the legislature and given additional authority by the revised state constitution of 1901 had systematically and successfully disfranchised most Alabama black men, and no Alabama woman of any race could exercise that basic democratic right.[14] The idealized image of the "southern lady" as pure, innocent, dependent, appropriately aloof from the gritty political hurly-burly, and, of course, always white still held sway around the turn of the century, even though this picture was a greatly distorted one. Only a few unusually progressive Alabama white women chose to address the issue of woman's suffrage, and Frances Griffin, one of those who did, characterized votes for women—white women exclusively, she hoped—as "a way out of the Negro difficulty." Not one white male journalist in the state openly espoused equal rights for women, and yet, in spite of this exceedingly inhospitable political and social climate, members of the Tuskegee Woman's Club began actively discussing the subject.[15]

Tuskegee Institute was situated in the heart of Alabama's Black Belt, far from any progressive urban center. To identify themselves with their region, "the badge worn by members of the Tuskegee Woman's Club," the NACW journal, *Woman's Era*, reported in 1895, "is a gold pin in the unique form of the state of Alabama, having a 'Black Belt' of enamel across the center with initials of the club and a star to mark the situation of Tuskegee." For many years, Margaret Murray Washington, wife of the famous Booker T. (the institute's principal and arguably the country's most politically influential African American), served as the chapter's president. By and large, its members were educated women who had attended Alabama State, Fisk, Atlanta University, Howard, Hampton, Tuskegee Institute itself, and normal schools as far distant as Massachusetts. Membership included neither students nor women from the town or surrounding agricultural hinterlands. By most prevailing standards, members of the Tuskegee Woman's Club were a privileged group of African-American women.[16]

Many of the club's concerns radiated from the domestic sphere, as did those of most other NACW chapters and a number of white women's clubs as well. Members addressed their attentions to a broad range of issues within the home, the classroom, and the community. They organized and led satellite groups of ministers' wives, "town girls," female students, and farm women. They discussed literature, religion, and history, opened a small lending library, advocated prison reform, and tried to educate the less well-situated women of the county about child and maternal health, education, hygiene, and nutrition. These matters, often referred to as "social uplift," represented a merging of the women's moral, material, and cultural concerns. The local club's work reflected the overall goals of the NACW and echoed its motto: "Lifting as We Climb." As an affiliated chapter, the club at Tuskegee Institute provided financial support for the parent organization and always sent delegates to its regional and national conventions. For many years, Margaret Murray Washington served as an officer of the NACW, and other Tuskegee women headed several subsidiary divisions as well.[17]

With greater or lesser degrees of commitment and intensity, most members of the club believed that women should have the right to vote. Their president, Margaret Murray Washington, concurred but somewhat softened her stand when she declared that "woman suffrage has never kept me awake at night." She was one of many African-American club women who devoted their greatest efforts to other concerns that they considered more pressing. On one occasion, the Tuskegee Woman's Club, in its entirety, officially took the position that "when the time comes for women to vote . . . the colored woman . . . will be educated along all lines enough to cast her vote wisely and intelligently." The club's active involvement in the suffrage issue began in earnest around 1897, when Adella Hunt Logan, a teacher and the wife of Tuskegee's treasurer, Warren Logan, initiated and then led regularly scheduled monthly discussions focusing on the importance of woman's suffrage and the progress of the movement. Logan also collected and maintained a substantial library of materials on the subject, which she readily shared with both club members and students alike.[18]

On occasion, the club also organized somewhat more comprehensive and formal "suffrage nights." One such event in early 1915 opened with an explanation of the "origin, development, and influence of the Woman's Suffrage Movement." The ensuing "lantern show" featured photographs of noted suffrage leaders, with each portrait accompanied by comments from a club member. "The picture of Sojourner Truth was greeted with especial applause," the institute's newspaper, the *Tuskegee Student,* reported. The leader of that evening's program told about Truth's participation at an 1852 convention. "When all sentiment seemed to be going against suffrage," the account continued, she "rose to address the audience, [and] by her magnetic personality and most unusual speech, she turned the sentiment back toward suffrage." The moderator then directly quoted Truth, who, more than a half century earlier, had stated that "if de fust woman God ever made was strong enough to turn de whole world upside down, all dese togedder ought to be able to turn it back and get it right side up again; and now since dey is asking to do it, de men better let 'em." Following that powerful quotation, Adella Hunt Logan rose to present the evening's featured paper, entitled "The Present Status of Woman's Suffrage," and the event finally concluded with the distribution of buttons and yellow streamers bearing the words "Votes for Women." [19]

Logan was the club's most vigorous proponent of woman's suffrage. Emily Howland, an enthusiastic white northern reformer and Quaker who visited Tuskegee Institute often and helped to support the school financially, had directed Logan's attention to the suffrage issue. In 1895, the first time that the NAWSA had held its annual national convention in Atlanta, that organization barred all African Americans—even including Susan B. Anthony's old friend and supporter Frederick Douglass—from its meetings. But Logan's interest was aroused when Anthony spoke that same week at Atlanta University, Logan's alma mater. "The people who feed and clothe you feel that they have a right to dictate to you," Anthony stated to a predominantly black audience on that occasion, then added, "some men even say to their wives, 'If you vote, you have to go elsewhere to live!'" Anthony's message inspired Logan, and later she wrote her friend Emily Howland, saying, "so few people look deeply enough into the woman problem to see that it is herself that the suffragist wants to free." [20]

Adella Hunt Logan developed an intense interest in the NAWSA, and Emily Howland sponsored and financed her life membership in that organization. Her role as an African-American member of the NAWSA, however, always was problematical. In late 1897, when Emily Howland's niece, Isabel, proposed Logan as a speaker for the upcoming convention in Washington, D.C., NAWSA president Susan B. Anthony's response to that request reflected both her assumptions about the inherent inferiority of black people and her unwillingness and inability to deal honestly and directly with the issues of race. Anthony's letter to Isabel Howland stated in part: "I would not on any account bring on our platform a woman who had a ten thousandth part of a drop of African blood in her veins, who should prove to be an inferior speaker either as to matter or manner, because it would so militate against our cause. . . . I do not in the slightest shrink from having a colored woman on the platform but I do shrink from having an incompetent one, so unless you know that Miss Logan is one who would astonish the natives, just let her wait until she is more cultured and can do the colored race the greatest possible credit."[21]

For many reasons, including political strategy and, most certainly, her own very apparent racial and class biases, Anthony was reluctant to have a little-known African-American woman appear on the platform at her organization's convention. In spite of this personal rebuff, however, Logan was neither discouraged nor deterred. She contributed annually to the NAWSA, attended at least one national convention, and wrote several articles for the organization's newspaper, *Woman's Journal,* which appeared under the deliberately cryptic bylines "A.H.L." and then "L.H.A." She also maintained her lasting admiration for the famed suffrage leader, and when Anthony died in 1906, Logan wrote her friend Emily Howland: "The death of Miss Anthony goes to my heart. Nearly all my life I have regarded her as the most wonderful of American women. It was such a privilege for me to know her."[22]

Adella Hunt Logan never considered herself anything but a "colored" woman, and she lived and worked as such within the African-American community, but because of her predominantly Anglo-American ancestry, she looked white. Her complexion was very pale, her nose narrow, her lips thin, her hair long and barely waved, and she used this somewhat deceptive physical appearance to her advantage as she pursued the political goals she championed for all women. In 1901, at the second NAWSA convention to be held in Atlanta, Logan arranged to have a private conversation with the organization's newly installed president, Carrie Chapman Catt. Afterward, Logan reported back to her friend Emily Howland that following her meeting with Catt, she discreetly entered the all-white general session, where she "could not resist the temptation to stay . . . a while, observing how the 'superior sister' does things." She further, and rather sarcastically, wrote, "you know a number of colored women would have done it more intelligently, and yet if they [the white suffragists] had known me [had known, that is, that she was not white], I would have been ordered out in no very gracious manner." Her correspondence with Howland reveals, beyond question, that Adella Hunt Logan engaged in the controversial and often condemned practice known as "passing," but at the same time, her comments clarify both her pragmatic reasons for doing so and her skeptical views of the racist attitudes

Adella Hunt Logan, suffrage leader and active member of the Alabama Federation of Colored Women's Clubs. (Photo courtesy of the Collections of the Herndon Home)

and behavior she observed within the woman's suffrage movement during her surreptitious attendance at an officially "all-white" event.[23]

Another discovery that may illustrate the ways that Logan moved between the distinctly separate worlds of African Americans and whites concerns some of her books. One of the possessions that she most treasured was a four-volume set of *The History of Women's Suffrage,* personally inscribed with warm regards from Susan B. Anthony herself, "because," Anthony wrote, "of my admiration of you and your work." These autographed editions turned up several years ago in the archives of Auburn University, just a few miles east of Tuskegee. In the early twentieth century, of course, that school at Auburn, Alabama, was a segregated white enclave. The Auburn University library has no acquisition records whatsoever for those particular books, leading to speculation that Logan might have loaned them to an unidentified white colleague in Auburn who had joined the local woman's suffrage club, which was organized in 1914.[24]

As an example of Tuskegee Institute's links with the wider world, Logan and others at the school had the opportunity to meet white suffrage proponents such as Julia Ward Howe. Howe visited the institute in 1894 in her capacity as a leader of the organization that the *Tuskegee Student* called the "Society for the Advancement of Women."[25] Members of the NAWSA came to the renowned school in Alabama's Black Belt as well, inspired by Booker T. Washington's prominence and encouraged by Anthony's colleague and Tuskegee's supporter Emily Howland. In early 1903, the school paper reported that "we are to be especially favored today with a visit by a number of the most prominent delegates in attendance at the National Suffrage Association which has been in session for a week at New Orleans." That convention in segregated Louisiana, of course, was closed to black women, just as the earlier ones that were held in Atlanta had been. The white suffragists who traveled to Tuskegee Institute on that occasion included Susan B. Anthony, Carrie Chapman Catt, Howland, and (according to the *Tuskegee Student*) "perhaps ten others." An assemblage of more than fifteen hundred individuals—"officers, teachers, families, and the entire student body"—welcomed the visitors by waving a "sea of snowy handkerchiefs." At the program's conclusion late that afternoon, all of Tuskegee Institute's female students "passed in review before Miss Anthony and received each a hearty hand shake."[26]

Logan gleaned what information she could from her sometimes deceptive relationship with the NAWSA and other outside contacts, and subsequently, she readily shared her knowledge and expertise with people at Tuskegee. She hoped not only to inspire her colleagues with the importance of the issue, but she wanted to inform and stimulate the students as well. With these goals in mind, she recognized and tried to take advantage of the value of participatory exercises for the school's young people. In early November 1900, for example, coinciding with President William McKinley's bid for reelection, she dropped Booker T. Washington a short note explaining that "my class in civics wanted to have a political parade tonight just after supper. I hope you do not object to such a demonstration." On that same occasion, Logan further asked whether "a few women teachers might be excused for a while from the faculty meeting [to] . . . chaperone the girls." "My plan is to make the meeting of an educative character and," she tactfully concluded, "we will try to keep reasonable order." The institute also debated against other schools for black Alabamians on, among many topics, the question of votes for women. At one such event, when Tuskegee was assigned the antisuffragist position, its team (fortunately or unfortunately) lost the debate.[27]

Beyond the gates of Tuskegee Institute, describing Alabama's white population as merely apathetic to the issue of woman's suffrage would be an understatement. Pervasive resistance prevailed during the century's early years. After a brief flurry of interest in suffrage during the early 1890s, virtually all attempts to gain the franchise for women ceased for more than a decade. Another indicator of the low level of support that woman's suffrage enjoyed among Alabama's white population in this period is that for several years the NAWSA's widely circulated newspaper, *Woman's Journal,* had just seven subscribers in the whole state, and three of those were at Tuskegee Institute. Furthermore, in 1900, Adella Hunt Logan became the state's first and only life member of the NAWSA. The next Alabama woman to acquire a life membership did so thirteen years later.[28]

Nonetheless, while the vast majority of white people in the state either ignored or openly opposed woman's suffrage, active discussion continued at Tuskegee Institute. And during these years when students debated the issue and the Tuskegee Woman's Club held regular monthly sessions on the subject, African-American women around the country not only advocated suffrage from within those clubs, which addressed themselves to a broad range of reform interests, but also formed separate organizations exclusively devoted to the matter of votes for women. Among these groups were Washington D.C.'s Colored Women's Franchise Association, the Topeka Colored Woman's Suffrage Association in Kansas, and the Colored Women's Suffrage Club of Los Angeles. Similarly focused associations also sprang up in cities such as Memphis, Boston, Charleston, New York, St. Louis, and New Orleans.[29]

Speaking for herself and representing Tuskegee Institute and particularly its woman's club, Adella Hunt Logan also presented a number of lectures on suffrage during the early years of the twentieth century. None of the texts of these talks has survived, but program listings document her regular appearances at the Alabama Federation of Colored Women's Clubs, the Southern Federation of Colored Women's Clubs, and the NACW national conventions between 1900 and 1914.[30]

In addition, Logan wrote two articles about suffrage directed toward a national audience. The first, "Woman Suffrage," was published by the *Colored American* magazine in September 1905. On that occasion Logan argued that "all governments derive their just powers from the consent of the governed." "The power that coerces," she continued, "that controls without consent is unjust." She firmly believed that suffrage was an issue that especially should concern African-American women, and she stated: "If white American women with all their natural and acquired advantages need the ballot, that right protective of all other rights; if Anglo-Saxons have been helped by it—and they have—how much more do black Americans, male and female, need the strong defense of a vote to secure their right to life, liberty, and the pursuit of happiness."[31]

Logan's second article, "Colored Women as Voters," appeared in 1912 as part of a wide-ranging colloquium on woman's suffrage featured in the NAACP's magazine, *Crisis*. In that forum, she argued that black women would be well prepared to vote once they had the opportunity, because "more and more colored women are studying public questions and civics." "As they gain information and have experiences in their daily vocations and in their efforts for human betterment," she went on, "they are convinced . . . that their efforts would be more telling if [they] had the vote." "But without a vote," Logan continued, a woman "has no voice in educational legislation, and no power to see that her children secure their share of public school funds." She further suggested that African-American women clearly were prepared to prove themselves good citizens. In states where women already had the ballot, Logan wrote, the black woman "is reported as using it for the uplift of society and the advancement of the State." "Women who see that they need the vote see also that the vote needs them," she concluded, adding that "colored women feel keenly that they may help in civic betterment."[32]

Writing from her home deep in Alabama, Logan addressed a national readership through these articles, but members of the black educated class also traveled to Tuskegee in substantial numbers. A large group of influential African Americans, for example, gathered at the institute to attend a conference of the National Medical Association (NMA) in August 1912.[33] In those years, that organization included not only physicians, but also virtually every African-American dentist and pharmacist in the country. Booker T. Washington, other Tuskegee officials, and members of Alabama's host delegation greeted and addressed the visiting group, and the stimulating three-day agenda included lectures, clinics, discussions on public health, preventive medicine, infant and child care, surgical techniques, and "modern" dentistry. These symposiums, of course, directly reflected the purposes, goals, and interests of the NMA and they were predictable components of any such medical conference. In addition, however, one unexpected and unrelated event presented by the institute's Hospital Aid Society highlighted the convention's welcoming pageant.[34]

Not coincidentally, perhaps, the "directrix" of those opening ceremonies was Tuskegee's new head of the women's physical education program, Ruth Logan, who was Adella Hunt Logan's oldest daughter. The gala pageant featured first aid demonstrations, tableaux representing "Education" and "Prevention of Disease," and folk dancing as well, but the afternoon's pièce de résistance was a rousing "Suffragette Parade." To support the student marchers, all of the visiting dignitaries and conference participants received program inserts printed with the words for a "sing-along" entitled "Just as Well as He," intended to be sung to the tune of "Coming through the Rye." The clever, though sometimes awkward, lyrics included the stanzas:

> If a body pays the taxes,
>   Surely you'll agree
> That a body earns the franchise
>   Whether he or she.
>
> Every man now has the ballot;
>   None you know have we,
> But we have brains and we can use them
>   Just as well as he.
>
> If a home that has a father
>   Needs a mother too,
> Then every state that has men voters
>   Needs its women too.

Man now makes the laws for woman,
Kindly too, at that,
And they often seem as funny
As a man-made hat.[35]

Not only the suffrage demonstration at that particular NMA convention but also other efforts that originated at Tuskegee Institute and
concerned gaining the franchise for women reverberated far beyond the
small group of Tuskegeeites who belonged to the local woman's club.
Within the school itself, information about woman's suffrage was disseminated to a younger generation of students, who learned about the
positive operations, as well as the shortcomings, of American democracy
in lectures and through participatory exercises and debates. Also, club
members—Adella Hunt Logan especially—lectured all around the country, primarily under the aegis of the NACW and its subsidiary components. In addition, Logan wrote articles about the importance of votes for
women, which reached a wider audience through national publications
such as the *Colored American* and *Crisis* magazines. And finally, of
course, because Alabama's Tuskegee Institute served as a magnet for
national organizations, people from the school could vigorously advocate woman's suffrage at large gatherings of influential African Americans and hopefully rally broader support for the cause.

During these years, Adella Hunt Logan had a protegée at Tuskegee, a
young teacher named Bess Bolden Walcott, who arrived at the institute in
1907 from Oberlin College, which she described as a "hot bed of suffrage
activity." Logan and Walcott's mutual concern with equal rights for
women helped to forge a strong bond between them. In 1898, Logan had
written a poignant letter to her friend Emily Howland saying that she
hoped someday to "see my daughter vote right here in the South," but
she died in 1915 at the age of fifty-two, five years prior to passage of the
Nineteenth Amendment. Nonetheless, some of the seeds planted by
Logan and other members of the Tuskegee Woman's Club survived even
in the politically infertile soil of Alabama's Black Belt. Although Adella
Hunt Logan did not live to see her daughter vote, Bess Bolden Walcott
remembered well her own first vote in 1920.[36]

Superior political negotiator that he always was, Booker T. Washington had managed to establish some tenuous agreements based on
mutual self-interest between his institute and the white-controlled town
of Tuskegee—which otherwise, of course, was hardly a mecca of racial
enlightenment. As a result of Washington's efforts, however, Tuskegee
was one of the few municipalities in Alabama where some African-

American men (though only those associated with the institute who managed to acquire both property and an education) could vote even during the most repressive period of Jim Crow rule.[37] When the time came, therefore, a small but determined number of women from the school were prepared to follow their male colleagues' example.

In 1920, shortly after the Nineteenth Amendment had become the law of the land, Adella Hunt Logan's friend Bess Bolden Walcott and three female associates from Tuskegee Institute buggied the short distance into town. "When the four of us went in to register," Walcott recalled in 1982, when she was in her late nineties, "the clerk said to me, 'Miz Walcott, I wish the white ladies in town here were as interested in voting as you women from out at the Institute.'"[38] This determination to exercise the franchise was one of the important and lasting legacies of Adella Hunt Logan and the Tuskegee Woman's Club, which had helped to build a solid foundation for suffrage among African-American women in the Deep South.

Ironically, the statement made by that somewhat unexpectedly welcoming white courthouse clerk in Tuskegee, Alabama, also illustrates one problem that African-American women faced and, paradoxically, may have generated themselves in the period after 1920. A number of white southerners correctly feared that many white women cared about voting far less than black women did, although two decades earlier, even Logan had expressed her own concerns that they were "a very needy class of women who are slow to believe that they might get any help from the ballot."[39] But when voting rights for women became a reality, African-American women in many communities attempted to register and vote in proportionately larger numbers than their white counterparts. In response to this perceived challenge to their hegemony, many southern whites employed the same kinds of exclusionary tactics that they had long used to keep black men politically powerless: physical and economic intimidation, poll taxes, educational and "character" requirements, and, finally, the "white" Democratic primary. Many southerners never wanted to see any females become enfranchised, black women least of all, but when all American women supposedly acquired the right to vote based on gender, African-American women still encountered massive barriers to equality because they were black.[40]

The Nineteenth Amendment to the Constitution gave women the right to vote in 1920, but very few black women in Alabama and elsewhere throughout the South were able to exercise the franchise and to take advantage of that hard-won privilege for more than another four decades. The obstacles to voting that they had once faced as women had come down, but the almost insurmountable barriers they came up against because of their race remained rigidly in place—often enforced by stringent and even brutal methods—at least until the great changes brought about by the titanic efforts of African Americans in the civil rights movement and passage of the historic federal civil rights acts during the second American revolution of the 1960s. During that turbulent decade, Alabama's black women recognized the importance of acquiring and exercising the franchise, and many of them, in fact, may have worked even more diligently to achieve their objectives than had some pioneering members of the Tuskegee Women's Club more than half a century earlier.[41]

7

From Parsonage to Hospital
Louise Branscomb
Becomes a Doctor

NORMA TAYLOR MITCHELL

When thirty-year-old Louise Hortense Branscomb came home to Birmingham, Alabama, in 1931 to open her private practice of obstetrics and gynecology, she faced a bleak prospect. The economy of the United States was still spiraling downward in the greatest depression in the nation's history. Among America's industrial cities, none was suffering more than Birmingham, which President Roosevelt later called "the worst hit town in the country."[1]

Even without the havoc of the Great Depression, Birmingham's class consciousness, racism, sexism, and violence made it an uninviting place for a professional woman. During her seven years of medical training in Baltimore, Philadelphia, England, Ireland, and France, colleagues had questioned the wisdom of Branscomb's plan to return to "'Bad Birmingham,' the city of minerals and murder" to practice medicine. Of the eight women in her medical school class, she would be the only one to establish a practice in the Southeast.[2]

Developments in the American medical profession also made her prospects bleak. In the late nineteenth century, the significant woman's medical movement had pried open the medical profession for women, establishing women's medical colleges and achieving medical coeducation at schools such as the University of Michigan and Johns Hopkins University. Optimistic expectations about the future of women in medicine had seemed well founded as the new century began.[3] These developments, however, reached their peak in 1910, when women physicians represented 6 percent of all the physicians in the nation. From that time, the percentage would shrink, declining to 4.4 percent in 1930 and not climbing back to "the magic 6 per cent" until 1950. In his report on American medical education for the Carnegie Foundation in 1910, Dr. Abraham Flexner noted the decrease already evident in the numbers of women applying to medical schools. Some leaders in women's medical education, however, continued to talk and write hopefully about the future for women doctors.[4]

When Louise Branscomb decided to seek medical education in 1924, she was aided by the achievements and the optimism that were the legacy of the nineteenth-century women's medical movement, but she would study and practice medicine amidst the worsening realities for twentieth-century women physicians. Beginning their medical careers at this transition point, she and another female medical student at Johns Hopkins who had observed the bitterness of some alumnae pledged to each other that they would never become "bittah" women doctors.[5]

Despite her strong resolve, young Dr. Branscomb's homecoming to Birmingham was bleak for personal as well as for professional reasons. In 1931, she and her large family were mourning the loss of her father. The Reverend Lewis Capers Branscomb, a distinguished Methodist minister in the North Alabama Conference, had died the year before in a Jasper hospital of complications from injuries in an automobile accident. Louise's daughterly sorrow was deepened by her unrealistic but powerful feeling that as a physician she should have been able to prevent her father's death.[6]

Amidst all these discouragements, Dr. Branscomb set out to establish her medical practice. To help her, she had outstanding resources. Her decision to become a doctor had been her independent choice, made not as the fulfillment of a childhood ambition or at anyone else's urging, but on her own in a three-year period after her graduation from the Woman's College of Alabama in Montgomery.[7] While she taught school in Russellville, Alabama, and Dallas, Texas, and then did graduate work in biology at Barnard College in New York, she carefully considered the alternatives for her life. One of these alternatives, becoming a traditional southern wife and mother, was a real one for her, since she had several suitors. Although she had never been a "belle," she was a lively and lovely young woman, who had many friends, such as Tupper Lightfoot, son of a wealthy Methodist banking family in Brundidge, Alabama. She had seen the satisfactions, as well as the burdens, of married life in her parents' home. Neither then nor later did she decide never to marry. Instead, she judged that it was not yet the right time for her to marry; life as a young single woman held so much exciting promise that she did not want to cut it short.[8]

By this time, Branscomb evidenced the ability, which was to characterize her the rest of her life, to interact creatively with her large family as well as many other people without allowing them to pressure her as she made major decisions. Branscomb primarily credits her father with nurturing her independent judgment and her self-esteem. From the time she was ten or eleven years old, he had engaged her in serious discussions of private and public issues, talking to her as if she were "a person who had good sense."[9] The diaries that she kept from the time she was thirteen until she graduated from college reveal her development into a self-confident woman who thought for herself and who aspired to high achievement.[10] In the mostly male medical profession, she expected that she would find the kind of intellectual stimulation and respect that she knew in her relationship with her father.[11]

Growing up in a Methodist parsonage, Branscomb absorbed her parents' deep concern to be of service to other people. In the family tradition, that commitment to service was associated with Louise Branscomb's birth. On Monday, March 25, 1901, a severe storm hit Birmingham, killing nineteen people, injuring more than one hundred, and causing widespread property damage. During that terrifying day, twenty-four-year-old Minnie McGehee Branscomb, pregnant with her first child, went into labor unexpectedly and gave birth to a girl, named Louise Hortense. Mrs. Branscomb's husband of one year, the pastor of St. John's Methodist Episcopal Church, South, missed much of the crisis in his own home because he was out helping the families of two of his parishioners who had been killed in the storm.[12] Devoted to his congregation, Louise Branscomb's father took his role as a pastor seriously. Branscomb recalls that when she discussed her intention to become a doctor with her father, his initial opposition eventually gave way to a conclusion that she had had a divine calling to medicine, as he had had to the pastoral ministry.[13]

To her vocation Branscomb brought physical stamina developed in swimming and playing basketball. Years later, reflecting on her decision to become a surgeon, she noted that the operating room promised a professional blend of the teamwork and excitement that had exhilarated her on the basketball courts at Central High School in Birmingham and at the Woman's College of Alabama.[14]

To the practice of medicine Branscomb also brought the self-confidence of having achieved a medical degree from Johns Hopkins

University, probably the most prestigious medical school in America at the time. Having chosen medical coeducation rather than a woman's medical college, she prepared to swim in the mainstream of the male-dominated medical profession rather than in what she perceived to be the backwaters of a separate female medical profession. From the beginning, Branscomb was, in the terms used by a major historian of women physicians, an assimilationist, not a separatist. Although she had welcomed the recent extension to American women of the right to vote, she did not think of herself as a participant in the women's rights movement. Fifty years later, she would be a leader in the women's liberation movement, but as a young professional woman in the 1920s, she had no interest in joining separate women's medical organizations.[15] Yet she owed her opportunity for an excellent medical education partly to the nineteenth-century women's medical movement. The applications of Branscomb and of seven other women who entered Johns Hopkins Medical School in 1924 received fair consideration, because at the school's opening in 1893, it had received a vital contribution of $400,000, raised by a group of prominent women. In return, the women had secured the pledge that Johns Hopkins would consider the applications of women on the same terms as those of men.[16]

Louise Branscomb also owed her opportunity for her excellent medical education partly to her family. When she decided to go to medical school, her older half-brother, Harvie, who had been a Rhodes Scholar and was now a seminary professor, agreed to lend her the money. But when their father heard of this plan, he insisted on paying his daughter's expenses. The generous income that he had long received from his prestigious positions in Alabama Methodism, the habits of frugality that he and his wife had practiced, and the wise investments that they had made in the Stockham Pipe and Fittings Company of Birmingham gave L. C. and Minnie Branscomb the means to help Louise and all of their children pursue their educational goals.[17]

Branscomb's justifiable pride in winning admission to Johns Hopkins, one of the three coeducational medical schools to which she applied, was somewhat deflated after she arrived in Baltimore. At a dinner party, she learned that the scholarly reputation of her half-brother, Harvie, had tipped the decision in her favor among the highly competitive applicants.[18]

When Branscomb returned to Birmingham in 1931 to establish her medical practice, her large family and many friends continued to support her. She moved in with her mother and her sister Allene and brother

Lamar. For the next thirty years, she and her mother would usually make their home together. As a widow, "Miss Minnie" devoted herself to caring for their home and to being a helpful companion to "my daughter, the doctor," at the same time that she respected her daughter's independence. Always an expert manager, Mrs. Branscomb helped her daughter in many practical ways. Other members of the family were also supportive, although they sometimes threatened Louise's independence. Brother Lamar initially insisted on accompanying her to night calls until she convinced him that she could and would take care of herself.[19]

The Branscomb name opened doors for her. In her professional contacts, she benefited from her late father's excellent reputation in Birmingham and throughout Alabama. At the same time, her disagreement with some of his ideas, which had begun to emerge long before she went to medical school, was no longer constrained by his strong, sometimes dominating, presence. Although she had absorbed her father and mother's deep commitment to Christian service, she had long ago moved away from the bold evangelical piety that had marked her father's Methodism. As a teenager, she had confided to her diary, "I've thought of being a missionary. . . . But I can't keep close enough to the father myself." She had also expressed resentment of her father's refusal to allow her and her siblings to attend dances. And when her four-year-old sister Emily died from burns, she wrote scornfully of the interpretation that her death was God's will. This explanation, made at Emily's funeral by her father's close friend, Bishop James H. McCoy, and by her father himself in an article for the *Alabama Christian Advocate*, violated Louise's understanding of God. Thus by the time Louise established her medical practice in Birmingham, she had developed a Christian faith and practice different from L. C. Branscomb's, and with his death, she was free to go her own way.[20]

As Branscomb began practicing medicine, Birmingham's male medical doctors, trained in many specialties at the best medical schools in the nation, gave her professional courtesies. Several became her mentors. In 1931, before Branscomb returned to Birmingham, Dr. Howard Kelly, one of the "big four" faculty members at Johns Hopkins, paved the way for her acceptance by the city's medical community. A renowned gynecologist and a prominent member of the Southern Medical Association, Dr. Kelly invited Branscomb to attend the association meeting in Birmingham as his guest and introduced her to his colleagues. Since she had worked in his clinic in Baltimore the previous summer, he could give convincing firsthand testimony to her competence.[21]

The eight women of the Johns Hopkins Medical School class of 1928, pictured in 1925. Louise Branscomb appears seated, at left. Sadie Sue Veazey from Bessemer, Alabama, one of Branscomb's roommates at Johns Hopkins, sits next to her. (Photo courtesy of N. T. Mitchell)

When Branscomb arrived in Birmingham, two other women were practicing medicine there, although neither was in private practice. One of them, Melson Barfield-Carter, a radiologist, proved especially supportive. Practicing a specialty necessary to other doctors, and married to Birmingham's first cardiologist, Henry Carter, Barfield-Carter was in the inner circle of the medical community. She shared valuable information with the new woman doctor. As Branscomb struggled to pay her office rent in 1931–32, when her practice brought only four dollars the first month and her mother lent her money to pay her bills, she learned from Barfield-Carter what no one else had told her—during the depression, realtors were giving most doctors a moratorium on paying office rents.[22]

Right away, she also found an empathic colleague in Dr. William Cowles, head of the outpatient department at Hillman Hospital. Hillman was a public hospital for indigent patients, which had been enlarged just two years before Branscomb had returned to Birmingham. When she applied for admission to Cowles's staff there, he gave her a sensitive interview, seeking her opinion on a difficult diagnosis he faced. Drawing on her work at Johns Hopkins, she told him that his patient had "Cullen's Sign," an indication of a ruptured ectopic pregnancy. Impressed by her astuteness, Dr. Cowles not only admitted Branscomb to practice in his department but gave her a unique pledge of professional support. Assuring her that any young physician starting out in practice would need more experienced help at times, he promised that he would be available to help her "day or night."[23]

Soon after opening her practice, Branscomb also sought admission to the in-patient staff at Hillman Hospital. The head of this staff was Dr. John Wesley Simpson, a son of one of her father's closest friends, the former president of Birmingham-Southern College. Dr. Simpson surprised her by advising her to seek letters of recommendation from wives of several prominent Birmingham business and civic leaders. Protesting that she wanted to be admitted on the basis of her credentials not her connections, she nevertheless listened to the realistic pediatrician, who told her to get on the staff any way she could and then demonstrate her professional competence. Among the women who wrote letters for her were the wives of the presidents of the Tennessee Coal and Iron Company, Birmingham's foremost corporation, and the Stockham Pipe and Fittings Company, whose dividends had enabled her parents to give her a Johns Hopkins medical education.[24]

Meanwhile, her private practice grew slowly. Her first office, in the Protective Life Insurance office building at First Avenue North and 21st Street, was a single room divided by a partition into an examining room and a waiting room. She soon moved into another office in the Brown-Marx Building on 20th Street and First Avenue North, where she shared a waiting room with a male doctor, who was a nose and throat specialist. Both of these offices were within a mile of Hillman Hospital. Serving a few black as well as white patients, she complied with southern custom and the preferences of her office mate by having her black patients wait in a separate room. Later in her career, during the late 1940s, when she had an office entirely to herself, she would abandon the racial segregation of her patients.[25]

Among her patients were many public school teachers, to whom she gave a professional discount, and ministers' wives, whom she charged nothing. Although she attracted some prominent women from out of town as her patients and a few from Birmingham itself, her patients never came primarily from the city's rich "over the mountain" women. Like other women doctors, for many years she was not able to charge anyone as much for her services as male obstetricians/gynecologists did. Beginning her practice as a woman's doctor in the depression decade of decreasing numbers of marriages and a declining birth rate, she did not notice a scarcity of babies to deliver, only a scarcity of money to pay the doctors who delivered them.[26]

Nearly all her early obstetrical patients were white, because black women's babies were usually delivered by nannies or midwives. Most of her patients in the 1930s delivered at home because they could not afford hospitalization. One of the hardest parts of her obstetrical practice was finding patients' houses, especially at night. In home deliveries, no nurse was usually present, and the doctor did everything needed for the woman in labor, with whatever help family members and friends could give. Often she sat beside a woman in labor all night. These home deliveries, in which she was the only medical person present, were a great contrast to the home deliveries she had done at Johns Hopkins with several other medical personnel. Whether Branscomb delivered a baby at home or in a hospital, there was no anesthesiologist, and she usually administered the drop ether herself. In using ether dropped onto a handkerchief or napkin and held over the laboring woman's nose, she was employing an anesthetic technique developed in the late nineteenth century and widely employed thereafter, not only because of its effectiveness in pain relief but also because of its simplicity. By usually administering the ether herself, rather than having an assistant do it, as many doctors did, she was exercising professional care in what could be an inexact and dangerous process.[27]

Even before she had many patients, her obstetrical practice kept her on call all the time and made her feel tied down. She would have liked to have had a partner in practice, but she was never able to find one, since male physicians were not interested in a partnership with a woman. She always found it awkward to arrange for another obstetrician to substitute for her, so that she could have an evening or a weekend free. While male doctors would agree to substitute for her, they would rarely ask her to substitute for them. As a result, she was reluctant to ask for their help.[28]

In addition, many of her patients, both obstetrical and gynecological, came to her precisely because she was a *woman* doctor, and they did not want to be referred to male substitutes. Thus the issue of gender in the thinking of both her male colleagues and her female patients hindered her efforts to get some help with her practice. Often she felt isolated and alone professionally. Rarely did she participate in the easy camaraderie that she thought many of her male colleagues shared.[29]

Although Branscomb practiced alone and initially even kept her own books, she soon found a lively coworker in Anne La Susa, who became her secretary and office assistant. An Italian Catholic from a family of fourteen children, the vivacious young Anne, who also played drums in a dance band, enlivened the medical office and refrained from passing judgment on the Methodist doctor's contraceptive advice to her patients.[30]

The nature and development of Branscomb's practice in the 1930s are illustrated by her relations with the women of the Jones family of Huntsville Road in Birmingham. As Methodists, the Joneses were well acquainted with Louise Branscomb and her family long before she opened her medical practice. The Joneses' father, Charles Alford Jones, owner of a wholesale hay and feed company, knew and respected the Reverend L. C. Branscomb and introduced his three daughters to Louise when they were teenagers. The Jones girls visited in the Branscomb parsonage and continued their girlhood friendships with Louise at the Woman's College of Alabama in Montgomery, where Louise became Elizabeth Jones's sophomore and junior "sister." Elizabeth Jones Baum recalls that at the college "Louise was so smart . . . we went to her instead of the encyclopedia."[31]

Fifteen years later, when the Jones women were married and pregnant, they turned to the young female obstetrician, whom they and many others called "Dr. Louise." Margaret Jones Rawls, the most shy of the Jones women, led the way. She regarded going to a female obstetrician, who was also a trusted family friend, as less embarrassing than going to a male doctor.[32] Like many people during the depression, Margaret and her husband had postponed having children because of the severe economic crisis. When she became pregnant, she was thirty-one years old and had been married nine years. Although her pregnancy was normal, her delivery in 1935 at the Norwood Clinic in Birmingham became dangerous to her and her baby. It put Dr. Louise's judgment, nerve, and skill to the test. The baby girl "was bruised about the face and neck by the forceps" and still carries the marks of the ordeal on her face. But she grew up with the family judgment that Dr. Louise had saved the lives of both mother and baby, and as a result, the physician was so loved and respected that she was "almost a deity" in the Jones family.[33]

The next year, 1936, Margaret's pregnant sister-in-law, Ethel Green

Dr. Louise H. Branscomb in the mid-1940s, when she had successfully established her practice of obstetrics and gynecology in Birmingham. The original photograph is inscribed to Anne La Susa of Birmingham, Dr. Brancomb's office assistant of many years. (Photograph courtesy of Anne La Susa Madonia)

Jones, planned to have her baby delivered by Dr. Louise at home because she and her husband did not have enough money for a hospital delivery. Still recovering from her own childbirth, Margaret had announced she would not be able to be present at Ethel's delivery. But going in the back door of her brother's house and unexpectedly finding her sister-in-law already in labor with Dr. Louise present, Margaret complied with the doctor's orders to assist her; she administered the drop ether at Dr. Louise's direction. When the baby girl was delivered, Dr. Louise said, "Catch!" and thrust her into Margaret's arms.[34]

The youngest of the three Jones sisters, Rosalind, went to Dr. Louise during her first pregnancy in 1937. Like her sister Margaret, Rosalind had a difficult and dangerous labor and delivery. For three days, she was in labor at South Highlands Hospital in Birmingham before her son was delivered. In 1990, she recalled: "I think if Dr. Louise had not been so smart, he would have been brain injured. She finally cut me . . . to keep him from being injured." After her ordeal, Rosalind felt "real close to Dr. Branscomb. I thought she was just wonderful." When she was again pregnant the next year, she had no reservations about having Dr. Louise as her physician.[35]

In the following years, Dr. Louise would deliver more babies to the Jones women and help them with other medical needs. When five-year-old Leah Marie Rawls, the baby born to Margaret in the difficult delivery of 1935, had her tonsils removed by the doctor whose office was across the hall from Branscomb's, she recovered in Dr. Louise's office. She recalls:

> After the surgery I was taken to a cot in a large closet/small room in Dr. Louise's office. The room was like a lab, had a sink in it, and some other things. I stayed there all day. I do not remember my Mother being there—only Dr. Louise and her nurse—and they would come in occasionally to check on me. I slept some, but I also remember that I had crayons and a coloring book and some toys and I entertained myself and was alone all day until my parents came and took me home. I remember it being a wonderful experience, lots of fun, and I was never afraid of being there alone because it was in Dr. Louise's office. . . . For our family, Dr. Louise was more than just a doctor.[36]

Being "more than just a doctor" to the Jones women and other women whose babies she delivered in the 1930s, Dr. Louise invited them and their children to an annual party, which she and her mother hosted in the home they shared.[37] Clearly, Dr. Louise derived deep satisfaction from her obstetrical practice. As she later wrote, "I have always loved to get in from an ob. case at that time of day [early dawn]. There is something very satisfying about that feeling of having sat thru the night with a woman to help her initiate that new life. . . ."[38]

While her private practice was growing, Branscomb became a physician to the State Training School for Girls at Trussville, Alabama, and an instructor in sociology at Birmingham-Southern College in Birmingham, with which her family had had a long association. These two positions added to her income, to her experience, and to her opportunity to influence young women's thinking about sex, marriage, motherhood, and family life.[39] So well respected was the instruction she gave that by the 1950s some parents sent their daughters to her for premarital examination and counseling. She gave her patients a copy of *Preparing for Marriage* by Paul Popenoe, published in 1938 by the American Institute of Family Relations. This publication emphasized the wife's need of and right to sexual satisfaction in marriage, the husband's responsibility to promote his wife's satisfaction, the importance of contraceptive knowledge and practice, and the role of "regular, well-spaced pregnancies" in promoting health and happiness. Branscomb's use of this publication shows that, like other liberal health professionals of the 1920s and 1930s, she had moved "beyond reproduction" in her thinking about the role of sex in women's lives. With her various female audiences, she shared her conviction that women, like men, had a capacity for and a right to sexual fulfillment within marriage.[40]

Undoubtedly, the most difficult part of Branscomb's early practice was surgery. By specializing in surgery, in addition to obstetrics and gynecology, she had entered a medical field almost entirely closed to women. Like most surgeons of her time, whether male or female, she went into practice with only about three years of clinical training, in contrast to what would later become the norm of seven years' training. Her work on the Hillman Hospital staff actually served as her continuing residency in surgery. In those early years, she often felt that she was "skating on thin ice" in the operating room, even though she was already a board-certified surgeon when she came home to Birmingham.[41]

In 1932, she was taken aback when Dr. Marye Dabney, a Hopkins graduate who now headed the obstetrics/gynecology department at Hillman Hospital and was the editor in chief of the *Southern Medical Journal,* asked her to show him how to do a new operation removing a woman's uterus through the vagina instead of through the abdomen. He assumed that she had done such surgery at Hopkins. Actually, she had only assisted in such surgery there, but she did not reveal that to Dr. Dabney. Instead, she put her self-doubts aside, did her homework, and performed the surgery with Dr. Dabney's assistance. Everything went perfectly.[42]

But everything did not always go perfectly in surgery. At Hillman Hospital during the depression, she and the other surgeons were often operating on women who sought help for long-neglected problems. These cases were frequently difficult, sometimes involving, as it was said, the removal of the woman from the ovarian cyst, rather than the other way around. Some male surgeons in Birmingham, one in particular, began saying that a woman could carry on an office practice and deliver babies but that she had no business in the operating room. Although they did not name Branscomb in such comments, they did not have to. She was the only woman surgeon in Birmingham.[43]

Branscomb had personally encountered sex discrimination before. At Johns Hopkins, she and her seven female classmates had been called "hen medics," a derogatory term widely used in coeducational medical schools. She had learned that male medical students would frequently try to compliment a female medical student by saying, "You're not like the other 'hen medics.'" In addition, the male urology professor resisted admitting women to his classes. Also, Branscomb later was denied a residency in a Baltimore women's hospital in favor of a male doctor who had a lower academic rank than she did. She was told that the female patients would feel safer at night knowing a male resident was on duty.[44]

But the criticism leveled against her as a surgeon in Birmingham affected her more deeply than these earlier experiences. To be criticized for her gender when she was struggling with surgical crises took a heavy emotional and physical toll. Instead of seeing surgery as an exciting challenge, she began to dread it. Recognizing that she faced a critical problem that often led women physicians to give up surgery, she flew to New York to seek professional counsel. With this help, she was able gradually to surmount her apprehensions as she continued her work in the operating room.[45]

She again received and accepted timely advice from a Birmingham colleague. Dr. James Monroe Mason, chief of surgery at Hillman Hospital, advised her to assemble her data on fifty patients as required for certification by the American College of Surgeons. Himself a Hopkins graduate, Dr. Mason had been one of the founders of the American College of Surgeons and was an influential supporter for a young doctor, especially a young woman doctor facing sex discrimination. In 1940, Dr.

Branscomb received certification from the college. Two years later, when she presented a paper on "Primary Dysmenorrhea" to the annual meeting of the Medical Association of the State of Alabama, she did so as a fellow of the American College of Surgeons.[46]

Clearly, Dr. Branscomb knew how to care for her own physical and emotional health, so that she could reach her goals. In her medical practice, her objective was to help other women also achieve and maintain their physical and emotional health, so that they could live their lives to the fullest. As she later remarked, "I wanted to make sick women well." Although her relationships with her medical peers were not altogether congenial and satisfying, she nearly always found her relationships with her patients to be so. She did not coddle women or treat them as children; rather, she tried to enlist them in the active care of their own health.[47] Rosalind Jones Carter, who continued to be Dr. Louise's gynecological patient for many years after the birth of her two children in the 1930s, remembers Branscomb as having "a lot of compassion" and also being "business-like."[48]

With this general approach to the medical care of women, Branscomb was convinced by the time she opened her practice in Birmingham that women should have the information necessary to control their own reproductive lives. As a medical student, she had become knowledgeable about contraception, especially the use of the diaphragm. Somewhat naively, she believed that her knowledge would be welcomed in the depression-racked city.[49]

Many of her patients in her private practice did welcome it. After Rosalind Jones Carter's second child was born in 1938, she and her husband decided that they did not have enough money to support more than two children. She sought Dr. Louise's help and was fitted with a diaphragm. Although "it was so uncomfortable that [she] did not always wear it," she never became pregnant again.[50]

As a staff doctor at Hillman Hospital, Branscomb faced more restraints in sharing her belief in and knowledge of contraception with patients than she did in private practice. Not long after she was admitted to the staff, she treated a patient with tuberculosis who needed to avoid another pregnancy and whom she wanted to fit with a diaphragm. Before doing so, she discussed the matter with Dr. Cowles, who told her to go ahead "quietly." But a nurse spread the word that Branscomb was dispensing contraceptive devices at the hospital, and doctors who opposed contraception for religious reasons, especially one prominent Roman Catholic obstetrician, objected.[51]

After Drs. Branscomb and Cowles were pressured into stopping the dispensing of contraceptives at Hillman Hospital, Branscomb became the doctor for one of the birth control clinics in the city financed by the Maternal Welfare Association, an organization established earlier by a group of Birmingham doctors and laypersons.[52] By 1938, over three hundred such clinics were operating in the cities of America.[53] In the 1940s, many of these clinics, including that of the Maternal Welfare Association, would become a part of the national Planned Parenthood Federation.[54]

Another Birmingham group that supported the birth control movement was the Junior League, an exclusive social and service organization of young matrons. Learning of Dr. Branscomb's commitment to birth control, the league invited her to address them on the subject. So impressed were the members with her message that they arranged for a newspaper reporter to interview her. Before the scheduled interview took place, however, Branscomb discussed it with her brother-in-law, Robert Cothran, also a physician in Birmingham. He warned her that she was about to make a serious mistake, which might ruin her career before it was fairly established. Not only would the medical profession consider such publicity unseemly, but her ideas would make her appear radical in a city where birth control was still a controversial issue. She took his advice and canceled the interview.[55] But she continued her volunteer service in the birth control clinic, serving a white and black clientele, until 1944.[56]

In those years, she would have liked to have applied for admission to the staff of St. Vincent's Hospital, one of the city's most prestigious medical centers, operated by the Roman Catholic Church. When she conferred with her friend Dr. James Mason, who was on the staff there, he told her frankly that there was no need to apply; she would never be admitted to St. Vincent's staff because of her views and practice on birth control. Nevertheless, when her patients wanted their surgery done at St. Vincent's, Dr. Mason arranged for her to do it there as his assistant. Ironically, the nuns of the Daughters of Charity, who ran St. Vincent's, went to Branscomb for their physical examinations. Like the Methodist Jones women and many other women in Birmingham, the nuns preferred her to male gynecologists. To the nuns she extended the same courtesy she gave to the wives of Protestant ministers—she charged them nothing.[57]

Contraception was not the only controversial issue on which Dr. Louise disagreed with some of her colleagues during the 1930s. At Hillman Hospital, she treated many black children from the slums of Birmingham for gonorrhea and syphilis. Informing herself about the dreadful conditions in which these children and their families lived, she began to question the medical community's silence on the issue. She soon learned that her colleagues had no intention of confronting the property owners and real estate agents who profited from the city's slums. Most doctors understood their role to be one of treating sick people rather than challenging the social and economic conditions that often caused their sickness. When she met her colleagues in social situations, where conversation went beyond immediate clinical concerns, she found she had little in common with many of them. More than gender separated Dr. Louise Branscomb from the camaraderie of the male medical community; her total social and political outlook set her apart. She was a liberal in a predominantly conservative medical profession.[58]

Her aspirations reached beyond the establishment of a successful medical practice "making sick women well." She increasingly yearned to make a sick society well. The reforming passion of southern progressivism in which she had been nurtured as a child and youth by her family and her church now coursed through her life during the Great Depression. Where her father had primarily opposed alcohol, she determined to fight poverty, ignorance, and injustice. As she later said, "I have always been more of a reformer than a scientist."[59]

Unable to work through the medical profession to change Birmingham's social and economic conditions, she nevertheless began what would become a major activity for the rest of her life—the practice of personal philanthropy. Gradually she took upon herself the task of combating social ills through her own efforts. Eventually, she would contribute up to 30 percent of her income to organizations and causes devoted to redeeming society. Always, the organization to which she gave the most was the Methodist Church, newly united north and south in 1939.[60]

As a young doctor, she had laid the foundation for her subsequent philanthropies by learning to manage her own money well. From her parents, she had learned the wisdom not only of frugality but also of shrewd financial investment. Even during the depression, while her income was still minimal, she engaged a woman friend in Montgomery as her investment broker.[61] Soon, however, she and other members of her family enlisted the financial talents of a Jewish broker in Birmingham, Mervyn H. Sterne, who in 1919 had cofounded the firm of Ward, Sterne and Company, an investment securities business. In 1940, the name was changed to Sterne, Agee and Leach, which is still used.[62]

Sterne was the kind of business counselor Dr. Branscomb needed. By the 1930s, he had already established a reputation for public-mindedness and service. At the very time Branscomb was opening her practice in the fall of 1931, he was directing the Community Chest Appeal, working "night and day raising money" and achieving an "outpouring of funds."[63] He helped Branscomb establish good business practices in her office, and he invested her money profitably. Although Sterne was more conservative than Branscomb on some political and social issues, he and his wife, Dorah, became her close personal friends.[64]

By the time the Japanese attack on Pearl Harbor had catapulted the United States into World War II, Louise Branscomb had practiced medicine in Birmingham for ten years. Her experience as a woman doctor in the 1920s and 1930s had been more difficult than she had foreseen when she made up her mind to go to medical school. Swimming in the mainstream of the medical profession, she struggled against an undertow of sexism and crosscurrents of social and political conservatism, which were stronger than she had expected. An heir of the optimistic nineteenth-century women's medical movement, however, she had managed to rise above sexism and other obstacles. With the steady encouragement of a large, loving, and respected family, she had proved herself to be the kind of "unusually strong-minded woman" who could enter medicine for the long run.[65]

But she had made sacrifices that most of her male colleagues did not have to make. She had been so busy and single-minded in establishing her career that she had not had much time or opportunity for a social life beyond her family and a small group of professional women in the Altrusa Club of Birmingham. She had never found the right time or the right person to marry.[66] The role expectations of the traditional southern marriage would have severely limited her fledgling medical career. Despite the supportive community she had in her family, her life as a doctor was often the "intimate and solitary struggle" that Regina Markell Morantz-Sanchez has described as characteristic of medical women in the early twentieth century. Her close friend Dorah Sterne would later recall: "In Birmingham, Louise had developed a flourishing practice. She was very serious and hard-working. . . . Being a minister's daughter and developing into a respected obstetrician and gynecologist had been a heavy load for her to carry!"[67]

By carrying that load, however, Branscomb had laid the foundation and set the direction for a long, creative life. Ahead of her stretched a medical practice that would continue until 1975 and would make her one of the South's notable professional women. Her zeal for reforming society's ills would lead her to service in North Africa and Europe as a U.S. Army doctor with the United Nations Relief and Rehabilitation Administration during 1944–45. On her return, she would make a midlife career decision to give up the obstetrical part of her medical practice so that she would have more freedom and time to devote to active participation in Methodism and other benevolent organizations and causes. As she began her ninth decade in 1991, she was serving on the Birmingham Housing Authority Commission, participating actively in various ministries of the United Methodist Church, and still practicing philanthropy. By this time, she was widely recognized as a leading "woman in mission" and as a "barrier breaker," particularly in racial and women's issues.[68]

The achievements of this later part of her life story, which remain to be researched and described in detail, were possible largely because she had not allowed the bleak prospects she had faced as a young medical doctor to defeat her. In her senior year of college in 1920, she had confided to her diary that "a person as young, as full of life as I am and one who has had the advantages that I have should be eager to get out in the world and *do* something."[69] By the 1940s, Dr. Louise had fulfilled her youthful ambition to "get out in the world" and had launched a long lifetime of *doing* something.

8

Loula Dunn
Alabama Pioneer in
Public Welfare Administration

MARTHA H. SWAIN

Loula Friend Dunn, Alabama's Commissioner of Public Welfare from
1937 to 1949 and the executive director of the American Public Welfare
Administration from 1949 to 1964, arrived to the profession too late to
be among the ranks of the first wave of pioneers in the field of social
work. Her generation of social work professionals drew their inspiration
from those earlier reformers who founded settlement houses, directed
associated charities, were deans of schools of social work, and even
headed federal bureaus. According to Clarke A. Chambers, the social
work historian who founded the Social Welfare History Archives, the
"plot line" of social work during the formative years was at variance
with that of other professions, notably teaching, law, and medicine. "In
extraordinary measure," he states, "social work was staffed and managed by a coalition of women and men at every level of practice and
leadership."[1]

By the end of the 1930s, when Loula Dunn rose to preeminence, that
"unique partnership" was weakened, the "equilibrium distorted." Men
had outpaced and now outranked women at the top administrative levels
in the field of social work and in the professional associations. Men were
predominant, too, in the state departments of public welfare, which were
responsible for the administration of federal relief agencies and the social
security titles that came in the wake of New Deal legislation.[2] When
Alabama's Loula Dunn began to achieve important appointments in public welfare administration in the mid-1930s, she was in a position unique
for a woman. It was her competent administration of public welfare in

Alabama during the New Deal era and World War II that awarded her a first-rank position among her peers within the profession. As the leader of the American Public Welfare Association (APWA) in the postwar era, she was a leading proponent of medicare and other extensions of the social security programs. She thus was one of a second generation of women pioneers in social work and welfare administration.

She was born in Grove Hill, Alabama, on May 2, 1896, to William Dickson Dunn and Minnie Savage Dickinson Dunn. Her grandfather represented Mobile County in the Alabama legislature from 1841 to 1844 and subsequently became the president of the Mobile and Northern Railroad. Her maternal grandfather, James Shelton Dickinson, established a law practice at Grove Hill following graduation from the University of Virginia in 1844, served in the Alabama legislature in 1853, and attended the Confederate Congress in Richmond from 1863 to 1865. Her father was the state senator from the Nineteenth District from 1901 to 1903.[3] Growing up in a family of four girls and four boys, the young Loula was closest to her sister Minnie. The two girls were in the same senior class, graduating in 1916. Classmates at Clarke County High School voted Loula the best "all round" girl and the graduate most likely to succeed. Loula, three years older than Minnie and twenty years old at the time of her graduation, had lost earlier years of schooling because of a thyroid deficiency. Once corrected, the problem never recurred. When Minnie left to attend Alabama College, the state-supported women's college at Montevallo, Loula remained at home and began teaching in the fall of 1916 at Center Point, a rural school near Grove Hill. Later she taught at nearby Leroy and then at Foley in Baldwin County, where Minnie and their younger brother Robert Horton Dunn also taught.[4]

Loula Dunn's experiences in the small schools, where she taught predominantly low-income, illiterate, and rural adults, affected her deeply. According to her, it was the gratitude expressed to her by a sawmill worker, whom she taught to write his name, that persuaded her to enter a field of social service broader than teaching. After one year in the classroom, she enrolled in 1917 in summer social work courses at the Alabama Polytechnic Institute. She continued to teach, but after attending the University of North Carolina in 1923, she left teaching to become a caseworker in the Foster Home Division of the Alabama Child Welfare Department. During the decade that followed, she advanced from caseworker to field representative to assistant director of the department.[5]

Loula Dunn was fortunate to enter an agency whose leader, Lorraine Bedsole Bush, was a major advocate for children's welfare in Alabama. In

1903, Alabama had become the first state to enact a child labor law, and a subsequent statute in 1907 strengthened the regulations. A decade later, Bush, a Clarke County native and the deputy factory inspector of Alabama charged with enforcement of the child labor law, took a leading role in the legislative campaign to create the state Child Welfare Department. After lawmakers authorized the department in 1919, Bush became its director.[6] She became Loula Dunn's mentor as well. In 1923, the year that Dunn joined the department, the legislature created county child welfare boards with authority to select county welfare superintendents. That same year, the functions of the privately run Alabama Children's Aid Society were transferred to the state Child Welfare Department, thus establishing the department as the single statewide agency with responsibilities for social services to children and families. The progressive legislators who were wise enough to create a sound child welfare system did not, however, provide the means to finance it properly. Even so, the department, under the competent direction of Bush from 1919 to 1924 and from 1926 to 1935, achieved national acclaim for its work.[7] Frank Bane, the first executive director of the APWA (1932–35), attributed Alabama's "forward looking" child welfare programs to "personalities," primarily Bush (who had become Lorraine Bush Tunstall) and her young assistant, Loula Dunn.[8]

Alabama's exemplary Child Welfare Department provided the personnel who would administer federal monies in 1932 under the Reconstruction Finance Corporation. When the governor, under the mandate of federal law, established the Alabama Relief Administration (ARA), he designated the state Child Welfare Department to serve as the ARA Social Service Division, responsible primarily for determining the eligibility and needs of applicants for federal assistance. Thus Tunstall and Dunn were brought into federal welfare administration. With the creation of the Federal Emergency Relief Administration (FERA) early in the New Deal in 1933, a reorganization of the relief machinery placed Thad Holt at the head of the ARA. Because the ARA was now the state component of a federal agency and subject to federal regulations, while, at the same time, Alabama Child Welfare Department officials were accustomed to operating under state rulings, conflicts between Tunstall and Holt over "turf" led to an almost impossible situation. In the standoff between the two, it fell to Loula Dunn to straighten out matters during the frustrating summer of 1933.[9] During that period, Dunn was asked to take more punishment than any human being should be asked to absorb, according to Aubrey W. Williams, a native Alabamian who was FERA's regional director for the southeastern states.[10] Not even Williams, however, could make peace between Holt and Tunstall. Tunstall left the ARA in October 1933 to return to duties solely related to the Alabama Child Welfare Department. Her replacement as the director of the Social Service Division of the FERA in the state was Loula Dunn. Inasmuch as Dunn was a personal friend of both Holt and Williams and was already recognized as a consummate administrator, Alabama settled down to a relief administration that became one of the least troublesome in the area under Williams's jurisdiction. He reported to Harry L. Hopkins, his superior, that the field staff, comprised mainly of a cadre of child welfare workers, was clearly "the best in his region."[11]

Williams and Hopkins both admired Dunn's administrative skills, and at their request, she left the Alabama post in October 1934 to become a regional supervisor for the FERA, with her headquarters in New Orleans. She soon won the attention of Washington officials for the candid reports she wrote on the relief work under way in the twelve states under her supervision. She described the obstructions in Birmingham, where the municipal director of public welfare refused to cooperate with the FERA to such an extent that she doubted that "any real progress" could be made in the city. In neighboring Mississippi, she was uneasy about finding competent leadership for the Social Service Division of the FERA in view of the hostile attitude toward out-of-state personnel.[12] She was eventually successful in establishing sound federal-state relationships in the administration of emergency relief.

One scholar has described the life of the federal field representative as "arduous . . . endless travel, long nights in cheap hotel rooms, and very little rest."[13] But Dunn persevered. She retained her position as a regional representative or field investigator under the new Works Progress Administration (WPA) at its creation in 1935. In the same year, the new Social Security Act mandated that all states have departments of public welfare, and Dunn was called upon by Frank Bane of the APWA to assist southern states in creating such departments.[14] The Alabama legislature readily responded in establishing the state Department of Public Welfare only thirteen days after the passage of the Social Security Act in 1935. It was that agency that Dunn would head two years later.

In the summer of 1937, Dunn went tarpon fishing with a group that included Governor Bibb Graves of Alabama. Graves persuaded her to return to her native state as the commissioner of the state Department of Public Welfare. "You told me that your middle name is Friend," he reminded her at the time of his offer. "Well, Miss Dunn, the poor people of Alabama need a friend, and I want you to come back here and help them." [15] As she assumed her duties in October, congratulations poured in both to her and to the state from leaders in the profession. Among them were Howard W. Odum, the noted scholar of sociology and himself the former chairman of the North Carolina State Relief Commission, and Christian C. Carstens, director of the Child Welfare League of America since 1921. To the latter Dunn wrote of her "real joy to be back in public welfare harness." [16]

Widely acquainted by 1937 with a number of notables in the field of social work through contacts established over the past fourteen years, Loula Dunn soon brought luster to her department by a series of leadership positions awarded her within professional associations. Child welfare workers particularly hailed her connections as promising for their programs when she was appointed to the Advisory Committee of Child Welfare Services of the U.S. Children's Bureau (1937–43) and to the national board of the Child Welfare League of America (1937–40). Later, in 1940, she was named vice president of the league. [17] By June 1938, she had been elected to the board of directors of the APWA in a balloting among members that also elevated Katharine Lenroot, the chief of the Children's Bureau, to the APWA board. A year later, Dunn was elected vice president of the organization, serving from 1940 to 1942. [18]

Meanwhile, in her capacity as president of the Alabama Conference on Social Work during 1938–39, Dunn enticed a number of national figures to Alabama to speak or conduct workshops. For the annual meeting in Huntsville in February 1939, she tapped Paul U. Kellogg, the longtime editor of *Survey Graphic* and *Survey Midmonthly,* who was attracted by the promise of seeing Tennessee Valley Authority social programs at work and learning firsthand of the current labor difficulties and negotiations in Huntsville. When Robert Lansdale, dean of the New York School of Social Work, encouraged Kellogg to go to Alabama to help bring recognition to the "good work which had gone on in that state," Kellogg consented to go. [19]

A year later, Dunn brought in Gertrude Springer, the associate editor of *Survey,* to meet with the field staff of the Alabama Department of Public Welfare. Springer, who wrote a sprightly column in the *Survey* under the pseudonym of "Miss Bailey," was one of Loula Dunn's closest personal friends. They shared candid views, professional "gossip," and visited each other regularly until Springer's death in 1953. After a visit to Texas in early 1941, Springer confided to Dunn, "You people [in Alabama] ought to be on your bended knees thanking God or somebody for the set up you have and the way it works." Upon holding Alabama's public welfare administration up to Texas officials, they had countered, "Oh, but of course Alabama has Loula Dunn." That circumstance, it seemed to Springer, was "the answer to everything."[20]

Dunn devoted much of her time, as all state commissioners of welfare were compelled to do, to public advocacy of the welfare needs of her constituency. To the Alabama county commissioners, meeting in Birmingham in July 1939, she affirmed her commitment to the principle of locally administered welfare services. While she ascribed Alabama's reputation for a sound welfare program to a salutary combination of local administration and state supervision, the stable structure was not enough to elevate Alabama from its low rank among the states in financial assistance to clients. In fact, the state was very near the bottom in its grants to the needy aged and blind and to dependent children. Uncertain appropriations made welfare administration a protracted struggle in Alabama.[21]

While official releases from Dunn's department make no references to race, it is highly probable that there were inequities in payments to black and white clients in Alabama, as there were in other southern states. Presumably, one of Dunn's beliefs, that there was a virtue in a mix of local administration with state supervision, sacrificed to local prejudices some level of protection for those individuals whom local welfare officials may have slighted. Racial matters are issues that cannot be determined until further research in payment records brings hard data to light.

"People, Politics, and Public Welfare" was the title of a major statement Dunn made to the National Conference of Social Work in 1941. She described it to her friend Gertrude Springer as a "very earthy kind of document," and she was a "little skittish" about its acceptance. She spoke at a time when the WPA was still in existence. The agency was always a source of rancor for politicians frustrated in their attempts to construct political machines based upon WPA relief rolls and employee patronage. Moreover, the new Social Security Board mandated that state departments of public welfare must adopt the merit system in employing all staff. That, too, rankled many politicians. Dunn described other confusing aspects of federal-state-local relationships that alienated elected officials. Since public welfare personnel could not "ignore the practicalities of campaigns and elections," many professional workers were left in a state of fear and inertia that "jeopardized" their contributions to improve social services delivery. Social workers distrusted politicians, while politicians scorned the "zealous spirit" and "reformist methods" of social workers. Dunn held it obligatory that public welfare administrators should "seek out the politician in an attempt to gain his respect and support for public welfare," while not yielding any of the administrative controls that should be lodged in a public welfare agency. In the American system, elected officials were "the warp and woof of democracy." Dunn thus lectured her colleagues on the necessity of coming to grips with the political institutions through which the voters channeled public welfare.[22] Observers knew that there was much more to the matter of getting along with state politicians. Dunn possessed skills that won for her the respect and support of the elected officials of Alabama and proved beneficial for her department when wartime demands for social services strained budgets and personnel as much as had the Great Depression.

By January 1941, Dunn's associates in public welfare were already alarmed about the effects of defense preparations upon Alabama and were eager to visit the state to observe developments. Social workers anticipated that rural and agricultural areas in the state would be rapidly transformed into urban and industrial societies with all their attendant ills. Gertrude Springer, the "roving reporter" for Survey Associates, traveled to Alabama, as did Fred Hoehler, the APWA executive director. Loula Dunn's own priority at the onset of Alabama's war efforts was adequate public welfare services for children, as burgeoning populations tested the limits of social services in defense communities and as trailer cities mushroomed on the outskirts of towns inundated by new inhabitants. Migrations of families focused concerns of social workers upon inadequate housing, crowded schools, and the lack of recreational facilities. One of the greatest needs Dunn identified was that of day-care centers for children of mothers who worked in defense installations. Strapped by a lack of funds, nonetheless, by September 1941, Alabama was able to place child welfare specialists in thirty-two of its sixty-seven counties to help organize nursery schools and recreational centers and to work as liaisons with school attendance, child labor, and juvenile court officers. In an address to the Child Welfare League of America one month before Pearl Harbor, Dunn pointed to the special obligations that society owed to its children, many of whom "were born in the worst of the depression, and just as they reach 'the age of reason' find themselves passing through another critical period."[23]

Wartime issues of *Alabama Social Welfare,* the official journal of the state Department of Public Welfare, frequently addressed the issue of day care and adequate juvenile services. In 1942, the agency created the State

Loula Friend Dunn (1896–1977), Alabama Commissioner of Public Welfare, first woman executive director of the American Public Welfare Association. (Courtesy of Bowling Library, Judson College)

Advisory Committee on Day Care to coordinate community efforts where defense installations were located. Since the national social work spotlight tended to fall on whatever Loula Dunn did about services for children, Kathryn Close, a writer for *Survey* magazine, sought out details on the Alabama experience with day care. Dunn was happy to report that Alabama had been spared "squabbling" because of the cooperation the statewide advisory committee had achieved between the state Department of Public Welfare and the WPA nurseries. At this point, the nurseries were still functioning under the supervision of Mary Weber, the state director of the WPA Community Service Program.[24] However, in 1943, Congress abolished the WPA. Dunn wrote Close in the summer of 1943 of the "disheartening story" that issued from the liquidation of the last of the WPA nursery, school lunch, and clothing projects that had provided assistance since 1935 to dependent groups under the sponsorship, in most cases, of the state Department of Public Welfare. Although Congress through the Lanham (or Community Facilities) Act appropriated funds for day-care centers for children of women employed in war industries, many communities stood to lose nursery centers because they could not meet the stipulations of the Lanham Act regarding defense-related need for day care.[25]

Loula Dunn's wartime concerns for Alabama assumed national proportions when the APWA enlisted her to serve on a panel of state welfare directors to testify in January 1942 before the congressional committee chaired by Representative John H. Tolan of California. The subject of inquiry was the effect upon housing, health, and welfare of migration to defense-impacted areas. She knew the Alabama experience firsthand, particularly at Childersburg, a rural hamlet of five hundred persons in December 1940, which swelled to a population of more than nineteen thousand within a year as construction workers descended on the totally unprepared town to build the Alabama Ordnance Works. All community functions—housing, health and sanitation, traffic and law enforcement, child welfare, education and recreation—were woefully inadequate both in the construction phase of the gigantic plant and in its operating phase when the population leveled off at six thousand. Thus Dunn pleaded for the swift and "friendly hand" of the federal government to reach into communities such as Childersburg through its network of wartime services and national agencies.[26]

Even as welfare needs reached crisis proportions in Alabama's civilian "war zones," Dunn's agency had its continuing responsibilities to its mainstream clients. Her annual report of the Alabama Department of Public Welfare, which was praised by *Survey* magazine in February 1943, described the distress inflicted upon recipients of categorical assistance. The already meager grants to the needy handicapped and aged and to dependent children were being eroded by wartime inflation. "It took war to clarify the broader functions of Public Welfare, especially in the Field of the Social Services," Dunn told Tennessee social workers, pointing to the fact that there had been no previous war in which there had been a network of welfare agencies reaching into every American community. Possessing neither the "excitement of the front line" nor the "glamour of the uniform," public welfare administrators and workers were major combatants in the war. As a result of the wider responsibilities they had assumed, Dunn believed the profession would acquire a "new maturity."[27] First as a member and then as chair of the APWA War Services Committee, Dunn understood the wider implications of manpower problems, the employment of children (particularly in agriculture), and the limitations imposed on welfare programs by tire, gasoline, and automobile rationing. Furthermore, she believed, it was incumbent upon public agencies to coordinate their emergency welfare services with those of the Red Cross and the federal Office of Civilian Defense. To facilitate cooperation in her own department, she added a training supervisor to help county units develop programs to use volunteers.[28]

At the onset of World War II, Loula Dunn's activities took on an international character when she went abroad as an invited representative of the United States. At the invitation of the Canadian Welfare Council, twelve Americans spent a week in Toronto and Ottawa in July 1941, assisting that nation in coordinating welfare work, caring for soldiers' dependents, and dealing with matters concerning the armed forces of Canada and the United States. Dunn, one of only two state welfare officials in the party, was included because she was vice president of the APWA and because Alabama had a mammoth defense program under way. In addition, British fliers were in training at Maxwell Field near Montgomery.[29]

Three years later, she toured the British Isles as a member of a team of public welfare administrators selected by the United States Office of War Information (OWI) at the request of the British Ministry of Information. Since Dunn was by then president of the APWA, she was encouraged to make the British trip by Fred Hoehler, the APWA executive director from 1936 to 1943, who was then in London to direct operations of the Office of Foreign Relief and Rehabilitation. The presence in England of such a close associate made the trip seem less formidable to Dunn, who only recently had been hospitalized for orthopedic treatment of recurring back problems related to an automobile accident in 1935.[30]

Dunn was in England from March 23 to April 18, 1945, discussing with her British hosts American accomplishments and problems in her specialized fields—maternal and child welfare, the place of welfare planning in state and local governments, and the operation of federal aid in the United States. Dorothy Crook, the OWI official in London who planned Dunn's itinerary, included British day nurseries, canteens, wartime emergency maternity homes, a workers' hostel, and a number of installations under the jurisdiction of the Ministries of Health, Labour, and Education.[31] The trip proved to be hazardous when a robot bomb knocked Dunn to the floor in her hotel room and killed more than a hundred people in a nearby block. Her empathy for the British people expanded when she attended a "beautiful and moving" memorial service at St. Paul's Cathedral following the death of President Franklin D. Roosevelt.[32]

One week after her return, Dunn attended by invitation a meeting of the Social Security Board in Washington to report on her observations of British welfare administration and conditions. She described with obvious admiration the plans of the British Ministry of National Insurance to provide all citizens protection in case of sickness, unemployment, accident disability, maternity, and old age. She found government postwar planning to be more advanced than that in the United States. Like Eleanor Roosevelt, who had reported to the Social Security Board as well on her trip to England in 1942, Loula Dunn's implication was that the United States could learn from the British experience. She did observe, on the other hand, that, in the United States, social work standards and training for social workers were more highly developed than in Great Britain.[33]

Dunn's wartime work included a stint in 1942 as one of three women enlisted by the commanding general of the Fourth Corps Area to interview applicants for commissions in the Woman's Army Auxiliary Corps. Women in the military, however, represented numerically the smallest group of women whose war work concerned Dunn. In her commencement address at Alabama College in May 1944, she focused on the heavy responsibilities war had placed upon women in Alabama. Women working on railroads and in shipyards, aircraft plants, and munitions factories had become commonplace. "Employers who in earlier years would have been shocked at the very thought of women workers now are concerned only as to where to find them," she remarked. The war had proved to women that careers and marriage were not incompatible and that work did not diminish the femininity of women. She pointed also to contributions of women who kept homes and reared children under war conditions and in the absence of husbands and fathers. When peace came, she hoped that the women of Alabama, as homemakers, as professional careerists, or as both, would enter the field of public service. Six years later, when a *Look* magazine interviewer asked Dunn for her opinion on the need for women in public service, she retorted, "Well, I could make a long speech about that." She already had, in 1944, at Alabama College.[34]

When Dunn assumed the two-year presidency of the APWA in 1944, she remained Alabama's welfare commissioner. Her national stature in professional circles added authority to her long advocacy of welfare in Alabama, and she spent extended periods of time on the road speaking to groups as diverse as fraternal and civic clubs of both men and women, church auxiliaries (Protestant and Catholic), and collegiate assemblies. Wartime restrictions on long-distance travel tended to keep her primarily in Alabama, but still she found herself "somehow making too many speeches [and] just getting garroulous [*sic*]." From 1944 to 1946, Dunn made thirty speeches in state and out, including the obligatory greetings to the APWA regional conferences from Oregon to California to Connecticut and her customary annual reports to the Alabama Association of County Commissioners. Her personal and professional friendship with Frank Bane, by then the director of the Council of State Governments, meant that he often lent his good offices and used his vast prestige among the nation's governors to assist Dunn in reaching both them and Congress in her efforts as the APWA president to achieve legislation to extend welfare services under social security.[35]

In 1948, in her ninth appearance before the Alabama county commissioners, the group responsible at the grass roots for welfare administration in the state, she provided a sober look at the limitations on public welfare in Alabama. The state's per capita income of $733 in 1946 had placed it fourth from the bottom of all states. Moreover, as an agricultural state, a large segment of its population was not covered by the social insurance provisions of the Social Security Act. With the end of the war, the decline of war industries, and the lessening of job opportunity for unskilled workers and disabled persons, the number of needy persons had increased. Dunn attributed the large incidence of disabled breadwinners to the long absence in Alabama of adequate medical care and general hospital facilities.[36]

Expenditures for the fiscal year ending in September 1948 were projected at $22,500,000 ($12,800,000 federal, $5,000,000 state, and $4,700,000 local), but the sum fell far short of meeting the needs of welfare supplicants. In June 1948, the statewide monthly average for 83,147 cases (representing 118,933 persons) amounted to only $21.02.

By far the largest group (77.82 percent) receiving financial assistance were the aged (over sixty-five) but in that respect Alabama did not differ from other states. The second-largest group receiving aid were the 10,634 families with dependent children (totaling 28,915). Although little money was available for adequate grants, Dunn could point to Alabama's Adoption Act, proclaimed as one of the best in the nation, and to the state's well-rounded child welfare statutes. Three other groups made up the remaining case loads: the blind (1,105), handicapped (6,035), and a small group temporarily unable to care for themselves (140 persons). More than a litany of statistics, Dunn's report was a forceful plea for understanding among county administrators that "one impoverished county affects all Alabama, and the economy of this State colors that of the entire nation." "We can never fail to be mindful," she added, "that an investment in human resources is made by every taxpayer who supports the welfare service."[37]

It was fortunate for the APWA that in the immediate postwar years a state welfare commissioner with Dunn's compassion, energy, and astuteness became its president. In addition to her personal characteristics, she brought to her office a keen understanding of the toll taken on society's less fortunate individuals by high living costs, low income, inadequate medical care, and limited social security benefits. She assumed the presidency just as the nation completed a full decade of public welfare as an integral function of government. Editorializing to the APWA membership in January 1945, she pointed to the new needs demonstrated by war conditions—adequate housing, recreation, education, day care, and nutrition—even as wartime employment lessened relief pressures. In January 1944, while vice president of the APWA, she had testified before the Senate Committee on Education and Labor supporting the extension of social security coverage.[38]

In August 1945, Dunn was in Washington again, this time to speak before the Senate Committee on Banking and Currency on Senate Bill 380, a measure to establish a national policy and program of full employment. She cited the falling employment levels in Alabama where, only one week before VJ Day, the claims load for unemployment benefits was already steadily rising, and economic upheavals and disruptions were spreading throughout the state. In Childersburg, Alabama's prototypical defense town, 98 percent of the workers expected to lose their jobs in the near future. There had been an approximate increase of 140,000 in the number of employed women in Alabama from April 1940 to May 1945, many of whom were the sole support of their families. Now most of them faced losing their jobs. "Full employment planning," Dunn insisted, "should take into account not only the need for some of these women to work, but also the value of their skills to the labor market." Unemployment had already reduced families to subsistence living little better than that afforded by relief grants. The APWA, she testified, "stands firmly on the belief that every able-bodied American should have a suitable and useful job." And thus, she told the congressional committee, her organization supported a federal "full employment" act that would unite private, state, and local enterprise to marshal the manpower resources of the nation.[39]

In other testimony before the Senate Banking and Currency Committee, Dunn described the impact of the decline in postwar employment upon children. Alabama mothers formerly employed in war industries were applying for aid-to-dependent-children benefits in growing numbers. Neither Alabama nor any other state could afford to have its children returned to the physical and psychological deprivation of the prewar depression economy. Nor could the nation permit "bleak and spiritless youth [to be] disinherited before they are given a chance to live decently."[40]

Dunn became a true disciple of national planning for general welfare in the postwar years, particularly as Congress turned to social security amendments and revision. She thought it imperative that public welfare professionals "educate" Congress to achieve their age-old "double purpose"—the relief of immediate need and the prevention of future dependency. She called upon Kathryn Close, a writer for the most widely read journal among social welfare enthusiasts, *Survey Graphic,* to inform the general public about the concerns of her colleagues. When Dunn was invited to write the editorial for the APWA's journal, *Public Welfare,* for November 1948, she responded with a piece based on the tenet that "public welfare belongs to all the people."[41] And that was the thrust of her statement to the House Ways and Means Committee in April 1949, as Congress debated further revision of the social security system.

Again Dunn spoke to the lawmakers on the basis of her knowledge of Alabama. The proportion of the state's resources allocated toward "human well-being" compared favorably with the national average (2.21 percent compared to 2.27 percent), she told the committee. Nonetheless, because of gaps in prevailing social insurance programs, Alabamians, like citizens of other poor states, were at a disadvantage. The social insurance title of the Social Security Act was deficient because too many workers were not covered (particularly in agriculture) and because unpredictable risks such as disability were not included. In Alabama, more than half of the public welfare cases were attributable to the disability of the breadwinner. Yet another problem stemmed from the fact that too few people had earned wages above marginal subsistence in their working years to enjoy social insurance. The Alabama experience, where there were nearly five times as many aged public assistance recipients as there were aged beneficiaries of old age and survivors insurance (OASI), pointed to an inequity that would persist until Congress extended OASI coverage.[42]

At least as early as 1945, professional colleagues and personal friends began to offer Loula Dunn's name for new jobs opening within the federal government. When there was a pending vacancy in the Federal Security Agency, her name was put forward as a possible administrator, but she did not apply and was not a serious candidate.[43] Four years later, she won the endorsement of the entire Alabama congressional delegation to be the new Cabinet Secretary of Welfare, an office requested by President Harry S. Truman in his annual message to Congress on January 6, 1949. The new Cabinet department never materialized during the Truman years, and Dunn's appointment was perhaps never more than a figment of the imagination of *Mobile Press Register* boosters and other enthusiastic Alabama admirers.[44]

On the other hand, Dunn could have become in 1946 the first dean of a projected University of Alabama Graduate School of Social Work. Although Dunn joined in the efforts to recruit recommendations and nominations for the post, it was her name that surfaced most often. Her friend Fred Hoehler strongly urged her to consider the deanship. "No amount of thought on people available could convince me that anyone else in the country could do a better job on the organization of the school and assuring its acceptance through the State," he wrote her. When she expressed serious reservations because she had no "academic equipment," Hoehler countered, "So far as your academic qualifications are concerned, you have everything sufficient and a great deal more in your practical experience."[45] After some months of preliminary discussion, university president Raymond R. Paty formally offered the new deanship to Dunn in October 1946; she hesitated to accept partly because Paty was leaving the university. She wrote Hoehler privately that "the time has come for me to think of a change of work." Should she remain in the South, she thought the position of dean to be "the best vantage point from which to work." But by December, Paty had left the university, and an acting president chosen from the faculty was in place, so Dunn eventually declined the post.[46]

In 1949, Dunn left Alabama for Chicago and the executive directorship of the APWA. The APWA had been formed in 1930 at a meeting of the National Conference on Social Work by a group of public welfare officials. They had determined at the conference the previous year that their particular concerns as public welfare workers functioning in the public realm in a new era of emergency relief made it prudent that they form a separate organization. A grant from the Spelman Fund of the Rockefeller Foundation enabled the APWA to hire Frank Bane as an executive director in 1931. Under a succession of directors, the association had promoted its professional outreach program. It had also advocated passage of the Social Security Act of 1935 and faithfully monitored congressional revision of the law that had given new vitality to the whole field of public assistance and general welfare.[47] By 1948, however, the APWA was troubled by grave problems—a precipitant decline in membership, factionalism among constituent groups, discord between the Chicago office and the Washington office, and a potentially death-dealing financial crisis because of the expiration of the Spelman grant. That same year, the director, Howard Russell, resigned, effective July 1, and a selection committee was named to recommend his successor to the general membership.[48]

Raymond Hilliard, the committee chairman, confided to Fred Hoehler that at the committee meeting in mid-May, "Loula Dunn appeared to stand out." Hoehler responded that the decision "was just the recommendation I would have made." Dunn knew by July 1 that the job could be hers, but she expressed reservations to many old friends and associates, both seeking their advice about accepting the offer and soliciting a pledge of support should she assume the office. To Gertrude Springer, as always, she was frank about what she knew would be "a terrific job" beset with "manifold problems" relating to money, personnel, and relationships with both federal agencies and the states. Despite the fact that she had been toying with the idea of leaving Alabama, she knew what a "wrench" it would be to do so. "I find my roots are deeper than I realize," she confessed. But the Alabama situation had become more difficult than ever. Enumerating the headaches, she divulged that "our Legislature is in . . . a snarl," that "the Governor [James E. Folsom] and the Legislature are hopelessly crossed up," and that "present inadequate appropriations will be cut." The APWA salary, expected to be $12,500 per annum, was double her Alabama pay. Even at that, she added, "I could not walk out of Alabama while it is in the heat of its legislative program even though I think they are going to wear me down at the rate they are going." To Frank Bane, she had written in March of that year of "our turbulent state," and no doubt she poured out her frustrations to him when they met at professional meetings that year.[49]

Throughout the month of June, Dunn was in almost daily touch by telephone or letter with colleagues whose opinions she trusted as to her ability "to do the job." She probed them also as to "how APWA can get on its feet during the next several years." While at the annual meeting of the National Conference of Social Work in Cleveland, she talked with a number of APWA members and returned to Alabama encouraged that her appointment would go well with the leadership and the rank and file within the association. She realized more and more that, unless she intended to remain in Alabama "the rest of [her] working years," it was expedient "to consider other work opportunities" (she was then fifty-three years old).[50] Her contacts were lavish in their urging that she accept the offer, certain to be made formally in early July. "Loula could get more money than anyone else," Charles E. Merriam, the famous University of Chicago political scientist, told Fred Hoehler in reference to the APWA's dire straits. Elizabeth Wickenden wrote from the Washington office of the APWA, from which she conducted field studies, that "it is extremely important that we have a person with your breadth of vision and your particular talents."[51]

Louis Brownlow, probably the foremost public administration figure in the country, assured Dunn that she was "the person who can and will restore the Association to the great prestige it once enjoyed." Herbert Emmerich, director of the Public Administration Clearing House, took a loftier approach when he advised Dunn that, with the postwar boom over, welfare would become a "major front" on the national scene. He was certain that the failure of the nation to assume "human responsibilities at home" would imperil its world leadership. It was left to a Catholic dean at Loyola University in New Orleans to counsel Dunn that "for a woman in public office it is vital for her to extend her sphere of influence or activity." The indomitable "Miss Bailey" was forthright: "Lissen, Loula, you'll never know what the next door leads to if you don't go through this one."[52] Springer knew of the loss Alabama would suffer if Dunn left. When she had called upon Frank Bane to endorse Dunn for the Survey Associates Award in 1949 (a recognition that went to someone else), she had described the job Dunn had performed for the past twelve years. She had engaged in "developing a sound public welfare program in Alabama, in steadily advancing the standards of public assistance, personnel and administration and in gaining local community understanding and acceptance of modern social work procedures." Bane responded that no one else had contributed "more constructively at the grass roots" in advancing public welfare as an effective public service.[53]

As the end of June approached, a second round of letters echoed the views of the earlier exchanges. Dunn again was frankest with Gertrude Springer. "It would be one hellish job for a year or two but that would be . . . no novelty to me." Meanwhile, associates had written of their willingness to help her approach major funding sources to tap the much-needed dollars vital to the survival of the APWA program.[54] It was while Dunn was vacationing on the Alabama gulf coast the second week in July that the APWA board of directors officially acted upon the committee recommendation and voted unanimously to offer Dunn the position as director to begin on September 15, 1949.[55] After a lengthy conference with Governor Folsom, Dunn telegraphed her acceptance on July 18 and then formally submitted her resignation, effective September 19, to the governor and transmitted a gracious statement to the state Board of Public Welfare. She described the strengths of the Alabama system of welfare administration and also the imperatives of simplifying and stabilizing the financing of public welfare so that "people in equal need can receive equal aid." Alabama coworkers were reconciled to their loss, but even so, "voices were lowered and a hush came over the building at 421 South Union" as word spread of the resignation.[56]

The state board immediately named Kitty Clyde Austin, Dunn's administrative assistant, acting commissioner.[57] As the news was heard around the state, the leading newspapers editorialized about the honor paid the state by Dunn's elevation to the new post. It was "handsome evidence of her standing in the welfare field," said the *Montgomery Advertiser,* while the *Mobile Press Register* engaged in self-adulation for having already designated her for higher office some weeks previous when rumors had circulated about the new Cabinet post for welfare matters. The Montgomery *Alabama Journal* reflected that "Alabama will miss her talent, her genius, and her charm." There were discordant notes, however, from the conservative Birmingham-based *Alabama Magazine,* which sniffed that Dunn had typified "the new American principle that it is a right, not a privilege, for needy citizens to live in comfort on public money."[58]

While congratulations poured in from APWA members and constituencies ("Swell Lady," Frank Bane wired), including a cordial note of welcome from Katharine Lenroot, chief of the Children's Bureau, Dunn struggled with the details of transition and preparation to move to Chicago.[59] In addition to leaving an apartment in Montgomery that had been her home since 1937, Dunn was under great personal stress for a period of two weeks from the end of July until early August because of a sudden, critical illness and hospitalization in Birmingham of her sister. Dunn was at Minnie's bedside for much of the time, and it was not until mid-August that she was able to make a brief weekend trip to Chicago to confer with interim APWA director Guy Justis and the office staff. Finally in late August, she escaped to a favorite retreat, Bacon's-by-the-Sea on the northwestern Florida coast. She was finding it harder than she anticipated "to pull up [her] roots."[60]

When Loula Dunn left Alabama in September 1949, she left behind a department of public welfare with a reputation, according to *Survey* magazine, as "one of the most progressive, not only in the South but in the country as a whole." Its comprehensive and modern system of child welfare services were attributable to the "nurture" provided by Dunn, dating from her tenure as assistant director of the Alabama Child Welfare Department. She left behind, also, numerous adult Alabamians who remembered her work over the years. Allen Rankin, writing in the *Montgomery Journal,* added a touch of pathos to his column on her leavetaking: "Up in Bibb County two small children had been deserted by their parents. They shivered, were lost and bewildered, in a cold house. Suddenly a lady appeared out of nowhere. She took off her coat and wrapped them in it and told them to come with her. Today those children have grown up. They are a credit to the state. More important they are happy."[61]

A comprehensive look at Alabama newspapers throughout the 1930s and 1940s doubtless would point to pockets of resistance among the press and the public citizenry of the state to Dunn's advancement of public welfare. As would be expected, tributes to Dunn in professional journals and those pouring in from longtime associates are nothing short of hagiographic, as were those when she retired from welfare administration fifteen years later. It is unrealistic to think that Loula Dunn had no faults or limitations, but whatever they may have been, critics remained silent in the public record.

Dunn's achievements in her fifteen years as the first woman director of the APWA were considerable. Almost immediately she alleviated the severe financial crisis by personally going to the Rockefeller Foundation and other funding sources. While the association had been important in the development of national social policy and programs, participation by individuals, agencies, and state welfare officials had not been extensive.

Within a short time, through Dunn's structure of state membership committees and national recruitment campaigns, the APWA boasted five thousand individual and nine hundred agency memberships.[62] Dunn knew hundreds of people on a first-name basis and drew upon them to promote lay participation in APWA conferences and to develop staff expertise in medical care, aging, child welfare, and other aspects of the APWA program.

Throughout the 1950s and 1960s, she involved state and local welfare leaders directly in drafting major social legislation. Often she brought state welfare directors to Washington, where she joined them to meet with congressional leaders and Department of Health, Education, and Welfare (HEW) officials. When crucial legislation lay before Congress, she was quick to mobilize the states. Eveline Burns, who had been a practitioner in social security planning and was then on the faculty of the New York School of Social Work in 1949, recalled that Dunn "had her state boys organized every time the two-year period came up" (i.e., Congressional biennial deliberations on social security issues). Former social security commissioner Charles I. Schottland added that she could "corral the states at a moment's notice of any fight."[63] Associates credited much of the expansion of public assistance, survivor's benefits, and health care provisions of social security to her political astuteness and timing. She herself was proudest of her endeavors as a member of the Consultant Group on Social Security in 1953, the Advisory Council on Public Assistance in 1953, and the important Advisory Council on Social Security Planning in 1964–65.

The latter was Dunn's last service as APWA director. At her retirement in June 1964 at the age of sixty-eight, Wilbur Cohen, then the assistant secretary of HEW and an APWA board member, remarked, "The trouble is that you can't replace 'Miss Loula.'" She could, he added, "work with localities, states, HEW, and Congress."[64] "Loula was an absolutely tremendous person," Cohen believed. "I would say," he said, "Miss [Frances] Perkins and Loula Dunn were the two most important women in the history of social security."[65]

"Miss Loula" had personal qualities that added to her effectiveness. While she was tenacious, she was at the same time nonthreatening, charming, and attractive. Maurine Mulliner, the longtime secretary of the Social Security Board, compared her to Mississippian Ellen S. Woodward, whose path often crossed that of Dunn over a period of twenty years of federal welfare and social security administration. "That nice soft southern accent didn't nearly reveal how tough and aggressive these ladies could be in getting what they wanted." She worked twenty-hour days, traveled to all regional conferences, and was on the telephone constantly conferring with the APWA board of directors. "Quick on the uptake and repartee," she was extremely well liked by most people. Dunn's gentle manner and gracious gestures were great assets in her work. It was a style, the *New York Times* said, that explained why in the field of social welfare, "where often women are resented," Dunn had been able to gain a top post and "the men have been the first to cheer her on."[66] While she directed the APWA, she was the only woman director of any national organization located in Chicago at "1313," the East 60th Street address of a complex of national public administrative associations.[67]

Dunn was the recipient of many honors, including the APWA's coveted W. S. Terry, Jr., Memorial Merit Award, given her in 1965, the year after she retired as director. To the customary description of her labors in the field of public welfare administration, the citation lauded the "personal essence" of her efforts, described as an "acute political sensitivity . . . rich sense of humanity in every individual, deep respect for the inherent dignity of each person, and a ready faculty for humor." Upon retirement, she moved to an apartment in Georgetown to be near her brother Robert and several nieces who all lived in the Washington, D.C., area. In June 1976, a gala reception was given in Washington in her honor on the occasion of her eightieth birthday, where she welcomed associates with open arms, said to be the "gracious gesture recognized as her trademark."[68] A summer later, she died on June 27 at the Georgetown University Hospital of congestive heart failure. She was buried in Evergreen, Alabama, survived by Robert, of Alexandria, Virginia, and Minnie, then living in Montevallo, Alabama. Loula Dunn had finally returned home, as her good friend Gertrude Springer had predicted she would. "Life will carry Miss Loula far afield but wherever it takes her some corner of her warm and generous heart will be forever Alabama."[69]

Many Alabamians who mourned Dunn's passing and remembered her life likely agreed with Alabama senator John Sparkman who told his Senate colleagues, "I knew Loula Dunn and had the pleasure of working in cooperation with her. She was really irreplaceable."[70] Posthumously, in 1982, Loula Dunn was named to the Alabama Women's Hall of Fame in ceremonies at Judson College in Marion. It was an honor she shared with an earlier inductee, her sister Clarke Countian, Lorraine Bedsole

Tunstall. Dunn was memorialized at the ceremonies by an official of the Alabama Department of Pensions and Security, who paid tribute to her as a "force for high quality services and in leading a statesmanship fight for better things for all people."[71] Loula Dunn was, indeed, an Alabama pioneer in public welfare administration.

9

Stepping Out of the Shadows into Politics
Women in the Alabama Legislature, 1922–1990

JOANNE VARNER HAWKS

In July 1919, when the Alabama legislature was considering whether or not to ratify the woman suffrage amendment recently passed by Congress, Senator James B. Evins pleaded with fellow legislators not to force women "from the quietitude of our homes into the contaminating atmosphere of political struggle."[1] With these words, he described a traditional southern belief that politics was an area of public responsibility where men should stand in the limelight while women remained in the shadows. He also evidently expressed the opinion of the majority of his colleagues, who proceeded to vote against ratification. Their rejection proved temporary, however, since action in other states ensured the adoption of the amendment, enfranchising Alabama women along with the rest of the nation.

Alabama women soon indicated that they were interested not only in voting but also in holding public office. In the election of 1922, three women ran for seats in the Alabama legislature. One, Hattie Hooker Wilkins of Selma, was elected.[2] When asked why she felt women should serve in the legislature, Wilkins, a veteran of the Alabama Woman Suffrage Association supported in the campaign by the League of Women Voters, said she agreed with the "one fundamental reason claimed by woman's suffrage . . . that . . . [women] belong, by rights, there . . . because they represent at least half of the population. It is right," she said, "that both men and women's viewpoints be heard and considered before the state's lawmaking bodies."[3] Wilkins said she hoped and believed that soon every county would be represented by men and women.[4]

Her hopes proved vastly overoptimistic. During the next fifty years, five women served in the Alabama legislature, and by 1990, the total had reached only twenty. It was not until 1969 that two women served at once, and the nine women serving between 1983 and 1986 formed the largest group to hold office together. Even by southern standards, these numbers were small. By 1989, only Louisiana had fewer women in office (three) or a smaller cumulative total (nineteen). While women composed 17 percent of all legislators in the country, they made up only 5.7 percent of the Alabama legislature. None of the southern states that made up the Confederacy attained the national average.[5]

Yet, in spite of the small number, Alabama's women legislators are hard to categorize. Although there are certain similarities—almost all are Democrats, most come out of a tradition of some kind of public involvement, and many of them have been teachers—each one seems distinctly individual. Paradoxically, they appear at the same time to characterize the eras in which they lived and to stand apart from many of their cohorts.

Hattie Hooker Wilkins, Alabama's first woman legislator, exemplified this paradox. In many ways, she was a typical middle-class matron of the 1920s. The announcement of her candidacy in 1922 described her as a woman whose "most signal accomplishment [was] that of wife and mother, and maker of a beautiful home."[6] Yet her activities extended far beyond that realm. As early as 1910, the young mother had become a charter member of the Selma Suffrage Association. With the encouragement of her husband, manufacturer Joseph G. Wilkins, she worked for woman suffrage as a member and officer of the local and state association. She was also involved in club and church work in Selma.[7]

During her legislative campaign, the forty-seven-year-old woman expressed her desire to serve the best interests of her "state, its women and its people."[8] During her one term in office, she headed the committee on public health and offered bills relating to public health, education, children, and the local concerns of her district.[9]

After Wilkins retired, almost a decade passed before another woman served. Her successor, Sybil Pool, was a very different personality. A single woman, she professed to prefer hunting to housekeeping.[10] After graduating from college, Pool returned to her hometown, Linden, where she taught violin and held several secretarial positions. In 1936, when she was thirty-two years old, she served as legislative clerk for Clint Harrison, Marengo County representative. When he became a member of the Alabama Public Service Commission, the county Democratic Executive

This portrait of Hattie Hooker Wilkins hangs in the offices of the Alabama Department of Archives and History. (Photograph courtesy of Alston Fitts)

Committee chose her as his successor. This appointment initiated a thirty-four-year career in state government, which included three terms in the legislature, two terms as secretary of state, one term as state treasurer, and four terms as a member of the Public Service Commission.[11]

Pool appeared to pick her way carefully through the minefields of Alabama politics. Described as a "girl" and a "comely young blonde" when she first entered office, she garnered the respect of her colleagues through her "unobtrusive but keen interest, coupled with clear understanding."[12] She played a quiet role in the legislature, neither introducing bills nor participating in debates. She communicated with her constituents during visits home and expressed her opinions to her colleagues outside the sessions.[13] She moved into new positions carefully in order not to jeopardize her career. In 1953, she considered races for governor, U.S. senator, and Alabama public service commissioner. Ultimately she chose the public service position, considering her likelihood of victory more certain.[14] At the end of her long career, she was lauded as "an authentic pioneer who accomplished what she did with charm, competence and shoe leather."[15] She seemed to have understood what was possible for a woman politician in her time and place.

After Pool left the legislature in 1944, almost two more decades passed before Clara Stone Fields [Collins] was elected in 1962. Fields was well qualified by background and experience to be a legislator. Daughter of a longtime county treasurer, sister of a former legislator, widow of the former chair of the Mobile County Democratic Executive Committee, and herself a member of that committee, she was familiar with Alabama politics. A one-time teacher active in civic affairs in Mobile, she became a successful insurance underwriter after the death of her husband.[16]

The strange position women legislators of that era, especially those who served without female colleagues, found themselves in was indicated by two designations Fields received during her first term. The Capitol Press Corps selected her as one of three outstanding freshman representatives, while her colleagues named her "Sweetheart of the House."[17] Men legislators tended to make a big to-do about how they were to address the group now that a woman was included. Should they say "Mister Speaker, Gentlemen of the House, and Mrs. Fields," or should they refer to her as "gracious lady," or "Sweetheart of the House?"[18] When Fields remarried in 1964, changing her name to Collins, she confused the issue even further.[19]

Determined not to be handicapped by her gender, Fields approached her responsibilities seriously. To avoid being considered a "typical woman," she said she arrived early for all meetings and talked in session only when she had something important to say.[20] When she felt the need to speak out, however, she was not reticent, and she often succeeded in gaining passage of measures she favored. Throughout her tenure, she supported progress in education and conservation and jury service for women.[21] As a lifelong resident of Mobile, she was attuned to issues of concern to that coastal area, including tourism, operation of the docks, water pollution, and the seafood industry. She learned to prepare herself and maneuver carefully to accomplish her purposes.[22]

In 1964, Fields ran unsuccessfully for a congressional seat against two seasoned veterans. She remained in the legislature until 1970, when she was unseated by a male challenger.[23]

Before Fields's term ended, Kylie T. Berryman of Lawrence County entered the legislature by succeeding to the seat left vacant by the death of her husband, Robert R. Berryman. Because she had often accompanied him to Montgomery and was familiar with legislative procedure and the issues her husband supported, the state Democratic Executive Committee selected her to fill his seat.[24] Only one special session occurred after her appointment, and she retired at the end of the term to return to teaching.[25]

By 1970, the number of women interested in political office was beginning to rise. Eleven women ran for seats in the Alabama legislature, but only Retha Deal Wynot of Gadsden was successful.[26] Wynot, a fifty-year-old teacher and guidance counselor who had been active in the Democratic party, had some definite ideas about what she hoped to accomplish. She wanted "to improve education, to strengthen Alabama insurance laws, and to correct weak laws governing bad checks, small loan companies, and laws relating to families and children."[27]

As the lone woman legislator in a period when more discussion of women's rights was occurring, Wynot could not avoid being questioned about equal rights, abortion, and other current issues. In an interview during her first year in office, she declared that she was no "women's libber." "I enjoy being a woman and am not interested in liberating myself," she said.[28] She also said she believed the present abortion law was adequate and that a more liberal law would be misused.[29] The following year, she sponsored a bill to create an Alabama Women's Commission "to seek out ways to expand and promote job opportunities, rights and responsibilities for women."[30]

When the Alabama legislature was faced with the issue of whether or not to ratify the federal equal rights amendment, Wynot expressed support for this "most misunderstood, but most important piece of legislation."[31] She defended the amendment by saying "no woman will be forced to do anything . . . we simply want to offer protection to women who do want to pursue careers [and] . . . guarantee women the right to seek whatever status or role they want in society."[32] She called the logic of the opposition "nonsense" and "political hogwash" and challenged claims that ERA was a radical effort, arguing instead that it "was borne out of a desire for dignified, nonmilitant, educated women to get the chances they need in society."[33]

But less than a month later, Wynot expressed "grave misgivings" about the amendment and hoped that the legislators would put off consideration until they could get a better sense of public opinion on the issue. She now described it as a hot, divisive issue that had been hurt by the support of a "radical bunch of rabble-rousing women." She said her personal preference would be to divide the issue, because she strongly supported some parts and had serious questions about others.[34]

While Wynot equivocated on the volatile equal rights amendment, she spoke out in behalf of educational rights for all children, strong legislation against air pollution, a better mental health program, and other changes she felt were needed.[35] In 1974, she ran for the position of state auditor. When Bettye Frink defeated her, Frink appointed Wynot her executive assistant.[36]

Retha Wynot may have equivocated on equal rights, but Marilyn Quarles did not. An avid opponent of abortion and the equal rights amendment (ERA), she did not hesitate to make her position known.[37] A forty-five-year-old high school guidance counselor from Springville, Alabama, Quarles entered the legislature in 1974, after defeating three male opponents, including the incumbent.[38] In 1977, she was part of an Alabama group that attended the International Women's Year convention in Houston, Texas. "There she saw with her own eyes the 'lesbians and homosexuals,'" who she felt were seeking superiority rather than equality.[39] Back in Montgomery for a legislative session in early 1978, she "lit into the libbers and ERA," gaining a spirited response from her colleagues, who "whooped and . . . hollered and . . . egged her on."[40]

Even though Quarles opposed the ERA, she supported women's right to be officeholders. In fact, she believed they could be more effective than men, although they had to work harder to do it, since "men generally . . . [did] not accept women in any other role except as a 'lover' and wife or homemaker."[41] She objected to the way male politicians used their power. In 1978, in discussing the legislature, she commented, "People would be down there with pitch forks if they knew how the power plays were being played."[42] When she ran for lieutenant governor that year, she campaigned on a pledge that "a woman can't do any worse."[43] Failing in that bid, she tried to reenter the legislature in 1982 but missed the runoff by eleven votes.[44]

In assessing her own success as a legislator, Quarles said she had entered the legislature "to help solve problems facing our people."[45] She hoped to be "an impetus between the legislative process and people of Alabama."[46] She believed she was instrumental in the passage of "model legislation," such as the "white cane act" for blind people, thirty-year retirement for teachers, a state kindergarten program, a law concerning teacher-student ratio, establishment of an ethics commission, and a sunshine law.[47] On occasion, her histrionics attracted the attention of the press.[48]

In 1977, Quarles was joined in the House by Shelby Dean Ward, a thirty-eight-year old Opelika housewife and businesswoman, elected to fill an unexpired term.[49] Ward ran as an independent, but once elected, she identified herself with the Democrats. When asked why she wanted to serve in the legislature, she responded that she felt "women are more conscious of the concerns of people."[50] Measures she supported included visitation rights for grandparents, revision of inheritance laws, funding of sickle cell clinics, funding for abused spouse shelters, and authorization for governments to burn garbage to produce energy.[51] Ward, who was backed in her initial bid by the Alabama Education Association, was reelected to one full term before being defeated in 1982.[52]

Also elected in a special election in 1977 was Louphenia Thomas, a cosmetology instructor from Birmingham, the first black woman to serve in the Alabama legislature.[53] Thomas, a veteran of twenty years of Democratic politics, had worked to elect blacks to county and city posts. In 1968, she had managed the campaign of seven blacks seeking seats on the Fairfield city council; six were elected. Although originally she had not considered seeking office for herself, she commented after her election, "It is gratifying to have been able to reach another milestone in the political arena."[54] She hoped that her example would motivate other women to enter politics.[55] Her objective in the legislature, she said, would be "to broaden the scope of women's opportunities in governmental affairs."[56] An appointment by the Speaker of the House, Joe C. McCorquodale, to serve on the fifteen-member Alabama Women's Commission (created in 1971 to review policy and legislation affecting women) provided her an arena in which to work toward that goal.[57]

Another particular area of interest was adequate funding for education, including predominantly black colleges. An accomplishment that gratified her was an appropriation of $2 million for a black college.[58]

In 1978, Thomas ran for reelection against William Fred Horn, the opponent she had defeated in 1977. She was unable to retain her seat.[59] She had, however, left a legacy she wanted to be remembered for: "the courage to put forth the effort to break this barrier" that had kept black women out of the legislature.[60]

Thomas was the first of six black women legislators elected during the period under consideration. Small in number, they still made up 30 percent of all Alabama women legislators, the largest percentage of black women in any southern legislature. All but one were elected from predominantly black districts in Birmingham or Jefferson County. The one exception, Yvonne Kennedy, represented a Mobile district.

Women's interest in legislative office continued to build, and their success in gaining election increased. In the 1978–82 term, five women were seated. Three white women, two Democrats and one Republican, were elected in 1978, and two black women entered during the session. The white Democrats were Martha Jo Smith of Huntsville and Mary Stephens Zoghby of Mobile. The first Republican woman, and the only one to serve during the period under consideration, was Ann Bedsole of Mobile. The two black women, both Democrats, were Yvonne Kennedy of Mobile and Sundra Escott of Birmingham. With the exception of Smith, who served only one term, these women twice gained reelection and were still serving in 1990. These four and two who entered later were from the large metropolitan areas of Birmingham or Mobile. Only two of the eight women in office in 1990 were from other areas.

Martha Jo Smith of Huntsville was a young, single real estate broker and part-time college student at the time of her election in 1978.[61] In office, she aligned herself with the established leadership of the House and opposed the secretary of state's election reform efforts.[62]

Mary Stephens Zoghby of Mobile parlayed a strong backgound in public affairs and business into her successful bid for office. The first Catholic woman to serve, Zoghby was the wife and business partner of Mitchell Zoghby of Mobile. She was a member of several civic and business organizations, active in the Historic Mobile Preservation Society, the Opera Guild Auxiliary, St. Pius X Catholic Church, and the Democratic party. As a member of the 1978 class of Leadership Mobile, she served as group leader for a Drug Abuse Education and Prevention Project.[63]

In the legislature, Zoghby continued her work in several areas. During her first year in office, she sponsored successfully the Historic Preservation Authorities Act of 1979.[64] Other legislative interests included establishment of shelters for victims of domestic violence, day-care services, youth services, and reform of inheritance laws.[65] In 1981, the Alabama chapter of the National Association of Social Workers named her legislator of the year.[66] Over the years, Zoghby learned that passing legislation was often a long process. In 1989, she was still pushing her "10-year, one-woman crusade for tax reform," an effort to gain income tax exemptions for elderly persons.[67]

Ann Bedsole, also from Mobile, was the first Republican woman elected to the legislature. Describing her lifelong interest in politics, she said, "I worked in other campaigns even as a child."[68] In the 1960s, she became active in the Republican party, serving on the county and state executive committees and helping in the campaigns of Republican candidates.[69] At the same time, she was heavily involved in several women's organizations and other civic projects in Mobile. That experience convinced her that political power was necessary even for the realization of local goals. She observed, "When you work and try real hard to get something accomplished that's right for the community, you always come back to the fact that it happens in Montgomery or Washington."[70] In 1978, when her children were grown, Bedsole ran successfully for a seat in the House of Representatives. Four years later, she became the first woman to enter the Senate. When asked after her second election why she wanted to serve in the legislature, Bedsole answered in words reminiscent of Hattie Hooker Wilkins's response to a similar inquiry sixty years earlier. Bedsole said, "I think women have a right to a legitimate voice in the government. . . . For me, it was the right time and the right thing to do."[71]

She acknowledged that women legislators had to earn the respect of their male colleagues. She said in 1978 that she and the other women in the House "had a difficult time being taken seriously. We weren't mistreated or anything like that. The House leadership gave us the opportunity to be effective and do a good job. But they looked with a jaundiced eye for a year to see if the women could handle it."[72]

Bedsole appeared to pass muster. Even as the sole woman in the Senate and a Republican in a heavily Democratic body, she experienced a certain amount of success in bringing attention to issues she considered important and in passing legislation. Her particular concerns included education and other programs needed by children and youth, health care, reform of divorce laws, historic preservation, and the local needs of her district.[73]

Like Clara Fields [Collins], Mary Zoghby, and Ann Bedsole, another Mobilian, Yvonne Kennedy, came to the legislature out of a background of community involvement. Through her work in her church and sorority, the League of Women Voters, and civic and neighborhood groups, Kennedy said she encountered many issues that bordered on the legislative process and learned the importance of working with other people to accomplish goals.[74]

At the time of her election in 1979, Kennedy, recipient of a doctorate in the administration of higher education from the University of Alabama, was a federal grants officer at Bishop State Junior College in Mobile. Two years later, she became president of that institution.[75] Controversy arose over whether or not she should continue in the legislature. The board member who had selected her for the presidency said she had agreed to resign.[76] Kennedy said the matter was never discussed with her, and she had no intention of resigning.[77] It was pointed out in news coverage that three white presidents of junior colleges or trade schools who were legislators had not been asked to resign their seats.[78]

Kennedy retained her seat, but the controversy did not entirely cease. In 1987, when a merger of Bishop State and two technical colleges in Mobile was being discussed, Kennedy suggested that the other two schools should come under the control of Bishop State. An editorial critical of her proposal raised the old question of how she could run one college well and spend as much time in Montgomery as her legislative duties required. Kennedy regarded her positions as complementary rather than conflicting.[79]

As might be expected, many of Kennedy's legislative interests have been related to education. She has expressed concern for improvement of education from early childhood through institutions of higher learning. She has worked to secure funding for kindergartens, curriculum development, standardized testing, preparation of institutions to serve highly technical areas, and increase in the number of and better funding for public schools. She has also supported issues of benefit to her area, including commercial development, creation of more jobs, improvement of state docks, and historic preservation and restoration.[80]

Throughout her tenure, Kennedy has worked closely with the Black Legislative Caucus, serving at times as its chair. The caucus used its influence to bring about the reapportionment plan that had led to the special election of 1983. It has monitored state agencies and the legislature to increase appointments of blacks to positions of influence. In 1987, concern over the lack of assignments of blacks to important committees in the House and Senate led to a meeting of 150 black leaders at

Dexter Avenue King Memorial Baptist Church. Kennedy, acting chair of the Black Legislative Caucus, concluded that, "whether the selection process was motivated by racism or politics, the effect was the same" and therefore must be changed.[81]

As a black woman, Kennedy has been a double minority in the legislature, a status that she pointed out can have good and bad effects. It has motivated her to work hard and do her homework. "You don't get out there half-stepping, so to speak," she commented.[82]

In 1981, Sundra Escott also entered the legislature to fill an unexpired term.[83] At twenty-six, she was the youngest woman ever elected to the legislature. Yet in a sense, she was already a political veteran. Her "first real exposure to politics" came in 1978, when she was chosen to serve as an intern and later as an administrative assistant in the office of Governor Fob James. In the latter position, she was the education advisor's legislative liaison.[84] Escott was also active in several Democratic organizations, including Young Democrats, Metropolitan Democratic Women, and Jefferson County Progressive Democratic Council. When a vacancy arose in mostly black House District 45, Escott was encouraged to run by the Jefferson County Citizens Coalition and the local Progressive Democratic Council. She easily defeated five opponents in the Democratic primary and polled 2,185 votes against a Libertarian candidate, who received 19 votes in the special election.[85]

Escott wanted to make the legislature more responsive to ordinary people. She realized the importance of cooperation in attaining success. She aligned herself with her local delegation to promote the interests of Jefferson County. She worked with the Black Legislative Caucus to increase minority employment at the state level, to establish clinics for the treatment of sickle cell anemia, and to gain tenure for support personnel in schools. She joined with other women to establish shelters for battered women.[86]

Escott attributed the success of women legislators to their knowledge and professionalism. She believed women had earned the respect of their male colleagues. She also observed that men recognized the growing political power of women and realized they needed to cooperate with them.[87] Escott has maintained her political support and gained reelection three times.

Two other black women were elected from Birmingham districts in 1982, Pat Davis and Jarushia (Jeri) Thornton. Thornton, a forty-four-year-old law student and U.S. Army reservist, explained her desire to serve in the legislature as a result of her longtime "involvement in civic and community affairs at the grass-roots level."[88] For a dozen or more years, she had campaigned for other candidates. An opportunity to do legislative research and consulting work with local agencies whetted her appetite to become a lawmaker and to conduct local forums to familiarize citizens with the operation of state government. When the incumbent withdrew and another candidate was disqualified, Thornton ran unopposed.[89]

As a legislator, Thornton expressed her commitment to "better government . . . through better legislation, legislation that speaks to the needs of the people, legislation that will move us in the direction of an improved system or condition of living together as a community."[90]

But when the special election was called in 1983, Thornton was not able to convince her county executive committee that she was the person who should continue to represent them. Disappointed in her performance and desirous of a "more active supporter of the mayor's programs," they recommended as their nominee George Perdue, Jr., a senior auditor at the University of Alabama at Birmingham, a man experienced in business, politics, and civic affairs.[91] Undaunted, Thornton entered the race as an independent, claiming that she wanted to represent the interests of the people rather than the "power holders."[92] Despite her optimistic predictions that the people would stand behind her, she met defeat in November.[93]

Pat Davis was a junior college instructor at the time of her election. Active in community projects, the PTA, and voter registration drives, she acknowledged that she had always wanted to serve in the legislature. She found the office "as exciting as I thought it would be. I wouldn't trade it for all the tea in China," she said.[94] Concerns she hoped to deal with as a legislator included statewide unemployment, quality of education, needs of senior citizens and the handicapped, and the mass transit system.[95]

Davis appeared to be a legislator on the rise. In 1983, the Alpha Eta chapter of Iota Phi Lambda sorority honored her as a woman of distinction.[96] In 1987, she served as vice president of the National Black Caucus of State Legislators.[97] In the House, where she became a floor leader for Governor Guy Hunt and chair of the Utilities and Transportation Committee, she was regarded as a person who could get things done.[98]

But then it all began to come crashing down around her. In the summer of 1989, she was charged with asking John Stewart, president of United Mine Workers Local 1928, for a bribe of $25,000 in return for her support of a bill to require state utilities to purchase Alabama-mined coal.[99] As a result of an investigation dubbed "Coalgate," Davis and two other Jefferson County legislators were indicted for using their offices to extort money.[100] Stewart, who had reported Davis's request, cooperated with the FBI in videotaping the meeting in which he brought the money to Davis. On the tape, Davis was heard to say, "We've got our relationship. We're going to keep it. . . . Don't forget us when the special session starts. . . . Don't take care of anybody but me. The others, we'll take care of them."[101]

When the case came to trial, Davis was convicted on four of eight counts and sentenced to six and one-half years in prison and a fine of $76,800. She also lost her seat in the legislature, bringing her promising career to an end.[102] The judge who sentenced her called her actions a "'systematic and pervasive corruption' of the legislative process."[103] A member of the U.S. Attorney's office noted that she "had everything going for her, but she betrayed the people in her district and in the state."[104]

Pat Davis was the first woman legislator to get into any kind of serious trouble. Her conviction and apparent lack of remorse were no doubt disappointing to those who have admired the manner in which women legislators have conducted themselves and the serious, straightforward way most of them have approached their responsibilities.[105]

Another woman legislator, also a member of the Jefferson County delegation, was accused in 1989 of taking a political bribe. Bobbie Greene McDowell of Bessemer, one of four new women seated in the special election of 1983, was indicted along with two other legislators and one former legislator on federal bribery charges in an alleged scheme to buy legislative support for construction of a dog track in Bessemer.[106] McDowell had introduced a bill in 1988 to limit greyhound racing in Jefferson County to one facility in Bessemer. She later withdrew the bill when the *Birmingham News* reported that former state representative Hugh Boles of Concord had allegedly offered stock options to four legislators in return for their support. She said she took the action "because of the 'smut' surrounding this piece of legislation and because of the feeling by some of 'guilt by association.'"[107] When the bribery trial was held in November 1989, McDowell and one of her colleagues, John Porter, were acquitted.[108] McDowell called her trial a witch hunt, and her lawyer claimed the charges were politically motivated, an example of Republican politics, and an open season on blacks.[109] Comments surrounding the case would be disturbing to many citizens, for it was intimated that high-handed political behavior was typical of many officeholders. U.S. district judge Truman Hobbs commented after the verdict, "I despair for this state if this is commonplace. If this is the way this state is going to be run, I shed a tear for this state."[110]

The election of McDowell and three other new women in 1983, along with the reelection of five incumbent women, brought the total of women in the legislature to nine, the largest group to serve at one time. Besides McDowell, the other three newcomers in 1983 were Senator Frances "Sister" Strong and Representatives Beth Marietta and June Bugg. All but Strong were reelected in 1986. No new women were seated at that time. The only other woman to enter the legislature in the period under consideration was Jane Gullatt, elected to a vacated seat in 1989. Gullatt's entry, which coincided with Davis's departure, maintained the level of women in the legislature at eight, one less than the 1983–86 total.

Strong, a physical education and science teacher from Demopolis, ran unsuccessfully for a House seat in 1982. The following year, when a special election was called, the state Democratic Executive Committee, of which she was a member, nominated her for a new Senate seat. With her election she became the second woman, and first woman Democrat, in the Senate.[111] Strong hoped to bring more progressive representation to her area in order to improve schools, highways, and mental health facilities and to establish needed programs such as shelters for victims of domestic abuse.[112]

She was a stalwart supporter of positions she felt strongly about, even when it meant taking on stiff opposition. In 1985, despite the objection of the state superintendent of education, she maintained her support of a bill to allow teachers to transfer tenure when they moved from one school district to another.[113] In the same session, her opposition to a bill regarding oil and gas leases, which was supported by the governor, led to a threat that she would "lose her (National Guard) armories" if she did not fall into line. She "withstood intimidation" and refused to change her position.[114]

Strong, a "petite" woman with a "self-described 'fog horn voice,'" had a flare for the dramatic and sometimes for the ridiculous.[115] In 1986, she tried for the third time to get a bill through the Senate to set up the Alabama Turkey Hunters Hall of Fame in Linden. Waving her arms wildly, she pleaded with her colleagues to pass the measure, which she called her "re-election bill for Marengo County."[116] Greatly relieved when they finally agreed, she said, "I would have done anything to get it out. I would have stood on my head, flapped my wings and clucked if I had to."[117]

In 1986, she ran for reelection against Rick Manley, a Demopolis attorney portrayed in the *Alabama Journal* as "a veteran conservative legislator."[118] Manley accused her of being a puppet of the Alabama Education Association, the Alabama Democratic Conference, and the Alabama Trial Lawyers Association.[119] Strong responded with charges that he was "a puppet for the Farm Bureau and Joe McCorquodale's forestry interests."[120] In a hard-fought campaign, Manley defeated his "old nemesis."[121]

After her defeat, Strong continued her political involvement as a member of the state Democratic Executive Committee and the Demopolis City Council and as state chair for the Alabama Women's Political Caucus. Her position on several boards gave her input on issues she was concerned about.[122]

June Bugg, a college English teacher, made several political races before she won a House seat in 1983. In 1974, she ran unsuccessfully for the legislature, and in 1978, she lost a bid for mayor of her hometown of Gadsden. In the 1970s, she chaired a displaced homemaker session during Alabama's observance of International Women's Year (IWY). She attended the national IWY convention in Houston as an alternate and the White House Conference on the Family as a delegate. As these activities suggested, concerns about the needs of women and children were high on her political agenda. She was also interested in the development of the state to make it more competitive educationally, industrially, and economically. Believing that the "public's business ought to be kept public," she worked to strengthen Alabama's "sunshine law."[123]

In 1988, Bugg's colleague, Mary Zoghby, charged that the governor was trying to use intimidation to bring Bugg into line behind his program and had threatened to "stymie" a $300,000 water project granted to her district unless she supported the revenue measures recommended by his administration. Although Governor Hunt denied the accusations, Bugg acknowledged that Zoghby's report was accurate. Zoghby called "this kind of intimidation on a retired teacher . . . an unconscionable act. We are only bound by the conscience we possess and the will of the people we represent," Zoghby said. "We are not branch managers for the governor's office."[124] Such combative statements by women legislators have appeared to become more customary in recent years.

Beth Marietta, a Mobile attorney, also elected in 1983, believed she could provide "stronger but cohesive leadership" for her area.[125] Upon reelection in 1986, she became head of Mobile's ten-member delegation, chair of the newly formed Oil and Gas Committee, and one of Governor

Hunt's floor leaders in the House.[126] When her campaign for a vacated Senate seat failed in 1989, she remained in the House where she has been an energetic sponsor of legislation on a number of topics, some of which have been quite controversial.[127] She offered bills to require motorists to carry automobile liability insurance, to limit liability of architects and engineers in lawsuits over building defects, to allow joint custody of children, to reduce liability of bar owners, to provide a home port for the U.S. Navy in Mobile, to suspend driver's licenses of teenagers convicted of drug- or alcohol-related offenses, to allow a pregnant woman to arrange for her child's adoption before the birth and eliminate open access to birth certificates for adoptees, to ban future common-law marriages, and to bring about tort reform.[128] One of the controversial issues during her Senate bid was her cosponsorship of a bill requiring an environmental impact study on a planned $15 million sewage system in Mobile.[129]

The last woman elected to the legislature during the period under consideration was Jane Gullatt, who ran for a vacated seat in November 1989. Gullatt, a former mayor of Phenix City, campaigned for improved state funding for education, stronger financial commitment to local schools, and provision of medical and health care assistance.[130]

With a total of only twenty women legislators since 1922 and eight in office in 1990, it is easy to understand why a 1990 feature article in the *Montgomery Advertiser* was entitled "White Males Dominate Offices." The author, Steve Prince, noted that Alabama's population of over four million was composed of about 26 percent blacks and 52 percent women. Yet, he continued, "state elective office is an old boys' network, with a scattering of women and blacks among them."[131] In a real sense, women and blacks have remained in the political shadows.

Yet what have the women who have chosen to step out of the shadows into the glare of legislative office been able to accomplish? Certainly they have proved, slowly but surely, what Hattie Hooker Wilkins asserted seventy-eight years ago: that they have a right to be there. And through the years, they have come to be regarded more as professional colleagues than as mascots or pets. No longer does the press refer to them as girls or comely young blondes, as Sybil Pool was described in the 1930s.[132] Nor do their colleagues elect them "Sweetheart of the House," as Clara Fields [Collins] was dubbed in the 1960s.[133] Far less print is devoted to their appearance, attire, or decor, although feature articles occasionally refer to their homemaking skills or lack thereof.[134]

Also in more recent years, they have begun to gain what Bradley Moore, professor of political science and public administration at

Auburn University at Montgomery, referred to as "the power of incumbency,"[135] that is, the power to remain in office once elected, either by defeating opponents or appearing strong enough to turn back would-be challengers.

All but one of the women in office in 1990 have served two or more terms. Ann Bedsole and Mary Zoghby have had the longest tenure, three full terms each. Of the nine women elected after them, only three have left office, two by defeat and one by resignation. One of those defeated fell to a former male legislator bent on making a comeback. Five have been reelected, and a sixth began her first term in 1990.

These women were gradually gaining the perquisites of longevity and positions of responsibility in their chambers. In 1990, three were committee chairpersons and two others vice chairpersons. When the 1986–90 legislature was organized in 1987, Governor Hunt chose three of the women as floor leaders.[136]

However, their numbers remained so small that their leverage was limited. Only 1 of 35 Senators was female; only 7 of 105 Representatives. Their total of 5.7 percent was far below the modest national average of women legislators, which was 17 percent. Only Louisiana and Kentucky had smaller percentages (2.1 percent and 5.1 percent, respectively).[137] Moreover, for a variety of reasons, the women chose not to organize a women's caucus and therefore lacked that formal means of taking a stand or exerting pressure as the Black Legislative Caucus has done.

Some of them felt that, given their small numbers, a women's caucus would be more detrimental than beneficial by setting them apart and limiting their maneuverability. An even more basic deterrent was that the women tended to be very different from one another, having their own individual agendas and priorities, and often turning up on opposite sides of the fence on many issues.

Yet, as Yvonne Kennedy observed several years ago, there were "commonalities" that drew the women together, including "education, jobs, battered wives, child abuse and neglect, senior citizens, and historic preservation."[138] Moreover, the presence of women in the legislature tended to sensitize male colleagues to certain issues that all-male bodies might have treated differently or failed to deal with at all. In some cases, women influenced the passage of legislation; in other cases, they drew attention to the fact that on certain issues men and women tend to have different perspectives.

A recent highly controversial issue on which a majority of the women took a stand contrary to the majority views of their chambers was the abortion issue. This was not a man-versus-woman issue but an issue that set woman against woman and man against man. Yet, in a very political atmosphere, where keeping silent or straddling the fence might have been easier, several of the women legislators were forthright about their positions, and most voted against some of the restrictions.[139] When a 1990 bill to regulate abortion clinics passed the Senate Judiciary Committee with a vote of seven to two, Ann Bedsole led the opposition to the measure because she felt it would "stop legal abortions in Alabama and result in the death of untold poor women."[140] The bill would not stop abortions, she said; it would only stop safe abortions. Women with money would go outside the state to obtain abortions, while poor women would have to seek unsafe, illegal abortions in Alabama.[141] She characterized another bill that would prohibit abortion except to save a woman's life as an attack on women. "I was really shocked at the tenor of it," she said, "and I don't really know how to explain it, but I felt that I was personally being attacked, that it was an attack on women."[142]

Seventy-year-old representative June Bugg objected to having such an important issue discussed in the highly political atmosphere of legislative committees, especially committees composed mainly of men. "If there is any place this problem does not belong, it is in a legislature during an election year," she said.[143] "I cry for Alabama's women, whose health, happiness and destiny are a political problem over which they have very little control."[144] Bugg suggested that the issue should be submitted to the public. "'The only fair way I know is to let the women of Alabama vote their conscience in the privacy of the ballot box,' she said. 'We have an election for bingo. Surely women deserve as much.'"[145]

Bedsole's and Bugg's comments led to a stinging retort from the bill's House sponsor, Representative Greg Beers of Birmingham, who said he was "tired of the liberal women legislators somehow feeling that they are the only people elected to office who can speak for the women of Alabama."[146] He noted that at least half of the twenty-five thousand people who marched to Montgomery to demonstrate against abortion were women.[147]

The women's willingness to speak out on such a controversial issue indicated that they had come of age politically. Where earlier women often kept silent, made equivocal statements, or took safe positions, some of the more recent women legislators were speaking out on measures they felt strongly about, even when they knew their views would be unpopular with a significant portion of the electorate.

Given their small numbers, the influence of the women has resulted

generally from their personal capabilities and their mastery of the legislative milieu. In an article about these Alabama women, written several
years ago, I concluded that the common threads linking them were their
"self-confidence, the boldness to challenge a system that did little to
encourage their participation, and a desire to effect change through the
political process."[148] More recent women possessed this same self-
confidence, combined with even more political savvy or knowledge of
how to use the legislative process to accomplish their goals. Some have
learned how to operate effectively within the give-and-take atmosphere
of the legislature. They formed alliances to achieve their purposes with
various groups such as other women, local delegations, the black caucus,
or ad hoc groups that formed around a particular issue. Some of these
configurations were more permanent, such as affiliation with local delegations or, for the black women, the black caucus. Others were more
kaleidoscopic, forming and reforming to meet special needs. Effectively
used, they enhanced the influence of the woman legislator, preventing her
from being as isolated as some of her predecessors were.

Small in number, Alabama's women legislators have nevertheless been
a force to be reckoned with. Despite the unfavorable publicity surrounding the trials of two of the women and the conviction of one, women
legislators in general have earned a reputation for being hardworking
and serious. Coming to the legislature from a variety of backgrounds,
they have brought professional expertise, knowledge of the issues, good
common sense, and a wealth of experience in working with others to
accomplish change. With their increasing longevity, experience, and self-
confidence, their stars would appear to be on the rise.

In summary, twenty women were elected or appointed to the Alabama
legislature between 1922 and 1990. Only one woman succeeded her
legislator husband. Six others were elected or appointed to fill unexpired
terms, while the remaining thirteen were seated in regular elections. Eight
served less than two full terms, and one began her first term in 1990.

Five women served alone for all or most of their tenures. The largest
group in office at one time was nine, seven in the House and two in the
Senate following the court-ordered election of 1983. In 1990, there were
only eight women, seven in the House and one in the Senate.

Only Sibyl Pool successfully used her position as a stepping stone to
statewide office. Three made losing bids for other state offices, and one
ran unsuccessfully for Congress.

Despite considerable diversity, many of the women have shared common experiences. All but one were Democrats. As might be expected, all

were involved in public affairs prior to their elections, either as business or professional women or as volunteers working in their communities through civil rights groups, women's organizations, political parties, or other special interest groups. Ten had experience as teachers or administrators in educational institutions, and their concern for changes in education appeared to be a motivating factor in their decision to run for public office. Seven hailed from the large metropolitan areas of Birmingham or Mobile, where their activities had provided them experience and a base of support that enabled them to run for office successfully. Interestingly, no women have been elected from the capital city of Montgomery.

In 1990, the Alabama legislature remained predominantly a white male body. Hattie Hooker Wilkins's dream of men and women representing each county seemed far from realization. Indeed, recent numbers would seem to indicate that few women or men shared that dream. Because of their sparse numbers and a disinclination to form a women's bloc, women have not been able to affect numerically the passage of many measures. What they have probably accomplished most successfully has been to focus attention on issues an all-male legislature might have tended to overlook and to bring women's perspectives to bear on measures under consideration by the legislature.

Most of the women have been creditable legislators. As the length of their incumbency increased, they began moving into committee chairmanships and other responsibilities that may position them to exert influence greater than their numbers in coming years.

Women in the Alabama Legislature, 1922–1990

Name and residence	Race	Marital Status	Occupation	Date and type of election	No. of terms	Additional comments
Hattie H. Wilkins Selma	W	M	Housewife; former teacher	1922 reg.	1	Club woman; did not run for reelection
Sibyl Pool Linden	W	S	Secretary; legislative clerk	1936 spec.	3	Appointed to vacant seat; elected to 3 other state offices; 34-year career
Clara Fields [Collins] Mobile	W	W	Insurance broker; former teacher	1962 reg.	2	Ran unsuccessfully for Congress 1964; defeated 1970
Kylie T. Berryman Moulton	W	W	Teacher	1969 spec.	1 –	Succeeded husband; served one special session; returned to teaching
Retha D. Wynot Gadsden	W	M	Teacher; guidance counselor	1970 reg.	1	Ran unsuccessfully for state auditor 1974
Marilyn Quarles	W	M	Guidance counselor	1974 reg.	1	Ran unsuccessfully for lieutenant governor 1978; legislature 1982
Shelby D. Ward Opelika	W	M	Housewife; husband's business associate	1977 spec.	1 +	Reelected to full term 1978; defeated 1982
Louphenia Thomas Birmingham	B	W	Instructor of cosmetology	1977 spec.	1 –	Civil rights activist; first black woman elected; defeated 1978
Martha Jo Smith Huntsville	W	S	Real estate agent	1978 reg.	1	Defeated 1982
Ann Bedsole Mobile	W	M	Housewife	1978 reg.	3*	Active in community affairs and Republican party; House 1978–82; Senate 1982– ; first Republican woman in legislature

Name	Race	Status	Occupation	Year	No.	Notes
Mary S. Zoghby, Mobile	W	M	Husband's business partner	1978 reg.	3*	Active in community affairs; first Catholic woman in legislature
Yvonne Kennedy, Mobile	B	S	Grants officer; later college president	1979 spec.	3*	Doctorate in higher education; active in community affairs
Sundra Escott, Birmingham	B	S	Insurance broker	1981 spec.	2*	Active in Democratic party
Pat Davis, Birmingham	B	M	Junior college instructor	1982 reg.	2	Active in voter registration and community affairs; convicted of bribery and ousted from legislature in 1990
Jarushia Thornton, Birmingham	B	S	Law student; U.S. Army reservist	1982 reg.	1 –	Lost seat in court-ordered election of 1983
Bobbie G. McDowell, Bessemer	B	M	Housewife	1983**reg.	2*	Active in Democratic party and community affairs
Beth Marietta, Theodore	W	M	Attorney	1983**reg.	2***	Ran unsuccessfully for state senate in 1989 and for circuit judge 1990
Frances W. Strong, Demopolis	W	M	Teacher	1983**reg.	1	First Democratic woman in senate; defeated in 1986
June Bugg, Gadsden	W	M	College professor	1983**reg.	2*	
Jane Gullatt, Phenix City	W	M	Former mayor	1989 spec.	1*	

*Remained in office in 1990.

**A court-ordered election was held in 1983 to effect reapportionment.

***Editor's note: Beth Marietta-Lyons ran unsuccessfully for a judgeship in November 1990. Lois Rockhold was elected to her legislative seat.

10

"Alive to the Cause of Justice"
Juliette Hampton Morgan and the
Montgomery Bus Boycott

SHERYL SPRADLING SUMME

Juliette Morgan was basically reserved and shy but could, in the words of her coworkers and friends, "rise to militancy for a righteous cause or speak out forthrightly for truth and justice." She was a deeply religious white intellectual who abhorred racial prejudice. As an Episcopalian and a member of the upper class in Montgomery, Alabama, she had the courage and the means to express controversial racial and political views and was often "the spokesman for a growing group of Progressive Southerners."[1] In 1955–56, she was one of a small number of white women in Montgomery to support publicly the boycott of Montgomery's buses by the city's blacks. Primarily through letters to the editor of the *Montgomery Advertiser,* she expressed strong integrationist views that marked her as unusual among white people in Montgomery at that time. While her privileged position in society gave her the opportunity to make a visible and significant dissent, it also made her a target for the special hatred directed at insiders who questioned the white establishment.

Born in 1914 to Frank P. and Lila Bess Olin Morgan, Juliette Hampton Morgan was a member of a family whose ancestors had lived in the South since the early seventeenth century and in Alabama since before the Civil War. As the only child in this wealthy and prominent Montgomery family, she was made aware of the importance of politics from an early age. Her father, a prominent politician concerned with the welfare of Alabama's blacks, was elected four times to the Alabama Public Service Commission and later served on the Interstate Commerce Commission.[2] Her mother, who prided herself on her English lineage and her place in southern society, had traveled widely in Europe, Asia, the Middle East, and Africa.

Juliette's parents had a stormy marriage. Although it is hard to say how aware she may have been of this in her early life, in her later years, her parents' problems troubled her greatly. According to a confidante, Juliette wrote many letters when she was living away from home "trying to keep her parents together."[3] She grew up knowing that all was not right with the world and wanting fervently to make it right.

Although Lila Bess Morgan spoke of her daughter in flowery terms of love, her behavior toward Juliette has been described as "mean as hell."[4] The young Juliette was made aware of her mother's expectations for her only child's future, which reflected the tension Lila Bess herself seems to have experienced between two views of womanhood. As an intellectual, Lila Bess desired an intelligent and well-educated daughter. This role Juliette had no trouble playing. But Lila Bess had other roles in mind for her daughter that were not among Juliette's priorities. In an article she wrote in 1920, when Juliette was about six years old, Lila Bess Morgan spoke of an antique French doll Juliette played with and said, "The doll has played many roles, from baby doll, school girl, sub-deb, debutante, to bride."[5] This sequence of events in the doll's play life seems to have paralleled the unfulfilled ambitions Lila Bess had for her daughter's real life.

Virginia Durr, a friend of Juliette Morgan and a fellow liberal dissenter during the boycott, has pointed out that there were limited choices for "well-brought-up southern white women." They could play the role of the southern belle and follow the stereotype, which included making a "good marriage." If they had an independent or creative streak, they could go quietly crazy, or they could rebel, abandon their privilege, and challenge this way of life.[6] Juliette Morgan would choose this latter way. In her adulthood, she would readily identify with the problems of Montgomery's black community, although she herself had relatively little contact with blacks. Perhaps she felt a kinship with their struggle to clarify their role in society because of her own struggle to find her identity as a southern woman.

Morgan's controversial actions later in her life were based on a sensitivity to injustice that was a direct result of her religious beliefs. Throughout her life, she displayed strong religious convictions. She was brought up as an Episcopalian, attended Sunday school regularly, and kept favorite religious poems and lessons in her scrapbook.[7] Later, the Federal Council of Churches' stand against segregation and discrimination would have a substantial effect on her ideas.

Mr. and Mrs. J. A. Olin of Heflin, Alabama, Juliette's maternal grandparents, also played a large part in developing her capacity for love and sympathetic concern. Her grandmother, whom she called "Big Mama," was especially important as a stable and affectionate adult figure in her early life. It was Big Mama who stood by Juliette when she and her mother had conflicts.[8]

The young Juliette was trained in etiquette and dance to prepare her for the roles and responsibilities of a young socialite. When only six, she performed a solo dance at a recital. Juliette proved to be much more than a socialite, however, contrary to the stereotype of Alabama society girls in the decades of her childhood and adolescence.[9] During her years as an elementary school student, Juliette participated in a well-rounded variety of activities while receiving all A's in her schoolwork. As a student at Lanier High School in Montgomery from 1926 to 1930, she continued to do excellent academic work as well as develop a great love and talent for the theater.[10]

The increasingly intellectual and religious Juliette found a role model in a friend of the family, a Mrs. McIntosh, who lived in New York City and was very active in the Young Women's Christian Association. The summer that Juliette spent in the McIntosh home immediately after her high school graduation gave her significant contact with a woman involved in a woman's organization for social change.[11]

Morgan entered the University of Alabama in the fall of 1931. While an undergraduate student, she served on the Women's Student Government Council, was selected for the university's theatrical group, and joined the Kappa Kappa Gamma social sorority. In 1933, she was elected to Phi Beta Kappa and Mortar Board and completed her undergraduate work in English. She continued her studies at the University of Alabama, receiving her master's degree in English in 1935. She stayed on at the university as a teacher of English until 1938.[12]

Making her first public statements in the *Montgomery Advertiser* in May of 1932, while still an undergraduate student, Morgan wrote a letter in defense of formal training in home economics. In this letter, she argued that motherhood was such an important role that it warranted special training. She wrote in support of adding a federal department of child welfare, saying that "the child crop is the biggest, most fragile, and most carelessly produced crop in America."[13] The fact that she was so concerned about the welfare of children was an expression of her feeling of obligation to be a force for social justice.

In 1938, she returned to Montgomery, and in the summer of that year, she was again using the public opinion section of the *Advertiser*. In July, she answered the letter of a woman whom she referred to as "Mrs. Yankee," in which she asserted that while southern women were, perhaps, a bit too complacent, many northern women were at the other extreme. She wrote that "they mistake the means for the end . . . and thereby make a fetish of washing their own dishes and chasing their own dust and being, oh, so righteous and busy." She went on to say that "Southern Womanhood" as an illusion or a romantic ideal is a dangerous notion, but that it is not true that "all Southern women whine and . . . do nothing but loll around and complain and drivel triviata [*sic*]." In fact, she said, she knew of one southern woman who could discuss the theory of Einstein before breakfast—that woman was her mother.[14] Such staunch defenses of the southern woman and the South in general would later be problematical for her enemies who wished to brand her as a traitor to the South.

From 1939 to 1942, Juliette Morgan taught English at her alma mater, Lanier High School. Finding teaching to be "a 24-hour job," she left that job to become a reference librarian at the Montgomery Public Library. After five years in this position, she went to work at a downtown book-store in 1946.[15] During these years, Morgan was just as interested in political problems and as outspoken about her views as ever. She was concerned with wartime and postwar diplomacy. In 1943 alone, she wrote letters to the *Advertiser* pertaining to the need for more coopera-tion among members of the United Nations, the need to fight rising isolationism in the United States, the value of the lend-lease program with Great Britain, and the urgency of the renewal of the Reciprocal Trade Agreements Act.[16]

It was while she was in her early thirties that Juliette Morgan began to focus on the problems of southern blacks. In a letter to the *Advertiser* in October of 1946, she made it clear that she was totally opposed to the Boswell Amendment being debated in the state legislature. This proposal, which was passed in 1946 but was subsequently declared unconstitu-tional in federal court, would have given "practically unlimited power" to the governor and the board of registrars over who could and who could not vote.[17] Knowing the history of voting discrimination in the South, she perceived that this was an attempt on the part of demagogic politicians to deny blacks their right of suffrage.

Juliette Hampton Morgan. (Courtesy of the Alabama Department of Archives and History)

Anti–civil rights feelings in Alabama were building in 1948. The state's delegates to the Democratic National Convention that year included Gessner T. McCorvey and Horace Wilkinson. These men were instrumental in the walkout of southern delegates who were irate over the strong civil rights plank inserted in the party platform by President Truman. Soon thereafter the disaffected delegates formed the Dixiecrat party. In the *Montgomery Advertiser,* Juliette Morgan spoke of McCorvey and Wilkinson, saying, "One must ask of our brave bolters 'Little men, what now?' . . . It is hardly probable that any man of presidential calibre would accept the nomination under the restrictions against civil rights that they will stipulate."[18]

This same year in a letter to the *Advertiser,* she made her first public connection between civil rights for blacks and Christian morality. She said, "It is significant that the Federal Council of Churches has taken an emphatic anti-discrimination stand. . . . It is becoming increasingly hard for many Southerners to reconcile our pattern of discrimination with the clearest and most unequivocal [*sic*] passages in the New Testament."[19] Thus Juliette Morgan, whose racial views were unusual in her local religious community, identified with a more racially progressive element in the national Christian church that gave her courage.

The controversial writer Lillian Smith was a southern dissenter with whom Juliette Morgan identified and in whose writing she found support for her own ideas. In 1949, Morgan wrote a review for the *Cleburne* (Alabama) *News* of Smith's controversial novel *Killers of the Dream.* In the novel, Smith tells of the heartache and bewilderment of a young girl growing up in the South who cannot understand racial segregation and therefore cannot accept it. Morgan said the book was "packed with thought and powerful arguments about racial questions."[20]

In 1952, Juliette Morgan took her first direct stand against discrimination in a letter to the *Advertiser.* She declared that "discrimination against minority groups can best be handled by a Federal commission." She condemned the so-called southern traditions and said state's rightists were for the most part more concerned with maintaining the status quo than securing basic human rights. Setting the issue down in stark terms of right versus wrong, she said, "Our Lord is against us if we consent to discrimination by color or place of ancestry."[21] The *Birmingham World,* a black-owned newspaper of limited circulation, reprinted her letter soon after its original appearance, with the comment that "Miss Juliette Morgan brings a new voice to the plea for simple justice for ethnic and exploited economic groups. She discusses with vigor, sensitive intelligence and fierce convictions . . . the tragic clinging on to the racial slogan by the Alabama Democratic Party."[22]

But few white people in Montgomery shared the perspective of the black editor, Emory Jackson. As Juliette Morgan wrote him, there were those in Montgomery who were "violently opposed" to her views.[23] She said she had faith, though, that those who were opposed could not remain so for long in the face of reason. Her sheltered and elitist upbringing had apparently blinded her to the powerful emotions behind the prejudices of many white southerners.

In 1952, Morgan returned to the Montgomery Public Library as head reference librarian, a job she dearly loved. The library and its interest had been important to her for many years. She believed that there was "an urgent need of a well-rounded library in the life of any community" and called for a higher pay for the library staff, money for more and newer books, and improvement of the library's cramped facilities. In a letter to the *Advertiser* in November of 1946, she had put the chief blame for the neglect of the library on its board of trustees. She said, "It is hard to believe that a group of citizens as able, prominent, and influential as the members of the board are could not have produced more tangible results if they had really had the interest of the library enough at heart." [24]

In addition to her work at the library, she became active in the Humane Society of Montgomery. In 1955–56, she served first as publicity director and then as secretary-treasurer for the society. She wrote many letters to the *Advertiser* publicizing activities of the Humane Society and bringing public attention to such matters as the inhumane methods used in the slaughter of calves. [25] In her work with the Humane Society, Juliette Morgan was once again expressing her sense of responsibility for correcting the world's evils and injustice.

Racist sentiment in Montgomery and throughout the South was heightened by the May 17, 1954, Supreme Court decision in favor of school integration. [26] Alabama segregationists were more determined than ever that full integration would not become a reality in their state. Moreover, the changing nature of Montgomery's population in the 1940s and 1950s was creating a large white lower-middle class whose political power was rivaled by an increasing number of blacks exercising their right to vote. [27] The increased hostility resulting from this situation was, of course, not confined to one particular economic segment of the white population.

An example of this increasing political power of blacks and the corresponding increase in segregationist fervor and demagoguery occurred in May of 1955. Police Commissioner Dave Birmingham, under pressure from his black constituents, hired four blacks to serve on the Montgomery police force. To ease the fears of segregationists worried that this might become a trend, white Police Chief Goodwyn Ruppenthal assured them that the blacks were "just niggers doing a nigger's job." [28]

Juliette Morgan responded passionately to Ruppenthal's statement in a letter to Mayor William Gayle. She said, "How low can we get? That remark . . . is sadistic in spirit. I really feel sorry for Mr. Ruppenthal. He must be a man of very limited opportunities and education. . . . Still I shudder to think that we are all more or less at his mercy. [His] remark reminds me of Shelley's wonderful description of such in *Prometheus Unbound*—'the dull sneer of self-loved ignorance.'"[29] Her comments increasingly tackled specific persons and their speeches and actions, rather than simply expressing her own thoughts. While certainly justified, her cutting analysis of the ignorance and pettiness of such remarks was the type of response that angered segregationists most.

When Montgomery's blacks began their boycott of the city's buses in early December of 1955, their goals were primarily to receive more courtesy from drivers, to have more black drivers hired on primarily black routes, and to have seating arrangements on the buses defined more clearly as "blacks from the back towards the front and whites from the front towards the back without insisting that a section always be kept clear for each race." As J. Mills Thornton has pointed out in his study of the boycott, "Although all the blacks were integrationists, the thrust of their efforts was so to reform the actual practice of segregation as to make it acceptable. . . . But the fears of Montgomery's segregationists were so aroused by the moderate demands that the blacks made that they stubbornly opposed them at every turn and were "by implication urging the blacks to seek the complete abolition of segregation in the courts."[30]

It was Juliette Morgan's belief in speaking out for social justice that led her to defend Montgomery's blacks against the mistreatment and humiliation they were subjected to on the city buses. Her daily rides on the buses provided her direct contact with blacks, which, though limited, was more contact than most upper-class whites had with blacks (other than her attendance at one or two interracial political meetings later in the movement, this appears to have been her only contact with blacks, and the record does not show that Morgan had any close black friends). She witnessed personally the ugly discrimination and abuse that frequently occurred. From the beginning, she wholeheartedly supported the boycott and its objectives. Within a week after it began, she was expressing support for it in the columns of the *Advertiser*. She likened the spirit of the boycotters to Gandhi's nonviolent resistance movement in India, and she said, "One feels that history is being made in Montgomery these days, the most important in her career."[31]

Her comments on Gandhi and his methods were quite significant in influencing an emphasis on distinctly Gandhian tactics within the movement being led in Montgomery by Martin Luther King, Jr. As King himself noted in *Stride toward Freedom,* it was after reading her letter in the paper that he called a meeting of the boycott leaders to discuss the possibility of using nonviolent direct-action methods. While Gandhi was one of King's early philosophical influences, he was by no means the major one, and were it not for Juliette Morgan's comparison, King might not have seized upon nonviolence itself as the major emphasis of his movement.[32]

In this same letter to the *Advertiser,* she made her position clear:

> I believe the Constitution and the Supreme Court of the United States constitute the supreme law of the land. I find it ironic to hear men in authority who are openly flouting this law speak piously of law enforcement.
>
> I also find it hard to work up sympathy for the bus company. I have ridden the buses of Montgomery ever since they have been running . . . and I have heard some bus drivers use the tone and manners of mule drivers in their treatment of Negro passengers. Three times I've gotten off the bus because I could not countenance such treatment of the Negroes. I should have gotten off on several other occasions. Twice I've heard a certain driver mutter quite audibly 'black ape.' I could not tell whether the Negro heard or not, but I did and felt insulted.
>
> It is interesting to read editorials on the legality of this boycott. They make me think of the famous one that turned America from a tea to a coffee drinking nation. Come to think of it, one might say that this nation was founded upon boycott.
>
> Instead of acting like sullen adolescents whose attitude is "Make me," we ought to be working out plans to span the gap between segregation and integration.[33]

This letter marks a turning point in courage for Juliette Morgan. In the past, her responses to the injustice on the buses had amounted to quietly leaving a bus in anger. But now she was pouring out her feelings in the newspaper—and calling segregationists lawbreakers in the process. Certainly she knew that the responses she would receive to these statements would be hostile. At the time the letter was published in December 1955, White Citizens' Councils had been organized throughout the South for some months with the purpose of preventing integration by using organized methods of coercion, intimidation, and violence. In January of 1956, twelve hundred people came to a Montgomery White Citizens' Council rally. A joint Mississippi/Alabama rally the following month drew ten thousand supporters who were encouraged to "organize and be militant."[34] Juliette Morgan's statements required great courage in the face of these developments.

Juliette Morgan, however, was not the only white person in the Montgomery community who had the courage to dissent. Clifford and Virginia Durr and Aubrey Williams were intellectual, upper-class whites influenced by Social Gospel teaching. But the Durrs and Williams had forged their ideas about racial democracy through work and social experiences outside of the South and through the integrated Highlander Folk School in Tennessee, which they helped to sponsor. In Montgomery, they showed their support for the black community through actions—the Durrs with legal assistance from Clifford's law firm and Williams with editorials in his *Southern Farmer* newspaper and his attempts to form an integrated farmer's union. The larger white community responded to this type of dissent with a pattern of reaction. First came economic retaliation when Durr lost most of his white clients and Williams lost most of his advertisers. Social ostracism came next, aimed not only at the dissenters but at their children and other family members as well.[35] Finally, when dissent continued, tactics of threats and harassment were used, but seldom acts of violence, as were used against blacks.

Virginia Durr has said that the crucial element for holding her and her husband's lives together in the face of such pressure was unflinching support from their family, even when the family did not agree with their views and actions.[36] This is in sharp contrast to Juliette Morgan's situation. Somewhat reclusive by nature, she was apparently uninvolved in the establishing of any social contacts that could lead to new friendships or, potentially, marriage (why she was uninvolved in this process is not made clear by the evidence, although it is possible she may have been negatively influenced toward the institution of marriage by her parents' problems). Increasingly cut off from casual social contacts, her only consistent companion was her mother, with whom she lived. The demanding and changeable behavior of Lila Bess Morgan toward her daughter left Juliette insecure about herself and was probably a factor in her extreme sensitivity to the public criticism she received for her views. Juliette did not have the family support crucial to dissenters through times of public scorn.

Most white progressives on the civil rights issue in Montgomery fell into one of two broad categories; they were clergymen or they were women. Perhaps these groups were especially significant as dissenting voices because they were not quite as vulnerable to the first retaliatory weapon of segregationists—economic pressure. A small but significant number of dissenting white women existed in Montgomery during the years of the civil rights struggle. The more deeply one researches the history of the boycott, the more one finds references to white women who supported it, although these references are often hidden in footnotes and afterthoughts in published accounts.[37] In December of 1955, the month the boycott began, several other white women expressed their views in the *Montgomery Advertiser* that the boycott was "a justifiable demand for simple decent treatment."[38] One of Montgomery's most prominent citizens, Clara Rutledge, wrote, "I have yet to find one white person who feels that it is right that a Negro be made to stand that a white person may sit."[39]

White and black women also worked together for social change. United Church Women, which had only recently become an integrated organization in the South, held integrated prayer meetings in black churches. Coretta King and other leading women in the black community attended, as did Virginia Durr, Clara Rutledge, and other white women (although not, apparently, Juliette Morgan). These meetings were discontinued when segregationists took the license plate numbers of those in attendance and published their names, addresses, and phone numbers. Harassing phone calls began, along with economic threats to their husbands. According to Virginia Durr, "Several husbands took out notices in the papers disassociating themselves from their own wives . . . they were scared of the repercussions to their businesses."[40]

During the boycott, some of these same women, along with others who were not as bold in their dissent, assisted blacks with rides to and from jobs in the white residential areas. Some, like Virginia Durr, would go out of the way to give rides to blacks who had extremely long walks, but, she said, in conversation "they wouldn't admit they were supporting the boycott." Other white women did not openly support the boycott but did provide transportation for their own maids. Even if done purely for selfish reasons, these actions did help the boycott's effectiveness. Mayor Gayle issued a plea to white women to stop giving their black maids rides. And the response? As Virginia Durr has said, "Well, you never heard such a roar of indignation in your life."[41]

One important progressive organization in Montgomery was the Council on Human Relations, which was mostly made up of clergymen and white women. It acted throughout the mid-fifties as one of the "voices of reason" in Montgomery and as an important source of support to dissenters isolated from the larger community. The Reverend Thomas Thrasher, rector of the Episcopal church Juliette Morgan attended, was one of the most visible and vocal of Montgomery's clergy and called for "kindness, forbearance, courtesy, and an awareness of the rights of all people."[42] Through the Council on Human Relations, he arranged meetings and helped conduct negotiations among the Montgomery Improvement Association (the organization created to run the boycott), the City Commission, and the bus company. Thrasher's actions and convictions were not appreciated by all of his church members, but Juliette Morgan praised him. Upon conclusion of the boycott, she said of him, "He has been outstanding in his fine work, in his article for *The Reporter,* in his appeal over radio and television when the court order for desegregation of the buses arrived here. . . ."[43] The article she referred to here was in the New York political magazine the *Reporter* and condemned the White Citizens' Councils, saying the answer to the tension and conflict between the races in Montgomery was patience in negotiation.[44]

Even within meetings of the Council on Human Relations, white dissenters could not feel entirely safe from community pressure. During the boycott, Juliette Morgan attended one meeting at which Martin Luther King, Jr., was the main speaker. During the address, she turned and saw a White Citizens' Council member in the audience. She said to Virginia Durr, who was seated next to her, "You know, I feel like somebody is pointing a gun at me."[45] She feared she would lose her job at the library for her views, and she turned out to be correct, because later she almost did.

Two Montgomery whites who were particularly resented by the larger white community at this time were federal district judges Frank M. Johnson, Jr., and Richard Rives. These judges were responsible for many decisions that upheld black civil rights claims, including the *Browder v. Gayle* decision in 1956 that called for desegregation of public transportation.[46] Judge Johnson, a native of northern Alabama, was appointed to the position in Montgomery in 1955, shortly before the boycott began. The reactions he received from the Montgomery white community to his rulings included the burning of a cross in his front yard, bags of hate mail, and the dynamiting of his mother's house, which was mistaken for his own. But like Virginia Durr, Johnson operated with "an intensely loyal group of people constituting the supporting personnel of the court" and was able to handle these negative reactions.[47]

Judge Richard Rives, unlike Johnson, had grown up in Montgomery and practiced law there before his appointment. Public hostility toward him was of a different nature. Reflecting on the resentment against Rives, Johnson has said, "He was one of them . . . and it was said by several

people, and probably in the newspaper, I think I recall, here in Montgomery, 'Richard Rives is one of our own, and we did expect more out
of him, and he's forfeited the right to be buried in Confederate soil.'
And that's how strong it was."[48] Like Judge Rives, Juliette Morgan was
"one of them."

However upset Juliette Morgan's segregationist enemies were with her,
it was difficult for them to characterize her as a radical agitator. She
certainly did not look like one. A delicate and frail woman of medium
height and fair complexion, she walked with a slump to her shoulders
and gave the impression of being meek, timid, and older than her true
age. As described by Joe Azbell, who was then the *Advertiser*'s city editor
and spoke with her several times during the boycott, she was "sweet-
natured and never offensive to anyone."[49]

Yet Juliette Morgan was quite a troublesome figure to many in
Montgomery during the most crucial and tension-filled months of the
boycott. In November 1956, the Supreme Court upheld the federal
district court's ruling, and on December 20, the court orders reached
Montgomery. As truly integrated bus rides began, there was rejoicing
among blacks and their white supporters. But this was soon followed by
a wave of fear, as a chain of bombings began that threatened lives,
homes, and churches in the black community.

In January of 1957, Juliette Morgan made her most emphatic condemnation of white southerners who would not accept the fact that their
"Southern way of life" must change. In a congratulatory letter to Buford
Boone, publisher of the *Tuscaloosa News,* on an antiracism speech he
had made to the Tuscaloosa White Citizens' Council, Juliette condemned
white men in particular for moral cowardice:

> There are many Southerners from various walks of life that know that
> you are right. They know the court is right. . . . Everyone who speaks as
> you do who has the faith to do what he believes right in scorn of the
> consequences, does great good in preparing the way for a happier and more
> equitable future for all Americans. You help redeem Alabama's very bad
> behavior in the eyes of the nation and the world.
>
> I had begun to wonder if there were any men in the state—any white
> men—with any sane evaluation of our situation here in the middle of the
> twentieth century, with any good will, and most especially any moral
> courage to express it.[50]

She made her criticisms even more offensive to her enemies by pointing
out that she was not someone whom they could dismiss as an outsider.

Perhaps in writing to the *Tuscaloosa News* rather than to the *Montgomery Advertiser*, Juliette Morgan did not anticipate the intense local attention her letter would receive. But it was this letter that brought her more public condemnation than she had ever before experienced. This was a time when tensions were extremely high and segregationists were facing what they perceived to be a failure. To be called cowards by someone like Juliette Morgan was more than they thought they should endure.

Immediately following the letter's publication, several members of the library board of trustees insisted that Juliette Morgan be dismissed from her job for her "criticism of city policy," because the library was funded by the city. Truman H. Hobbs, now a federal district judge in Montgomery, was at that time the only lawyer on the board and stopped the dismissal action with the argument that it would violate her First Amendment right to free speech. One other member of the board, Irene Munroe, sided with Hobbs on this matter.[51]

Consequently, Juliette Morgan was not fired from her job, but community pressure continued as people brought their books back to the library saying "that they didn't want anything to do with it while she was there."[52] These hostile actions, especially when they hurt the library she loved, distressed her greatly. The harassment continued to build as "young people threw rocks through her windows, insulted her on the streets and played tricks on her in the library."[53]

In March of 1957, her letter to the *Tuscaloosa News* was reprinted in the *States' Rights Advocate*, the monthly publication of the Montgomery White Citizens' Council, under the headline "Juliette Morgan Stays at Library," thus gaining even more attention from local segregationists.[54] Those who knew her at this time say that the continuing public criticism and threats "took a terrible toll on her."[55]

Two months later, Juliette Morgan took a leave of absence from the library and began seeing a Birmingham psychiatrist, who gave her shock treatments for "an acute anxiety attack." While in Birmingham, she stayed with her aunt, Roberta Morgan. In a letter to her mother, she expressed a sense of shame about her mental and emotional instability. She wrote, "I'm sure it was best for me to come on up here [to Birmingham]. It was about the only move to make and something had to give. I'm so sorry about it all. . . . Do what you can to keep me from appearing publicly any bigger fool than I am. Maybe I can live it down and pick up the pieces yet."[56]

But she was not able to "pick up the pieces." As Martin Luther King,

Jr., said, "Miss Juliette Morgan, sensitive and frail, did not long survive the rejections and condemnation of the white community. . . ."[57] Virginia Durr, who visited her on July 17 at her mother's home in Montgomery, said that Juliette was in such deep despair that she said "all she wanted was to die."[58] Later that same day, at the age of forty-three, Juliette Morgan took her own life. A note she left read, "Please let everything I have go to my mother. I can't go on."[59]

In the early days of the boycott, King gave a particularly inspiring speech in which he said that "there comes a time when people get tired of being trampled over by the iron feet of oppression."[60] The boycotters were tired of oppression. They chose to resist it with the weapon of protest. Juliette Morgan, too, was tired of oppression. She protested the oppression of others, but when she herself was oppressed and persecuted, she chose, finally, tragically, to try to escape it.

Following her death, one of her friends wrote to the *Montgomery Advertiser* that Juliette Morgan was "alive to the cause of justice as are few of us and had the courage of her convictions. . . . She was a flame that many cowardly people tried to extinguish, but she burned the brighter for it."[61]

Notes

Introduction
THOMAS

1. Anne Firor Scott, *The Southern Lady from Pedestal to Politics 1830–1930* (Chicago: University of Chicago Press, 1970).
2. Deborah Gray White, *Ar'n't I a Woman? Female Slaves in the Plantation South* (New York: W. W. Norton, 1985); Jacqueline Jones, *Labor of Love, Labor of Sorrow: Black Women, Work and the Family, from Slavery to the Present* (New York: Vintage Books, 1986).
3. Elizabeth Fox-Genovese, *Within the Plantation Household: Black and White Women of the Old South* (Chapel Hill: University of North Carolina Press, 1988).

1. Stewards of Their Culture
Southern Women Novelists as Social Critics
FOX-GENOVESE

1. Blanche Glassman Hersh, *The Slavery of Sex: Feminist-Abolitionists in America* (Urbana: University of Illinois Press, 1978); Carroll Smith-Rosenberg, *Religion and the Rise of the American City: The New York City Mission Movement, 1812–1870* (Ithaca, N.Y.: Cornell University Press, 1970); Jean Fagan Yellen, *Women and Sisters: Antislavery Feminists in American Culture* (New Haven, Conn.: Yale University Press, 1990).
2. For a preliminary discussion of the conservatism of antebellum southern women, see Elizabeth Fox-Genovese, "Social Order and the Female Self: The Conservatism of Southern Women in Comparative Perspective"; Barbara Jeanne

Fields, "Commentary," both in *What Made the South Different?*, ed. Kees Gispen (Jackson: University of Mississippi Press, 1990), 49–70.

3. Mary Kelly, *Private Woman, Public Stage: Literary Domesticity in Nineteenth-Century America* (New York: Oxford University Press, 1984); Jane Tompkins, *Sensational Designs: The Cultural Work of American Fiction 1790–1860* (New York: Oxford University Press, 1989). See also Joyce W. Warren, *The American Narcissus: Individualism and Women in Nineteenth-Century American Fiction* (New Brunswick, N.J.: Rutgers University Press, 1989), on the ways in which nineteenth-century American fiction made no place for women as individuals.

4. Alexander Cowie, *American Novel* (New York: American Book Company, 1948), 413; Jane P. Tompkins, "The Other American Renaissance," in *The American Renaissance Reconsidered*, ed. Walter Benn Michaels and Donald E. Pease (Baltimore: Johns Hopkins University Press, 1985), 35.

5. Tompkins, "Other American Renaissance," 35.

6. Tompkins, *Sensational Designs*, 185, 145.

7. Louisa S. McCord [L.S.M.], "Uncle Tom's Cabin," *Southern Quarterly Review* 23 (January 1853): 81–120. On Louisa McCord and on southern women's response to *Uncle Tom's Cabin* in general, see Elizabeth Fox-Genovese, *Within the Plantation Household: Black and White Women of the Old South* (Chapel Hill: University of North Carolina Press, 1988); Fred Lewis Pattee, *The Feminine Fifties* (New York: D. Appleton-Century, 1940); Cowie, *Rise of the American Novel*, 413; E. Douglas Branch, *The Sentimental Years 1836–1860* (New York: D. Appleton-Century, 1934). On the various women writers, see, among many, Kelly, *Private Woman, Public Stage;* Elizabeth Moss, *Domestic Novelists in the Old South: Defenders of Southern Culture* (Baton Rouge: Louisiana State University Press, 1992). Anne Goodwyn Jones, in *Tomorrow Is Another Day: The Woman Writer in the South, 1859–1936* (Baton Rouge: Louisiana State University Press, 1981), discusses Augusta Evans Wilson, but not the antebellum tradition as a whole. Ann Douglas, *The Feminization of American Culture* (New York: Alfred Knopf, 1977), focuses on the North.

8. For a general discussion of the reception of the novel, see Thomas F. Gossett, *Uncle Tom's Cabin and American Culture* (Dallas, Tex.: Southern Methodist University Press, 1976). See also Gillian Brown, "Getting in the Kitchen with Dinah: Domestic Politics in Uncle Tom's Cabin," *American Quarterly* 36, no. 4 (Fall 1984): 503–23; Tompkins, *Sensational Designs*.

9. Moss, *Domestic Novelists*, 31.

10. Francis Pendleton Gaines, *The Southern Plantation: A Study in the Development and Accuracy of a Tradition* (New York: Columbia University Press, 1924; reprint, 1962).

11. On the religious views of slaveholding women, see Elizabeth Fox-Genovese, "Religion in the Lives of Slaveholding Women of the Antebellum South," in *That Gentle Strength: Historical Perspectives on Women in Christianity*, ed. Lynda L. Coon, Katherine J. Haldane, and Elisabeth W. Sommer (Charlottesville: University of Virginia Press, 1990), 207–29. See also Jean E. Friedman, *The Enclosed Garden: Women and Community in the Evangelical South, 1830–1900* (Chapel Hill: University of North Carolina Press, 1985).

12. Caroline Gilman, *Recollections of a Southern Matron* (New York: Harper and Brothers, 1858), 107.

13. Ibid., 27.

14. Ibid., 70.

15. Ibid., 132.

16. Ibid., 71.

17. Ibid., 47.

18. Ibid., 47–48.

19. Ibid., 56.

20. Fox-Genovese, "Religion in the Lives of Slaveholding Women."

21. Gilman, *Recollections,* 71.

22. The Gothic tradition retained considerable resonance in nineteenth-century women's fiction. On the general phenomenon, see Judith Wilt, *Ghosts of the Gothic: Austen, Eliot, and Lawrence* (Princeton: Princeton University Press, 1980). For a specific example, see Charlotte Smith, *Emmeline: The Orphan of the Castle,* ed. Anne Henry Ehrenpreis (London: Oxford University Press, 1971).

23. The need for a father's participation in the education of sons frequently surfaces in the correspondence of slaveholding women whose husbands were too often absent on business or politics. See, for example, the letters of Anna Matilda King to Thomas Butler King, Thomas Butler King Papers, Southern Historical Collection, University of North Carolina, Chapel Hill. On gender conventions in general, see Fox-Genovese, *Within the Plantation Household,* 192–241, and Steven M. Stowe, *Intimacy and Power in the Old South: Ritual in the Lives of the Planters* (Baltimore: Johns Hopkins University Press, 1987).

24. Mrs. Mary E. Eastman, *Aunt Phyllis' Cabin; Or, Southern Life as It Is* (Philadelphia: Lippincott, Grambo & Co., 1852; reprint, New York: Negro Universities Press, 1968), 93.

25. Ibid., 71.

26. Ibid., 95.

27. Ibid., 24.

28. Ibid., 21.

29. Ibid., 19.

30. Mrs. Henry R. Schoolcraft, "The Black Gauntlet: A Tale of Plantation Life in South Carolina," in *Plantation Life: The Narratives of Mrs. Henry Rowe Schoolcraft* (1852–60; reprint, New York: Negro Universities Press, 1969), 93.

31. Ibid., 227.

32. Ibid., 306–07.

33. Ibid., iv.

34. Ibid., v.

35. For the fullest account of Evans's life, see William Perry Fidler, *Augusta Evans Wilson, 1835–1900: A Biography* (University: University of Alabama Press, 1951).

36. See Moss, *Domestic Novelists,* for an arresting reading of the pro-southern implications of *Inez.*

37. For a fuller development of my views on *Beulah,* see my "Introduction" to *Beulah,* ed. Elizabeth Fox-Genovese (Baton Rouge: Louisiana State University

Press, 1992), and my *Ghosts and Memories: Fictions of Black and White Southern Women* (Charlottesville: University of Virginia Press, 1993).

38. Henry Hughes, *Treatise on Sociology, Theoretical and Practical* (1854; reprint, New York, 1968). On Hughes, see Douglas Ambrose's excellent dissertation, "'The Man for Times Coming': The Life and Times of Henry Hughes," (SUNY Binghamton, 1991).

39. For a strong argument about southern women's alienation during the war, see Drew Gilpin Faust, "Altars of Sacrifice: Confederate Women and the Narratives of War," *Journal of American History* 76, no. 4 (March 1990): 1200−1228, and her "Introduction" to *Macaria*, ed. Drew Gilpin Faust (Baton Rouge: Louisiana State University Press, 1992).

40. For a fuller development of this argument, see Elizabeth Fox-Genovese, *Feminism without Illusions: A Critique of Individualism* (Chapel Hill: University of North Carolina Press, 1990). See also the excellent discussion in Jeanne Boydston, Mary Kelley, and Anne Margolis, *The Limits of Sisterhood: The Beecher Sisters on Women's Rights and Woman's Sphere* (Chapel Hill: University of North Carolina Press, 1988).

2. The Plantation Mistress
A Perspective on Antebellum Alabama
BOUCHER

1. Henry Watson to [sister] Julia Watson, January 26, 1845, Henry Watson Papers, Duke University, Durham, N.C.

2. George Fitzhugh, *The Sociology of Slavery* (Richmond: A. Morris, 1854; reprint, New York: Burt Franklin, 1965), 214−15.

3. Catherine Clinton, *The Plantation Mistress: Woman's World in the Old South* (New York: Pantheon, 1982), 109.

4. Ibid., 179.

5. Elizabeth Fox-Genovese, *Within the Plantation Household: Black and White Women in the Old South* (Chapel Hill: University of North Carolina Press, 1988), 30.

6. Ibid., 27.

7. Suzanne Lebsock, *The Free Women of Petersburg: Status and Culture in a Southern Town, 1784–1860* (New York: W. W. Norton, 1984), xv.

8. Jane H. Pease and William H. Pease, *Ladies, Women, and Wenches: Choice and Constraint in Antebellum Charleston and Boston* (Chapel Hill: University of North Carolina Press, 1990), 169.

9. This study of women in wealthy Alabama plantation families is part of a larger project focused on families that held one hundred or more slaves in 1860 Alabama (Ann W. Boucher, "Wealthy Planter Families in Nineteenth Century Alabama," unpublished Ph.D. dissertation, University of Connecticut, 1978).

10. Daniel Scott Smith, "Parental Power and Marriage Patterns: An Analysis of Historical Trends in Hingham, Massachusetts," in *The American Family in Social, Historical Perspective*, ed. Michael Gordon (New York: St. Martin's Press, 1978), 94−95. Smith found that 24.7 percent of daughters who came of

marriage age in the period 1821–40 and 1861–80 married out of birth order, if spinsters are included in the calculation. Examination of the marriage experience of sixty-seven daughters of thirty-one wealthy Alabama families indicates that 27 percent married out of birth order if spinsters are included.

11. Clinton, *Plantation Mistress,* 59–61.

12. Fox-Genovese, *Within the Plantation Household,* 207–9.

13. Boucher, "Wealthy Planter Families," 92–109.

14. Clinton, *Plantation Mistress,* 60.

15. Henry Watson to [mother] Julia Watson, November 30, 1843, November 15, 1844; Henry Watson to Frederick Peck, January 13, 1845, Watson Papers.

16. Henry Watson to [sister] Julia Watson, January 26, 1845, Watson Papers.

17. Lillian A. Pereyea, *James Luske Alcorn* (Baton Rouge: Louisiana State University Press, 1966), 3–5, 9, 21–22; Greene County, Alabama, Marriage Book B, 19.

18. Boucher, "Wealthy Planter Families," 92–100. Between 1840 and 1860, geographical proximity and wealth were the more significant factors, with kinship having a less important influence on marriage formation.

19. Clinton, *Plantation Mistress,* 164.

20. Fox-Genovese, *Within the Plantation Household,* 27, 29–30, 38–48, 192–241.

21. *Harriet Hawthorne, by her next friend Moses Waring, v. Joseph R. Hawthorne,* Wilcox County, Alabama, Proceedings of the Court of Chancery, unnumbered volume, 606–30; *Sarah Walker v. Laird Walker and George Bowie,* Dallas County, Proceedings of the Court of Chancery, vol. K, 433, 856–88.

22. Anne Firor Scott, "Women's Perspective on the Patriarchy in the 1850s," *Journal of American History* 61 (June 1974): 57–58, n. 22.

23. Clinton, *Plantation Mistress,* 6, 153.

24. Boucher, "Wealthy Planter Families," 46.

25. In a one-way analysis of variance, age at marriage proved to have a significant effect, an F ratio of 6.07, on completed fertility (Boucher, "Wealthy Planter Families," 136–41). Ansley J. Coale and Melvin Zelnik, *New Estimates of Fertility and Population in the United States: A Study of Annual White Births from 1855 to 1960 and of Completeness of Enumeration in the Census from 1880 to 1960* (Princeton: Princeton University Press, 1963), 36.

26. Fox-Genovese, *Within the Plantation Household,* 235–36.

27. Clinton, *Plantation Mistress,* 154–55.

28. Fox-Genovese, *Within the Plantation Household,* 112–13, 137.

29. Jessie Webb and James Webb, July 17, 1861, Walton Family Papers, Southern Historical Collection, Chapel Hill, N.C.; Sophia Watson to Henry Watson, May 13, 1848, Mrs. Henry Barnard to Sophia Watson, January 8, 1860, Watson Papers.

30. Sally McMillen, *Motherhood in the Old South: Pregnancy, Childbirth, and Infant Rearing* (Baton Rouge: Louisiana State University Press, 1990), 111–34.

31. Jessie Walton to James Webb, July 8, 1861, July 17, 1861, September 21, 1861, November 14, 1861, Jessie Webb to Mrs. Justina Walton, May 11, 1857, June 23, 1857, Walton Papers; Mrs. Julia Watson to Sophia Watson, May or

June 1847, Sophia Watson to Henry Watson, May 9, 1848, Henry Watson to Mrs. Julia Watson, December 25, 1851, Julia Watson to Sophia Watson, n.d., Henry Watson to Julia Watson, February 14, 1861, Watson Papers.

32. Jessie Webb to Mrs. Justina Walton, March 17, 1861, Jessie Webb to Mrs. Justina Walton and Louisa Creswell, June 25, 1856, Amelia Glover to Mrs. Justina Walton and Jessie Webb, February 23, 1854, Walton Papers; Sophia Watson to Mrs. Julia Watson, n.d. [1858–59], Watson Papers.

33. Sarah L. Fountain to Hannah Coker, September 30, 1836, Sarah L. Fountain to Hannah Coker, February 15, 1838, Sarah L. Fountain to Hannah Coker, December 6, 1838, in Fletcher M. Green, ed. *The Lides Go South . . . and West: The Record of a Planter Migration in 1835* (Columbia: University of South Carolina Press, 1952). Henry Watson to Miss Amelia Dresser, September 12, 1858, Watson Papers; Jessie Webb to James Webb, July 8, 1861, Jessie Webb to James Webb, November 14, 1861, Walton Papers; Eugenia Fitzpatrick to Benjamin Fitzpatrick, Jr., November 30, 1870, Ben James to Benjamin Fitzpatrick, n.d., Benjamin Fitzpatrick Papers, Southern Historical Collection, Chapel Hill, N.C.

34. Margaret Calhoun to Andrew Calhoun, December 18, 1853, Calhoun Papers, South Caroliniana Library, University of South Carolina, Columbia; Aurelia Fitzpatrick to Benjamin Fitzpatrick, Jr., n.d., Fitzpatrick Papers; Mary Louisa Hall to daughter [Laura Hall], February 7, 1855, Bolling Hall Papers, Alabama Department of Archives and History, Montgomery.

35. Clinton, *Plantation Mistress*, 165.

36. Fox-Genovese, *Within the Plantation Household*, 225–30.

37. Louisa Creswell to Jessie Walton, January 5, 1852; Louisa Creswell to Jessie Walton, August 14, 1853, Amelia Glover to Mrs. Justina Walton, October 23, 1852, Amelia Glover to Mrs. Justina Walton, February 23, 1854, Jessie Webb to Mrs. Justina Walton, September 10, 1853, Jessie Webb to Mrs. Justina Walton, June 25, 1856, Jessie Webb to Mrs. Walton, June 4, 1857, Jessie Webb to Mrs. Walton, December 8, 1857, Jessie Webb to Mrs. Walton, April 10, 1861, Walton Papers.

38. Sarah A. Crenshaw to Mary Louisa Hall, July 10, 1847, Hall Papers.

39. Fox-Genovese, *Within the Plantation Household*, 203.

40. Lebsock, *Free Women of Petersburg*, 44–45, 57.

41. Ibid., 37–48.

42. Ibid., 85.

43. Lawrence M. Friedman, *A History of American Law* (New York: Simon & Schuster, 1973), 185–86; Alabama, *Acts Passed at the Annual Session of the General Assembly* (1841), 75, 77, 79, 80, 93; Alabama, *Acts Passed at the Annual Session of the General Assembly* (1845), 25, 160, 179, 193, 198, 202, 232–33; Alabama, *Acts Passed at the Annual Session of the General Assembly* (1848), 79; Alabama, *Code of 1952*, chap. 1, art. 3, sec. 1994, 382.

44. Clinton, *Plantation Mistress*, 37, 85.

45. Marengo County Will Book A, 490.

46. Dallas County Will Book C, 200, 208.

47. Marengo County Will Book A, 378.

48. William R. Smith, *History and Debate of the Convention of the People of*

Alabama (Montgomery: White, Pfister, 1861), 369–71. This reference is cited in J. Mills Thornton III, *Politics and Power in a Slave Society: Alabama 1800–1860* (Baton Rouge: Louisiana State University Press, 1978), 306.

49. Thornton, *Politics and Power in a Slave Society*, 20–58.

3. White and Black Female Missionaries to Former Slaves during Reconstruction

DOSS

1. See, for example, Eric Foner, *Reconstruction: America's Unfinished Revolution, 1863–1877* (New York: Harper & Row, 1988); Sara M. Evans, *Born for Liberty: A History of Women in America* (New York: Free Press, 1989); Jean E. Friedman, *The Enclosed Garden: Women and Community in the Evangelical South, 1830–1900* (Chapel Hill: University of North Carolina Press, 1985); Janet Wilson James, ed., *Women in American Religion* (Philadelphia: University of Pennsylvania Press, 1980). The major study of northern-born common school teachers, male and female, in one state is Jacqueline Jones. *Soldiers of Light and Love: Northern Teachers and Georgia Blacks, 1865–1873* (Chapel Hill: University of North Carolina Press, 1980). Another valuable study of AMA teachers in one state is Randy J. Sparks, "'The White People's Arms Are Longer Than Ours': Blacks, Education, and the American Missionary Association in Reconstruction Mississippi," *Journal of Mississippi History* 54 (February 1992): 1–27.

2. Allis Wolfe, "Women Who Dared: Northern Teachers of the Southern Freedmen, 1862–1872" (Ph.D. dissertation, City University of New York, 1982), 6; Barbara Miller Solomon, *In the Company of Educated Women: A History of Women and Higher Education in America* (New Haven, Conn.: Yale University Press, 1985), 45.

3. Virginia Lieson Brereton and Christa Ressmeyer Klein, "American Women in Ministry: A History of Protestant Beginning Points," in *Women of Spirit: Female Leadership in the Jewish and Christian Traditions*, ed. Rosemary Ruether and Eleanor McLaughlin (New York: Simon and Schuster, 1979), 308.

4. Ibid., 307–8, 310.

5. See, for example, John Patrick McDowell, *The Social Gospel in the South: The Woman's Home Mission Movement in the Methodist Episcopal Church, South, 1886–1939* (Baton Rouge: Louisiana State University Press, 1982), 6–11. For a list of the major women's missionary societies in the nation and in the South, see Brereton and Klein, "American Women in Ministry," 305–6.

6. See James D. Anderson, *The Education of Blacks in the South, 1860–1935* (Chapel Hill: University of North Carolina Press, 1988), chap. 1. On the prewar quest for literacy, see Janet Duitsman Cornelius, *When I Can Read My Title Clear: Literacy, Slavery, and Religion in the Antebellum South* (Columbia: University of South Carolina Press, 1991).

7. Maxine D. Jones and Joe M. Richardson, *Talladega College: The First Century* (Tuscaloosa: University of Alabama Press, 1990), 2.

8. Richard B. Drake, "The American Missionary Association and the Southern Negro, 1861–1888" (Ph.D. dissertation, Emory University, 1957), 152, 154;

Joe M. Richardson, "The American Missionary Association and Blacks on the Gulf Coast during Reconstruction," *Gulf Coast Historical Review* 4, no. 2 (Spring 1989) 152–53; Leon F. Litwack, *Been in the Storm So Long: The Aftermath of Slavery* (New York: Random House, 1979), 452. For a full discussion of the AMA in the South, see Joe M. Richardson, *Christian Reconstruction: The American Missionary Association and Southern Blacks, 1861–1890* (Athens: University of Georgia Press, 1986).

9. Richardson, "American Missionary Association," 152; Mary F. Wells to George Edward F. Smith, February 18, 1867, American Missionary Association Archives, Amistad Research Center, Tulane University, New Orleans (hereinafter cited as AMA Archives). References pertain to microfilmed copies of the originals.

10. G. L. Putnam to E. P. Smith, November 9, 1868, AMA Archives; Report of Trinity School in Athens, Alabama, for January 1871, signed M. F. Wells, Report of Trinity School in Athens, Alabama, for February 1871, signed M. F. Wells, Report of Normal and A.M.A. School, Talladega, Alabama, for October 1870, signed Albert A. Safford, Report of Colored School in Eufaula for November 1870, signed John A. Bassett, William P. M. Gilbert to E. P. Smith, July 16, 1867, John A. Bassett to E. P. Smith, December 8, 1869, AMA Archives; H. Paul Douglass, *Christian Reconstruction in the South* (Boston: Pilgrim Press, 1909), 216.

11. Jones and Richardson, *Talladega College*, 22–23.

12. Ibid. The quotation comes from J. Peirce to E. M. Cravath, February 13, 1872, AMA Archives.

13. Ellen L. Benton to E. P. Smith, July 29, 1867; Miss J. E. Beigle to E. M. Cravath, October 29, 1870; M. F. Wells to E. M. Cravath, March 26, [1872]; D. L. Hickok to M. E. Strieby, May 13, 1878, AMA Archives.

14. Lucy Brown to M. E. Strieby, 1869, AMA Archives, quoted in Jones and Richardson, *Talladega College*, 10.

15. Alfred Jones to M. E. Strieby, May 27, 1878, AMA Archives.

16. D. L. Hickok to M. E. Strieby, December 10, 1878, E. C. Silsby to M. E. Strieby, October 4, 1877, E. C. Silsby to M. E. Strieby, October 24, 1877, Fletcher Clark to M. E. Strieby, March 1, 1878, George E. Hill to M. E. Strieby, February 18, 1878, George E. Hill to M. E. Strieby, January 7, 1878, AMA Archives.

17. *Baptist Home Mission Monthly* 10, no. 5 (May 1888): 125–26.

18. *Baptist Home Mission Monthly* 1, no. 8 (August 1889): 227.

19. Joanna P. Moore, *"In Christ's Stead": Autobiographical Sketches* (Chicago: Women's Baptist Home Mission Society, 1903), 136. The Women's Baptist Home Mission Society, organized in Chicago in 1877, and the Woman's American Baptist Home Mission Society, organized in Boston in 1877, worked independently until their union in 1909 under the latter name.

20. "Report of the Executive Board of the Women's Baptist Home Mission Society for the Year Ending April 30, 1883," in *The Women's Baptist Home Mission Society 1877 to 1882: Minutes of Annual and Special Meetings, and Annual Reports of Corresponding Secretary during the First Five Years* (Chicago: R. R. Donnelly & Sons, 1883), p. [11] of 1883.

21. Brereton and Klein, "American Women in Ministry," 309.

22. "Report of the Executive Board of the Women's Baptist Home Mission Society for the Year Ending April 30, 1882," in *The Women's Baptist Home Mission Society 1877 to 1882*, [66]; *Baptist Home Mission Monthly* 4, no. 3 (March 1882): 79.

23. *Women's Baptist Home Mission Society 1877 to 1882*, 1883, [p. 13], 1884, p. 9, 1885, p. 19. The quotation comes from the last citation.

24. WBHMS, Report of the Executive Board for the Year Ending March 31, 1886, p. 22, 1887, p. 26, 1888, p. 20, American Baptist Historical Society, Colgate-Rochester Seminary Library, Rochester, N.Y. (hereinafter cited as ABHS); ABHMS, Annual Report, 1887, pp. 100–101, 1888, p. 115, 1889, p. 111, ABHS; Stephen Nathaniel Reid, *History of Colored Baptists in Alabama* (1949), 63.

25. Moore, *"In Christ's Stead,"* 136; *Baptist Home Mission Monthly* 3, no. 1 (January 1881): 15; *Baptist Home Mission Monthly* 3, no. 3 (March 1881): 62–63.

26. "Report of the Executive Board of the Women's Baptist Home Mission Society for the Year Ending April 30, 1881," in *The Women's Baptist Home Mission Society 1877 to 1882*, [53].

27. *Baptist Home Mission Monthly* 3, no. 4 (April 1881): 88; *Baptist Home Mission Monthly* 3, no. 3 (March 1881): 63.

28. Woman's American Baptist Home Mission Society Report, 1878, and November 20, 1879, ABHS.

29. *Report of the Woman's American Baptist Home Mission Society, Presented at Saratoga Springs, May 30, 1879* (Saratoga Springs: Paul & Ritchie, 1879), 2; Report of the Woman's American Baptist Home Mission Society, Presented at the Second Anniversary, at Warren Avenue Baptist Church, Boston, November 20, 1879, p. 2, ABHS.

30. *An Appeal from the "Woman's American Baptist Home Mission Society"* (Woman's American Baptist Home Mission Society, 1878); *Fifth Annual Report of the Woman's American Baptist Home Mission Society with the Report of the Annual Meeting Held in Warren Avenue Church, Boston, May 9, 1883* (Boston: G. J. Stiles, 1883), 16, 17, ABHS.

31. U.S. Bureau of the Census, Thirteenth Census: 1910, Alabama, Enumeration District 133, sheet 1; *Minutes of the Seventeenth Annual Session of the Alabama Colored Baptist State Convention . . . 1884* (Selma, Ala.: Baptist Pioneer Printing, 1885), 10; Reid, *History of Colored Baptists in Alabama*, 62–63. Booth was sometimes spelled Boothe.

32. Jones and Richardson, *Talladega College*, 39–40, 256 (n. 59).

33. Moore, *"In Christ's Stead,"* 132–34, ABHS.

34. *Baptist Home Mission Monthly* 4, no. 4 (April 1882): 108.

35. Jones and Richardson, *Talladega College*, 11–12. For sources of quotations, see p. 250, n. 35.

36. E. L. Benton to E. P. Smith, August 26, 1867, AMA Archives.

37. M. F. Wells to M. E. Strieby, August 9, 1876, AMA Archives.

38. John B. Callis to Edwin Beacker, July 23, 1866, Huntsville, Alabama, Subdistrict, Letters Sent, vol. 63, p. 149, John B. Callis to C. Cadle, Jr., August 9,

1866, Huntsville, Alabama, Subdistrict, Letters Sent, vol. 63, pp. 170–71, Bureau of Refugees, Freedmen, and Abandoned Lands, Record Group 105, National Archives, Washington, D.C. The quotation comes from the second cited letter.

39. J. F. McGogy to Edwin Beecher, October 18, 1868, Greenville, Alabama, Subdistrict, Letters Sent, vol. 126, pp. 38–39, Bureau of Refugees, Freedmen, and Abandoned Lands, Record Group 105, National Archives, Washington, D.C.

40. William Fiske to George Whipple, March 14, 1866, AMA Archives.

41. J. E. Biegle to [E. M.] Cravath, October 29, 1870, AMA Archives.

42. Maria Waterbury to O. O. Howard, October 10, 1871, Maria Waterbury to E. M. Cravath, October 17, 1871, Maria Waterbury to E. M. Cravath, November 6, 1871, AMA Archives. The quotation comes from the last letter cited.

43. James F. Childs to E. M. Cravath, June 20, 1871, AMA Archives.

44. Charles L. Harris to Editor, "Alabama News," *Christian Recorder*, December 19, 1878.

45. Friedman, *Enclosed Garden*, 124.

4. Amelia Gayle Gorgas
A Victorian Mother
WIGGINS

Material for this essay came from research for a larger project supported by a grant from the National Endowment for the Humanities and a grant from the University of Alabama Research Grants Committee. The essay was written during a sabbatical leave, Fall 1989, from The University of Alabama.

1. William Crawford Gorgas (WCG) to Mary Gorgas, January 1, 1914, WCG to Jessie Gorgas, June 17, 1915, WCG to George Palfrey, February 24, 1913, William Crawford Gorgas Papers, University of Alabama, Tuscaloosa (hereinafter cited as WCG Papers, UA).

2. WCG to Mary Gorgas, January 1, 1914, WCG Papers, UA.

3. John Demos, *Past, Present, and Personal . . .* (New York: Oxford University Press, 1986), 31–35; Carl N. Degler, *At Odds: Women and the Family in America from the Revolution to the Present* (New York: Oxford University Press, 1980), 8–9, 26–30; Miriam M. Johnson, *Strong Mothers, Weak Wives: The Search for Gender Equality* (Berkeley: University of California Press, 1988), 231–32; Elizabeth Janeway, *Man's World, Woman's Place: A Study in Social Mythology* (New York: William Morrow, 1971), 7–8, 14–15.

4. Unidentified typescript in Gayle Family Papers, Alabama Department of Archives and History, Montgomery; Thomas L. Bayne to My Dear Children, October 6, 1870 (typescript), 15–16, Stanhope-Bayne Jones Papers, Manuscripts Collection, History of Medicine Division, National Library of Medicine, National Institutes of Health, Bethesda, Md.; Elizabeth Fox-Genovese, *Within the Plantation Household: Black and White Women of the Old South* (Chapel Hill: University of North Carolina Press, 1988), 1–28, and "Family and Female Identity in the Antebellum South: Sarah Gayle and Her Family," in *In Joy and in*

Sorrow: Women, Family, and Marriage in the Victorian South, 1830–1900, ed. Carol Bleser (New York: Oxford University Press, 1991), 16–18.

5. Sarah Haynsworth Gayle journal, February 19, 1831, June 1, 1834, Gorgas Family Papers, University of Alabama, Tuscaloosa.

6. Ibid., April 1, July 20, 1831, [May 1832?], November 6, 1833, March 16, 1834, November 5, 1835.

7. Sarah Gayle Crawford journal, June 27, 1849, Sarah Gayle Crawford and William B. Crawford Papers, University of Alabama, Tuscaloosa; Mary Tabb Johnston, *Amelia Gayle Gorgas: A Biography* (University: University of Alabama Press, 1978), 10–14; Frank E. Vandiver, *Ploughshares into Swords: Josiah Gorgas and Confederate Ordnance* (Austin: University of Texas Press, 1952), 37–38; Sarah Woolfolk Wiggins, "A Victorian Father: Josiah Gorgas and His Family," in *In Joy and in Sorrow,* 233–35.

8. Johnston, *Amelia,* 32–36.

9. Ibid., 37–79; Wiggins, "Victorian Father," 234–36.

10. Josiah Gorgas Personal Account Book, 1857–1875, June 13, 1873, Gorgas Family Papers; Johnston, *Amelia,* 80–102; Vandiver, *Ploughshares into Swords,* 287–305; Wiggins, "Victorian Father," 240–50.

11. Vandiver, *Ploughshares into Swords,* 308–14; Amelia Gorgas (AG) to WCG, June 20, 1879, October 2, 1879, December 28, [1879], [April 1880], Gorgas Family Papers.

12. Johnston, *Amelia,* 103–15.

13. [Josiah Gorgas], "Epistolary Gossipings of Travel, &c.," *Russell's Magazine* 5 (May 1859): 134–35.

14. The author has corresponded with a dozen descendants of Amelia and her sisters from California to Florida, and no portraits or photographs of Amelia before 1900 have been found. Amelia's mother described the child at two as an "urchin" who was so small that "everything appeared extraordinary in her" (Gayle journal, March 29, 1828). From an early age, Amelia seemed conscious that her success lay with her personality, not her appearance.

15. AG to Josiah Gorgas (JG), June 27, [1858], AG to My dear Milly [Amelia Crawford], September 27 [25], [1864], Gorgas Family Papers (many letters in this collection are undated, partially dated, or incorrectly dated; each date cited represents a separate letter).

16. Johnston, *Amelia,* 38–39, 42, 110–11. Anne's special place in the Gorgas family was demonstrated in 1881, when eldest son William Crawford escorted her to the wedding of one of the Gorgas daughters. Anne died a few weeks later and became the first to be buried in the Gorgas family cemetery plot in Tuscaloosa.

17. See Steven M. Stowe, *Intimacy and Power in the Old South: Ritual in the Lives of the Planters* (Baltimore: Johns Hopkins University Press, 1987), 170, for an analysis of this strong attachment to children.

18. AG to JG, May 30, June 6, June 11, 1858, Gorgas Family Papers.

19. AG to JG, July 4, June 18, 1858, June 27, [1858], July 15, July 4, July 24, 1858, [1858], June 18, 1858, Gorgas Family Papers (each date cited represents a separate letter).

20. Similar lavish maternal care for southern children despite the presence of

reliable nursemaids has been documented in Jane Turner Censer, *North Carolina Planters and Their Children, 1800–1860* (Baton Rouge: Louisiana State University Press, 1984), 36–39, and Ann Williams Boucher, "Wealthy Planter Families in Nineteenth-Century Alabama" (Ph.D. dissertation, University of Connecticut, 1978), 149–51.

21. AG to JG, March 18 and 20, [1866], Gorgas Family Papers.

22. Josiah Gorgas journal, September 8, October 10, 1867, Gorgas Family Papers.

23. Ibid., October 18, 1872, June 28, October 19, 1874, Gorgas Family Papers. For other examples see also WCG to Richard Gorgas, August 22, 1881, WCG Papers, UA; AG to WCG, August 6, 1884, April 26, 1885, October 7, 1886, Gorgas Family Papers. The diary of Amelia's sister, Mary Gayle Aiken (Aiken Family Papers, South Caroliniana Library, University of South Carolina, Columbia), provides no information on this subject.

24. AG to Marie Gorgas, March 13, 1894, Jessie Gorgas to WCG, October 3, 1894, AG to WCG, November 4, 1894, William Crawford Gorgas Papers, Manuscript Division, Library of Congress, Washington, D.C. (hereinafter cited as WCG Papers, LC); WCG to Jessie Gorgas, July 2, 1913, WCG Papers, UA; [Sarah Gayle Crawford] to Sallie [Crawford Hughes], November 3, 1895, Sarah Gayle Crawford Papers, Manuscript Department, Duke University Library, Durham, N.C.

25. WCG to Jessie Gorgas, September 3, 1919, WCG Papers, UA. The idea that the Gorgas household was home for Amelia's extended family persists among Gorgas relatives today. The first letter to the author from one descendant proudly opened with "I was born in the Gorgas House" (George Tait to Sarah W. Wiggins, May 14, 1989, Gorgas Family Papers).

26. AG to WCG, October 7, 1886, Gorgas Family Papers. In the post–Civil War South, the Gorgas family exemplified the elastic, extended planter families of the antebellum South described in Joan E. Cashin, "The Structure of Antebellum Planter Families: 'The Ties that Bound us Was Strong,'" *Journal of Southern History* 56 (February 1990): 55–70.

27. Crawford journal, January 28, 1854; Johnston, *Amelia,* 27–28, 30–31, 34; Gorgas journal, June 22, September 7, October 17, 1862.

28. Johnston, *Amelia,* 78; JG to [Jessie Gorgas], July 2, [1867], JG to My Dear Son [WCG], January 2, 1875, AG to WCG, [Fall 1875], Gorgas Family Papers; JG to WCG, January 18, [1875], WCG Papers, UA.

29. AG to My dear Children [Jessie and Mamie Gorgas], June 8, [1872], AG to WCG, [April 1880], December 3, 1884, Gorgas Family Papers; WCG to Jessie Gorgas, March 4, 1877, WCG to AG, October 3, 1884, WCG Papers, UA.

30. AG to JG, June 26, [1865], August 13, [1865], September 5, [1865], JG to AG, September 29, [1865], Gorgas Family Papers.

31. JG to Sister [Sarah Crawford], [July 1865?], Gorgas Family Papers.

32. Postscript of AG to JG, in Richard H. Gayle to JG, July 7, 1865, Gorgas Family Papers. For a superb study of the web of southern "connexions" and their importance, see Daniel E. Sutherland, *The Confederate Carpetbaggers* (Baton Rouge: Louisiana State University Press, 1988).

33. AG to [JG], [June? 1865], Gorgas Family Papers.

34. JG to AG, September 29, [1865], March 6, [1868], October 14, 1869, Gorgas Family Papers.

35. JG to AG, March 13, [1870], AG to JG, October 14, [1868?], Gorgas Family Papers.

36. JG to AG, January 25, 1876, Gorgas Family Papers.

37. AG to WCG, June 20, 1879, March 12, [1879], Gorgas Family Papers.

38. AG to [T. L.] Bayne, January 12, 1881, Gorgas Family Papers; Jessie Gorgas to WCG, September 30, 1916, WCG Papers, UA. When Josiah suffered his stroke, Amelia had been at Sewanee nursing her ill sister Mary. For a month Amelia had never left her sister's beside. Amelia hastened to Josiah, and in March, Mary and her son and daughter moved in with the Gorgases in Tuscaloosa (AG to WCG, February 27, [1879], March 16, [1879], Gorgas Family Papers).

39. Helen Gayle Locke, quoted in Jessie Gorgas to WCG, February 29, [1916?], WCG Papers, UA.

40. JG to AG, April 14, [1855], Gorgas Family Papers.

41. AG to JG, two separate letters of 1870, Gorgas Family Papers.

42. AG to JG, two separate letters of 1870 (one undated), Gorgas Family Papers.

43. AG to JG, [1870], JG to AG, [1870], Gorgas Family Papers.

44. AG to WCG, January 14, 1895, WCG Papers, LC.

45. Minnie Gorgas to Jessie Gorgas, January 11, 1878, Gorgas Family Papers.

46. J. W. Mallet to AG, March 1, 1887, J. W. Mallet to Jessie Gorgas, November 7, 1906, Gorgas Family Papers.

47. Gorgas journal, March 6, 1857.

48. Mary A. Gayle to AG, June 5, 1883, Gorgas Family Papers. The relationship of Mary Anne Gayle to the Gorgas family refutes the notion that genuine love could not exist between a slave and an owner. A Mobile florist annually decorated the graves in the Gayle family plot in Magnolia Cemetery on All Saints' Day. Each year on that day, he noticed that someone also had placed flowers at the grave of Amelia's father, John Gayle. On one occasion, he arrived at the Gayle lot to discover an elderly black woman, who identified herself as Mary Anne Gayle, a former slave of the Gayle family. She placed flowers there every year for twenty-five to thirty years after the death of Governor Gayle in 1859 (Hugh A. Bayne memoirs, Bayne-Gayle Papers [microfilm], Southern Historical Collection, University of North Carolina at Chapel Hill).

49. AG to JG, June 27, [1858], Gorgas Family Papers.

50. WCG to Richard Gorgas, January 4, 1913, WCG Papers, UA.

51. WCG to Jessie Gorgas, December 24, 1914, WCG to Richard Gorgas, January 4, 1913, WCG to Minnie Palfrey, December 18, 1914, WCG to AG, October 8, 1901, WCG Papers, UA.

52. WCG to Jessie Gorgas, June 17, 1915, WCG Papers, UA.

53. WCG to Richard Gorgas, January 4, 1913, WCG Papers, UA.

54. WCG to Jessie Gorgas, October 19, 1914, WCG Papers, UA.

55. JG to AG, November 16, 1854, Gorgas Family Papers.

56. JG to AG, July 1865, May 4, [1865], Gorgas Family Papers; Gorgas journal, November 19, 1865, February 11, 1866. See also JG to AG, January 23, [1866], Gorgas Family Papers.

57. AG to JG, undated fragment, Gorgas Family Papers.

58. AG to JG, July 29, [1865], January 28, 1866, Gorgas Family Papers.

59. AG to JG, June 26, [1865], Gorgas Family Papers; Gorgas journal, June 30, 1867. See also JG to AG, July 29, [1865], Gorgas Family Papers. Amelia would have laughed at the pronouncement of Bertram Wyatt-Brown, *Southern Honor: Ethics and Behavior in the Old South* (New York: Oxford University Press, 1982), 251, that southern mothers "were confined at home, resentful of their immobility, whether they knew it or not."

60. AG to JG, June 2, [18??], AG to Sarah [Crawford], December 4, 1864, AG to WCG, [Fall 1875], Gorgas Family Papers.

61. AG to WCG, August 6, 1884, Gorgas Family Papers. Amelia's Confederate sympathies died hard. From Baltimore in January 1866, she described to Josiah the scene in church where, at the prayer for the U.S. president, she said, "I . . . closed my own prayer book & held my *own head* erect." She noted that "a number of defiant looking little bonnets dotted the large congregation, showing a strong seceech element still existing in this charming city" (AG to JG, January [1866], Gorgas Family Papers). Planning to attend a friend's wedding, Amelia trimmed Willie's gray suit so that he would "appear as much as possible in the uniform of his lost but beloved Confederacy" (AG to JG, [January] 21, [1866], Gorgas Family Papers). In 1896, Amelia maintained her Confederate sympathies, as she demonstrated when she wrote one of her daughters that she anticipated a visit from an old friend who was "such a staunch, true Confederate" that she was "always glad of a war-talk with him." Few were left "to grieve" over the dark days of Lee's surrender, and Amelia acknowledged that she rather enjoyed "an occasional indulgence in the harrowing reminiscences" (AG to Maria Gorgas, February 9, 1896, Gorgas Family Papers). As Alabamians prepared for Confederate Memorial Day in 1901, Amelia excitedly reported local activities to Willie. If the weather was "favorable," she planned to make her "last appearance in memory of the 'lost cause,' so dear to my heart." After the veterans received crosses, widows were to receive one "to be inherited by the oldest living son, an anomaly in your case as you wear the U.S. uniform but you can hide the dear 'Con Cross' upon your heart" (AG to WCG, [April 22, 1901], WCG Papers, UA). The son was no less a staunch Confederate than the mother. "Let me have the Confederate cross," he replied to Amelia. "I will wear it on the outside of my full dress coat. Because I wear the blue now does not make me any the less an ardent Confed" (WCG to AG, May 3, 1901, WCG Papers, UA). In the twentieth century, Amelia still referred to herself as "an unreconstructed old rebel" (AG to [Maria Gorgas], [1904?], Gorgas Family Papers).

62. Marie D. Gorgas and Burton J. Hendrick, *William Crawford Gorgas: His Life and Work* (Garden City, N.Y.: Garden City Publishing Co., 1924), 17–18.

63. AG to Marie Gorgas, July 4, 1900, July 24, 1906, Gorgas Family Papers.

64. WCG to Jessie Gorgas, October 19, 1914, April 4, 1913, WCG Papers, UA.

65. WCG to Minnie Palfrey, December 18, 1914, WCG Papers, UA.

66. *Crimson-White*, undated clippings, Gorgas Family Papers.

67. *Crimson-White*, two undated clippings, Birmingham *Age-Herald*, undated clipping, Gorgas Family Papers; *New York Times*, June 19, 1916. Nothing in the Gorgas manuscripts suggests Amelia as an advocate of the admission of women to the university, nor do her letters mention that they were first admitted in 1893. Logic suggests that she knew the women's advocate Julia Tutwiler of Greensboro, but no correspondence between the two women has been found, and the Gorgas manuscripts do not mention Tutwiler.

68. Birmingham *Age-Herald,* undated clipping, Gorgas Family Papers.

69. AG to WCG, April 6, 1884, Gorgas Family Papers; AG to WCG, October 3, 1899, WCG Papers, LC.

70. AG to [T. L.] Bayne, January 12, 1881, Gorgas Family Papers.

71. WCG to AG, March 7, 1903, WCG Papers, UA.

72. R. E. Park, Jr., to Mary Gorgas, November 17, 1906, Gorgas Family Papers.

73. Hill Ferguson to AG, December 28, 1906, Gorgas Family Papers.

74. AG to WCG, February 1, 1907, WCG Papers, UA.

75. E. M. Harris to AG, December 28, 1906, Gorgas Family Papers. See also R. E. Park, Jr., to Harry S. Pritchett, November 17, 1906, Gorgas Family Papers.

76. O. D. Street to AG, December 27, 1906, Gorgas Family Papers.

77. George H. Denny to AG, undated, Gorgas Family Papers.

78. Hubert T. Davis to Mamie Gorgas, January 13, 1913, Gorgas Family Papers.

79. W. H. Mitchell to Jessie Gorgas, February 16, 1913, Tyler Goodwyn to Mamie Gorgas, January 6, 1913, Gorgas Family Papers; WCG to Jessie Gorgas, April 4, 1913, December 24, 1914, WCG Papers, UA. See also Frank McIntyre to WCG, January 6, 1913, WCG Papers, LC.

80. [AG to JG, early July 1865], Gorgas Family Papers.

81. Library Checkout Record Book for the School Year 1901–1902, University of Alabama Archives, Tuscaloosa.

5. White and Black Alabama Women during the Progressive Era, 1890–1920
THOMAS

1. This article has since been expanded into a book, *The New Woman in Alabama: Social Reforms and Suffrage, 1890–1920* (Tuscaloosa: University of Alabama Press, 1992).

2. Anne Firor Scott, in her path-breaking book, *The Southern Lady from Pedestal to Politics 1830–1930* (Chicago: University of Chicago Press, 1970), was the first to describe the progression of organizations that southern women joined.

3. Proceedings of the Woman's Christian Temperance Union of the State of Alabama, January 22, 1884, University of Alabama Library, Tuscaloosa.

4. Report of the Alabama Woman's Christian Temperance Union, Thirty-First Annual Convention, Birmingham, Alabama, October 26, 27, and 28, 1915,

Auburn University Library, Auburn, Ala.; James B. Sellers, *The Prohibition Movement in Alabama, 1702 to 1943* (Chapel Hill: University of North Carolina Press, 1943), 53.

5. Ruth Bodin, *Woman and Temperance: The Quest for Power and Liberty, 1873–1900* (Philadelphia: Temple University, 1981), 95–97.

6. Proceedings of the Woman's Christian Temperance Union of Alabama, January 22, 1884; Report of the Alabama Woman's Christian Temperance Union, October 26–28, 1915; Minutes of the National WCTU, 1906, Report of the Corresponding Secretary, 144.

7. Thomas McAdory Owen, *History of Alabama and Dictionary of Alabama Biography,* vol. 4 (Spartanburg, S.C.: Reprint Publishers, 1987), 1965; Anne Gary Pannell and Dorothea E. Wyatt, *Julia S. Tutwiler and Social Progress in Alabama* (Tuscaloosa: University of Alabama Press, 1961), 49–122.

8. Albert Burton Moore, *History of Alabama* (University, Ala.: University Supply Store, 1934), 814–15.

9. Minutes of the National WCTU, 1888, Report of the Department of Prison, Jail, Police, and Almshouse Work, 205–6; Pannell and Wyatt, *Julia S. Tutwiler,* 106–119; Julia Strudwick Tutwiler, Educator, Friend of Humanity, Public Benefactor, Memorandum Printed by Friends, n.d., Alabama Department of Archives and History, Montgomery; "Julia S. Tutwiler," *Alabama White Ribbon,* May 1916, p. 1.

10. Annual Report of the Mercy Home, December 1906, p. 7, Birmingham Public Library, Birmingham, Ala.

11. Edward S. Lamonte, "The Mercy Home and Private Charity in Early Birmingham," *Journal of the Birmingham Historical Society 5* (January 1978): 5–15; Minutes of the Board of Directors of the Mercy Home, January 24, 1893; Annual Report of the Mercy Home, December 1920, pp. 12–13.

12. Minutes of the National WCTU, 1887, Report of the Corresponding Secretary, 324, Report of Juvenile Department, xxxvi; *The Union Signal,* December 9, 1886, p. 11, November 24, 1887, p. 9.

13. Minutes of the National WCTU, 1890, Report of Department of Work among Colored People, 218; Minutes of the National WCTU, 1896, Report of Work among Colored People, 184.

14. Minutes of the National WCTU, 1897, Report of Work among Colored People, 275; Minutes of National WCTU, 1899, Report of Work among Colored People, 200; Minutes of the National WCTU, 1900, Report of Work among Colored People, 202; Minutes of the National WCTU, 1903, 12. "Do Everything" was the motto of the National WCTU.

15. Lura Harris Craighead, *History of the Alabama Federation of Women's Clubs* (Montgomery, Ala.: Paragon Press, 1936), 1:11–12.

16. Ibid., 26.

17. Ibid., 150, 177–78.

18. Ibid., 350.

19. Ibid., 93, 105.

20. David M. Weakley, "History of Alabama Boys Industrial School," Department of Archives and Manuscripts, Birmingham Public Library, Birmingham, Ala. Coming from the Tennessee Industrial School, Weakley served as superinten-

dent and his wife as matron of the school from 1905 to 1948. By the 1930s, their work had been widely acclaimed by social workers throughout the state. The University of Alabama granted Weakley an honorary degree in 1935.

21. Craighead, *History,* 350.

22. Mrs. Booker T. Washington, Synopsis of the Lecture on the Organizing of Women's Clubs, June 2, 1910, and Report of the Tuskegee Woman's Club, October 1909–May 1910, Booker T. Washington Papers 1909–1910, box 982, Manuscript Division, Library of Congress, Washington D.C.

23. Josephine T. Washington, "The Influence of Club Work in Alabama," *National Association Notes,* July 1904. This newsletter was the official publication of the National Association of Colored Women and is deposited at the Library of Tuskegee University, Tuskegee, Ala.

24. Washington, Organizing of Women's Clubs and Report of the Tuskegee Woman's Club; Gerda Lerner, *Black Women in White America: A Documentary History* (New York: Pantheon Books, 1972), 444, 453–56.

25. Quoted in Cynthia Neverdon-Morton, *Afro-American Women of the South and the Advancement of the Race, 1895–1925* (Knoxville: University of Tennessee Press, 1989), 133.

26. Mrs. Booker T. Washington, "The Tuskegee Woman's Club," *Southern Workman,* August 1920, p. 365.

27. Emmett J. Scott, "Mrs. Booker T. Washington's Part in Her Husbands [*sic*] Work," Booker T. Washington Papers, containers 6–7, reel 6; Neverdon-Morton, *Afro-American Women of the South,* 123.

28. Lerner, *Black Women in White America,* 437.

29. Ellen DuBois, "The Radicalism of the Woman Suffrage Movement: Notes toward the Reconstruction of Nineteenth-Century Feminism," *Feminist Studies* 3 (Fall 1975): 63–71.

30. Marjorie Spruill Wheeler, "Southern Suffragists and the 'Negro Problem,'" (paper presented at the First Southern Conference on Women's History, June 1988). Wheeler maintained that race was not the main motive, but that it supplied the strategy in the 1890s.

31. Aileen S. Kraditor, *The Ideas of the Woman Suffrage Movement, 1890–1920* New York: Columbia University Press, 1965), 163–218.

32. Sheldon Hackney, *Populism to Progressivism in Alabama* (Princeton: Princeton University Press, 1969), 147; *Official Proceedings of the Constitutional Convention of the State of Alabama, May 21, 1901, to September 3, 1901* (Wetumpka, Ala.: Wetumpka Printing Co., 1940), 1:464–71.

33. Pattie Ruffner Jacobs Scrapbook, 1911–1914, Department of Archives and Manuscripts, Birmingham Public Library, Birmingham, Ala.; Minutes of the Alabama Equal Suffrage Association, 1912–1918, Alabama Equal Suffrage Association Papers, Alabama Department of Archives and History, Montgomery; Lee Norcross Allen, "The Woman Suffrage Movement in Alabama" (M.A. thesis, Alabama Polytechnic Institute, 1949).

34. Minutes of the National WCTU, 1891, Report of the Corresponding Secretary, 255–56.

35. "The Alabama Convention," *Union Signal,* December 3, 1885, p. 8.

36. Craighead, *History,* 165, 177, 410.

37. Adele Logan Alexander, "How I Discovered My Grandmother," *Ms.,* November 1983, pp. 29–33; Paula Giddings, *When and Where I Enter: The Impact of Black Women on Race and Sex in America* (New York: William Morrow, 1984), 121.

38. Giddings, *When and Where I Enter,* 121; Adella Hunt Logan, "Colored Women as Voters," *Crisis* 4 (September 1912): 242–43. See also Cynthia Neverdon-Morton, "The Black Woman's Struggle for Equality in the South, 1895–1925," in *The Afro-American Woman,* ed. Sharon Harley and Rosalyn Terborg-Penn (Port Washington, N.Y.; Kennikat Press, 1978).

39. Jacobs scrapbook; Minutes of the Alabama Equal Suffrage Association, 1912–1918, pp. 1–7; Allen, "Woman Suffrage Movement," 17–22, 45–50.

40. Minutes of the Meetings of the Alabama Equal Suffrage Association, 20–110; Allen, "Woman Suffrage Movement," 23–45, 50–69.

41. Minutes of the Meetings of the Alabama Equal Suffrage Association, 44–45; Allen, "Woman Suffrage Movement," 42–43.

42. Minutes of the Meetings of the Alabama Equal Suffrage Association, 78–114; Allen, "Woman Suffrage Movement," 71–89, 139–60. See also Gillian Goodrich, "Romance and Reality: The Birmingham Suffragists, 1892–1920," *Journal of the Birmingham Historical Society* 5 (January 1978): 5–21.

43. Allen, "Woman Suffrage Movement," 161–70; *Woman Citizen,* October 2 and 30, November 13, 1920.

44. Allen, "Woman Suffrage Movement," 161–70; *Woman Citizen,* November 6 and 13, 1920, July 13, 1923.

45. Daniel Scott Smith, "Family Limitation, Sexual Control, and Domestic Feminism in Victorian America," *Feminist Studies* 1 (Winter–Spring 1972): 40–57. Smith used the phrase "domestic feminists" to describe a growing autonomy that he perceived nineteenth-century women to be developing within the home, most notably by limiting sexual intercourse with their husbands; his phrase, however, has wider application.

46. Karen J. Blair, *The Club Woman as Feminist: True Womanhood Redefined, 1869–1914* (New York: Holmes and Meier, 1980), 93–106.

47. D. S. Smith, "Family Limitation," 53.

48. DuBois, "Radicalism of the Woman Suffrage Movement," 63–71; D. S. Smith, "Family Limitation," 54.

6. Adella Hunt Logan and the Tuskegee Woman's Club
Building a Foundation for Suffrage
ALEXANDER

1. Adella Hunt Logan, "Woman Suffrage," *Colored American,* September 1905, pp. 487–89, and "Colored Women as Voters," *The Crisis,* September 1912, pp. 212–13. For more information on Logan's life, see "Adella Hunt Logan," in *Black Women in America: An Historical Encyclopedia,* ed. Darlene Clark Hine (Brooklyn: Carlson Publishing, 1993), 1:729–31.

2. This essay owes a great deal to Rosalyn Terborg-Penn's "Afro-Americans

in the Struggle for Woman Suffrage" (Ph.D. dissertation, Howard University, 1981), which remains the definitive work on this subject. Unless otherwise specified, general information about the involvement of African Americans in the suffrage movement has been gleaned from Terborg-Penn's work. Terborg-Penn first introduced me to the suffrage activities of my paternal grandmother, Adella Hunt Logan of Tuskegee Institute. She and a group of other historians—many of them female and many of them African American—are now addressing the critical roles of black women as reformers and activists. Because of this new body of work, the profession as a whole can no longer legitimately address these issues and report only activities within the white community. See also Adele Logan Alexander, "How I Discovered My Grandmother, and the Truth about Black Women and the Suffrage Movement" *Ms.*, November 1983, pp. 29–33.

3. Terborg-Penn, "Afro-Americans in the Struggle for Woman Suffrage," 31–39. In *Black Women in America*, see also "Maria W. Stewart," 2:1113–14, and "Sojourner Truth," 2:1172–76.

4. Terborg-Penn, "Afro-Americans in the Struggle for Woman Suffrage," 71–75, 104–5.

5. Ibid., 80–90, 95–97.

6. "National Association of Colored Women," in *Black Women in America*, 2:842–51; Ruby M. Kendrick, "'They Also Serve': The National Association of Colored Women, Inc., 1895–1954," in *Black Women in United States History*, ed. Darlene Clark Hine, vol. 7 (Brooklyn: Carlson Publishing, 1990); Dorothy C. Salem, *To Better Our World: Black Women in Organized Reform, 1890–1920*, vol. 14 of *Black Women in United States History*, esp. 26–27 and 41–43.

7. Salem, *To Better Our World*, 38–41. See also, in *Black Women in America*, "Lugenia Burns Hope," 1:573–79, "Addie Waits Hinton," 1:596–97, "Mary Eliza Church Terrell," 2:1157–59, "Ida Bell Wells-Barnett," 2:1242–46.

8. Mary Martha Thomas, *The New Woman in Alabama: Social Reforms and Suffrage, 1890–1920* (Tuscaloosa: University of Alabama Press, 1992), 123–31; *Woman's Journal*, April 4, 1903, December 12, 1913; *The Crisis*, September 1912, p. 199. Most of this issue of *The Crisis* was devoted to the topic of votes for women, which the journal's editor, W. E. B. Du Bois, strongly advocated.

9. Salem, *To Better Our World*, 127–29. *Woman's Journal*, March 15, 1913, reporting about black women marchers at the 1913 national suffrage parade, stated that "there were three in the college section, and a number among the teachers." A letter from Adella Hunt Logan to her friend Emily Howland read in part, "I am writing Mrs. Terrell [Mary Church Terrell] and a few other friends there [Washington, D.C.] encouraging them to take part if permitted—and I'm quite sure they will be welcomed by those in charge. It would seem to me a travesty to have a float of Indians and no Negroes in that great demonstration" (Logan to Howland, February 10, 1913, Emily Howland Papers, Cornell University, Ithaca, N.Y.).

10. Terborg-Penn, "Afro-Americans in the Struggle for Woman Suffrage," 121–22.

11. Ibid., 286–94.

12. Rayford Logan, *The Negro in American Life and Thought: The Nadir, 1877–1901* (New York: Dial Press, 1954).

13. "The Tuskegee Woman's Club, 1950–51" (includes that group's early

history), Margaret Murray Washington Papers, Tuskegee Institute Library, Tuskegee, Ala. (hereinafter cited as MMW Papers). Most information about the Tuskegee Woman's Club is found in this collection, some of it not specifically identified. Cynthia Neverdon-Morton has written about women's activities at Tuskegee Institute in "Self-Help Programs as Educative Activities of Black Women in the South, 1895–1925: Focus on Four Key Areas," *Journal of Negro Education* 51, no. 3 (1982): 207–21, and in *Afro-American Women of the South and the Advancement of the Race, 1895–1925* (Knoxville: University of Tennessee Press, 1989).

14. Thomas, *New Woman in Alabama*, 123.

15. Ibid., 125–26. Thomas points out that several white-controlled newspapers in the state did run separate columns that presented dissenting opinions written by white female suffragists. See also Lee N. Allen, "The Woman Suffrage Movement in Alabama, 1910–1920," *Alabama Review* 11 (April 1958): 83–99; *Woman's Journal*, May 22, 1901.

16. *Woman's Era*, October 1895, Mary Church Terrell Papers, Library of Congress, Washington, D.C. See also "Margaret Murray Washington," in *Black Women in America*, 2:1233–35. Louis J. Harlan, *Booker T. Washington: The Making of a Black Leader, 1901–1915* (New York: Oxford University Press, 1983), also includes information about the background of several of Tuskegee Institute's faculty wives.

17. *Woman's Era*, October 1895, Terrell Papers and MMW Papers. On a number of occasions, *Woman's Journal* carried notes about activities at Tuskegee Institute. On September 19, 1896, for example, it reported that the Tuskegee Woman's Club held "a weekly conference with over four hundred women, some of them walking sixteen miles to be present."

18. Salem, *To Better Our World*, 39; *Tuskegee Student*, June 5, 1909, June 28, 1913; "Tenth Annual Report of the Tuskegee Woman's Club, 1905," Booker T. Washington Papers, Library of Congress, Washington, D.C. (hereinafter cited as BTW Papers).

19. *Tuskegee Student*, April 3, 1915. The modern-day equivalent of the "lantern show" would be a slide presentation. Photographic images would have been projected onto a screen or the wall of a meeting hall, with illumination provided by a rudimentary electric projection device.

20. *Woman's Journal*, March 2 and 16, 1895, reported that during the previous month the Alabama suffragist Ellen Stephens Hildreth had visited Tuskegee Institute and also reported that Booker T. Washington was "doing wonders for the race." There is no indication as to whether or not she might have met Adella Hunt Logan or discussed woman's suffrage at that time. There are suspicions, but no proof, of Logan's possible interaction with white Alabama suffragists. Atlanta University, where Logan received her undergraduate degree in 1881 and an honorary M.A. in 1905, was one of the first schools for African Americans established in the South following the Civil War (Thomas, *New Woman in Alabama*, 124; *Bulletin of Atlanta University*, March 1895; Logan to Howland, March 6, 1906, Howland Papers). Emily Howland was a reformer and suffragist who may have been somewhat paternalistic but was, nonetheless, a genuine friend to African Americans, especially African-American women, as evidenced,

in part, by her extensive correspondence with Logan. See Judith Colucci Breault, *The World of Emily Howland: Odyssey of a Humanitarian* (Millbrae, Calif.: Les Femmes, 1974).

21. NAWSA Convention Proceedings, 1900, Schlesinger Library, Radcliffe College; Susan B. Anthony to Isabel Howland, October 5, 1897, Rachel Avery–Susan B. Anthony Papers, University of Rochester Archives. Ironically, Anthony herself, although an accomplished speaker, had far less education and arguably less "culture" than Logan did. The member of a well-to-do family who had been educated at Atlanta University, Logan had been teaching English, debate, and rhetoric for almost two decades at the time of the exchange between Howland and Anthony. Anthony's views and actions concerning African Americans have been widely debated. See, for example, Kathleen Barry, *Susan B. Anthony: A Biography of a Singular Feminist* (New York: Ballantine Books, 1988), and Ellen Carol DuBois, ed., *Elizabeth Cady Stanton, Susan B. Anthony: Correspondence, Writings, Speeches* (New York: Schocken Books, 1981).

22. Logan probably never became aware of the disparaging tone of Anthony's letter to Isabel Howland. Her two articles about NACW activities appeared in the *Woman's Journal*, January 26, 1901, and January 17, 1903. Logan, or someone close to her, must have sent other "news" items about her to *Woman's Journal*. On July 4, 1903, for example, the paper reported that Logan had received an honorary master's degree from Atlanta University, and on August 6, 1911, it acknowledged her contribution to a memorial fund honoring Susan B. Anthony (Logan to Howland, March 19, 1906, Howland Papers).

23. Logan to Howland, December 1, 1901, Howland Papers. In recent years, I learned from my mother that *her* mother (my maternal grandmother), who also looked white, accompanied Adella Hunt Logan (my paternal grandmother) to segregated, all-white suffrage meetings in the early 1900s (see Alexander, "How I Discovered My Grandmother"). Like a number of other suffrage leaders, Carrie Chapman Catt was torn between a tolerant personal philosophy on racial matters and espousing positions that she believed were more politically expedient. Catt stated, for example, that "it is little wonder that the North is beginning to question the wisdom of the indiscriminate enfranchisement of the Negro" (*Woman's Journal*, February 20, 1904), but a few months earlier (on April 25, 1903, in that same newspaper), she had responded to one of Belle Kearney's racist tirades by arguing that "the Anglo-Saxon is the dominant race today, but things may change. The race that will be dominant through the ages is the one that proves itself the most worthy."

24. The existence of these four volumes was revealed to me by Ann Gordon at the Susan B. Anthony Papers Project at the University of Massachusetts, Amherst. Vol. 1 of the *History of Woman Suffrage* was inscribed from Susan B. Anthony to Adella Hunt Logan on February 15, 1902. Librarians at the Auburn University archives showed me the actual books and provided information about the 1914 founding of the woman's suffrage club at their institution.

25. *Tuskegee Student*, August 24, 1894. *Woman's Journal* (September 9, 1894) also reported that Howe, president of the Association for the Advancement of Women, would spend a "day of visitation" at Tuskegee Institute.

26. *Tuskegee Student*, March 28, 1903, April 4, 1903.

27. Adella Hunt Logan to Booker T. Washington, November 3, 1900, BTW Papers; *Woman's Journal,* April 4, 1914.

28. Allen "Woman Suffrage Movement in Alabama," 87–93; Thomas, *New Woman in Alabama,* chaps. 6 and 7. The NAWSA Convention Proceedings show that Logan became a life member in 1900. Bossie O'Brien Hundley, a white Alabama suffragist, obtained her life membership in 1913.

29. Salem, *To Better Our World,* 38–41; Terborg-Penn, "Afro-Americans in the Struggle for Woman Suffrage," 21, 27.

30. Programs from a number of conferences held by the Alabama Federation of Colored Women's Clubs, Southern Federation of Colored Women's Clubs, and National Association of Colored Women, MMW Papers; *Southern Workman* 11, no. 43 (1912): 534–35.

31. A. H. Logan, "Woman Suffrage," 488–89.

32. A. H. Logan, "Colored Women as Voters," 213. It is significant that Logan, who was Booker T. Washington's next-door neighbor (and the wife of Warren Logan, Tuskegee Institute's second-ranking official), contributed to the NAACP's journal, *The Crisis,* which was edited by Washington's most outspoken nemesis, W. E. B. Du Bois. There are few examples of such open apostasy within Washington's inner circle.

33. The NMA was founded in the 1890s, when African-American medical practitioners were denied membership in the all-white American Medical Association (AMA). These practices of virtual racial exclusion by the AMA continued into the 1950s (NMA Convention Program, August 1912, BTW Papers).

34. *Tuskegee Student,* December 16, 1911, and December 14, 1912, reported that Adella Hunt Logan was president of the Hospital Aid Society. NMA Convention Program, 1912, BTW Papers.

35. NMA Convention Program, 1912, BTW Papers.

36. Bess Bolden Walcott, interview with the author, December 1982, Tuskegee, Ala.; Logan to Howland, January 24, 1898, Howland Papers. Logan's daughter referred to in this letter was the same Ruth who organized the "suffragette parade" in 1913. Adella Hunt Logan committed suicide at Tuskegee Institute in December 1915. After her mother's death, Ruth Logan married and moved to New York City, where she became a lifelong reformer and activist in Republican party politics (see "Ruth Logan Roberts" in *Black Women in America,* 2:986).

37. Receipt for payment of the poll tax in 1903 by my grandfather, Warren Logan, was found in the Warren Logan Papers, Tuskegee Institute Library, Tuskegee, Ala.

38. Walcott interview.

39. Logan to Howland, January 24, 1898, Howland Papers.

40. Terborg-Penn, "Afro-Americans in the Struggle for Woman's Suffrage," 319–22.

41. For a fine account of Tuskegeeites' participation in the civil rights movement of the 1960s, see Robert J. Norrell, *Reaping the Whirlwind: The Civil Rights Movement in Tuskegee* (New York: Random House, 1986). Also see James Forman, *Sammy Younge, Jr.: The First Black College Student to Die in the Black Liberation Movement* (New York: Grove Press, 1968), and Bernard Taper,

Gomillion versus Lightfoot: The Tuskegee Gerrymander Case (New York: McGraw-Hill, 1962).

7. From Parsonage to Hospital
Louise Branscomb Becomes a Doctor
MITCHELL

For assistance in the preparation of this paper, the author wishes to thank: Troy State University for a sabbatical leave in the spring of 1991; Melinda Bumbeloe of the Reynolds Historical Library, the University of Alabama at Birmingham; Virginia Durr of Montgomery, Ala.; Lucy Farrow, formerly of the Troy State University Library; Kathryn C. Knowlton of Birmingham, Ala.; Blanche Lockard of Brandon, Miss.; Mary R. McCarl of the Jefferson County (Ala.) Medical Society; and Joseph Mitchell of Troy, Ala.

1. Quoted in Leah Rawls Atkins, *The Valley and the Hills: An Illustrated History of Birmingham and Jefferson County* (Woodland Hills, Calif.: Windsor Publications, 1981), 144. See also Roger Biles, "The Urban South in the Great Depression," *Journal of Southern History* 56 (February 1990): 71–100.

2. Wayne Flynt, "Religion in the Urban South: The Divided Religious Mind of Birmingham, 1900–1930," in *From Civil War to Civil Rights, Alabama, 1860–1960: An Anthology from The Alabama Review,* ed. Sarah Woolfolk Wiggins (Tuscaloosa: University of Alabama Press, 1987), 258; Louise H. Branscomb, interview with author, November 18, 1989, tape recording and transcript in possession of author; Branscomb, interview with author, August 26, 1986, notes in possession of author. (Note: Unless otherwise indicated, all interviews with Louise H. Branscomb by author were conducted in Birmingham, Ala., and all tapes, notes, and transcripts of these interviews are in possession of author.) Sadie Sue Veazey from Bessemer, Ala., was a roommate of Branscomb at Johns Hopkins Medical School. For many years, women represented about 10 percent of each medical school class at Hopkins. See Thomas B. Turner, *Heritage of Excellence: The Johns Hopkins Medical Institutions, 1914–1947* (Baltimore: Johns Hopkins University Press, 1974), 16–17.

3. Regina Markell Morantz-Sanchez, "So Honored, So Loved? The Women's Medical Movement in Decline," in *"Send Us a Lady Physician": Women Doctors in America, 1835–1920,* ed. Ruth J. Abram (New York: Norton, 1985), 231–45; Regina Markell Morantz-Sanchez, *Sympathy and Science: Women Physicians in American Medicine* (New York: Oxford University Press, 1985), 232–34.

4. Abraham Flexner, *Medical Education in the United States and Canada: A Report to the Carnegie Foundation for the Advancement of Teaching,* Bulletin No. 4 (New York: Carnegie Foundation for the Advancement of Teaching, 1910; reprint, New York: Arno Press and the *New York Times,* 1972), 178–79; Morantz-Sanchez, *Sympathy and Science,* 279–80.

5. Branscomb, interview with author, November 18, 1989. Several works that discuss the increasing difficulty for women entering the professions after 1920 include: Nancy F. Cott, *The Grounding of Modern Feminism* (New Haven,

Conn.: Yale University Press, 1987); Penina Migda Glazer and Miriam Slater, *Unequal Colleagues: The Entrance of Women into the Professions, 1890–1940* (New Brunswick, N.J.: Rutgers, 1987); Lynn D. Gordon, *Gender and Higher Education in the Progressive Era* (New Haven, Conn.: Yale University Press, 1990); Patricia M. Hummer, *The Decade of Elusive Promise: Professional Women in the United States, 1920–1930* (Ann Arbor, Mich.: University Microfilms Research Press, 1979); Barbara Miller Solomon, *In the Company of Educated Women: A History of Women and Higher Education in America* (New Haven, Conn.: Yale University Press, 1985).

6. "Lewis Capers Branscomb," *Who's Who in the South* (Washington, D.C.: Mayflower, 1927), 101; "Dr. Branscomb Dies Following Auto Accident," *Birmingham News,* October 31, 1930; Branscomb, interview with author, November 18 and 19, 1989.

7. The Woman's College of Alabama later became Huntingdon College.

8. Branscomb, interviews with author, January 18, 1985, August 26, 1986, March 18, 1988, November 17 and 18, 1989, October 5, 1990; Branscomb, UNRRA application, Manuscripts Department, Perkins Library, Duke University, Durham, N.C.; John Phillip Johnston, interview with author, September 2, 1990, Brundidge, Ala., notes in possession of author.

9. Branscomb, interviews with author, November 18, 1989, March 3, 1990, October 5, 1990, March 12, 1991.

10. See Anne Virginia Mitchell's discussion of Branscomb's early life (1901–21) and of Branscomb's diaries in "Swimming in the Mainstream: Louise H. Branscomb, M.D., of Birmingham, Alabama" (master's thesis, University of North Carolina, 1991), 4–36.

11. Branscomb, interview with author, November 18, 1989.

12. "A Disastrous Cyclone Visits Birmingham and Vicinity," *Birmingham News,* March 25, 1901; Atkins, *The Valley and the Hills,* 94–95; Branscomb, interview with author, August 26, 1986.

13. Branscomb, interview with author, November 18, 1989.

14. Ibid.; Mitchell, "Swimming in the Mainstream," 4–5; Branscomb, interview with author, November 30, 1988.

15. Branscomb, interviews with author, August 23, 1985, September 2, 1985, November 18, 1989, March 3, 1990; Morantz-Sanchez, *Sympathy and Science,* 267–79.

16. Morantz-Sanchez, "So Honored, So Loved?," 231.

17. Branscomb, interview with author, July 31, 1987, November 18, 1989; Erna Oleson Xan, "Character Building Came First and Training Next in Father's Rule for Active Branscomb Sisters," *Birmingham News,* February 25, 1958.

18. Branscomb, interviews with author, July 31, 1987, March 3, 1990.

19. Branscomb, interviews with author, January 18, 1985, August 23, 1985, September 2, 1985, October 5, 1990, November 18, 1989; O. C. Weaver, "Louise as a Neighbor and a Church Member," speech given at Louise Branscomb Day, McCoy United Methodist Church, Birmingham, Ala., May 25, 1986, typed document, photocopy in possession of author, 2; Charles F. Zukoski, Jr., interview with author, September 4, 1990, Birmingham, Ala., notes in possession of author.

20. Branscomb, interviews with author, August 23, 1985, September 2, 1985, March 12, 1991; Mitchell, "Swimming in the Mainstream," 18–20, 32.

21. Branscomb, interviews with author, August 23, 1985, September 2, 1985, November 18, 1989.

22. Branscomb, interviews with author, August 23, 1985, September 2, 1985, July 31, 1987, November 18, 1989.

23. Branscomb, interviews with author, August 23, 1985, September 2, 1985, November 18, 1989; Howard L. Holley, *The History of Medicine in Alabama* (Birmingham: University of Alabama in Birmingham, School of Medicine, 1982), 57–59.

24. Branscomb, interviews with author, August 23, 1985, September 2, 1985, November 18, 1989; L. C. Branscomb, "Memoir of Rev. John D. Simpson," *Journal of the North Alabama Conference, Methodist Episcopal Church, South* (Birmingham: 1921), 80–82. Women played a significant leadership role in the early history of Hillman Hospital (see Holley, *History of Medicine in Alabama*, 52–56, 59, and the cornerstone of Hillman Hospital, which lists the "incorporators" of 1888, all of whom were women).

25. Branscomb, interviews with author, August 23, 1985, September 2, 1985, July 31, 1987, November 18, 1989; Anne La Susa Madonia, interview with author, June 6, 1991, Birmingham, Ala., tape and notes in possession of author.

26. Branscomb, interviews with author, August 23, 1985, September 2, 1985.

27. Branscomb, interview with author, March 3, 1990; Judith Walzer Leavitt, *Brought to Bed: Child-bearing in America, 1750–1950* (New York: Oxford University Press, 1986), 117–27.

28. Branscomb, interviews with author, December 13 and 14, 1986, July 31, 1987, November 18, 1989.

29. Ibid.

30. Branscomb, interviews with author, August 26, 1986, July 31, 1987.

31. Leah Marie Rawls Atkins to author, April 4, 1990, Auburn, Ala., typed letter, signed, in possession of author; Rosalind Jones Carter, interview with author, September 5, 1990, Birmingham, Ala., tape, transcript, and notes in possession of author; Elizabeth Jones Baum, interview with author, September 3, 1990, Birmingham, Ala., notes in possession of author.

32. Carter and Baum interviews.

33. Atkins letter; Carter and Baum interviews.

34. Ethelyn Jones Bellande, interview with author, September 2, 1990, Birmingham, Ala., notes in possession of author; Carter and Baum interviews.

35. Carter interview.

36. Atkins letter; Carter interview.

37. Carter interview.

38. Louise H. Branscomb diary, July 1944–June 1945, October 4, 1944, entry, photocopy in possession of Anne Mitchell, original in possession of Louise H. Branscomb.

39. Branscomb, UNRRA application. In 1944, Branscomb's salary at Trussville was $1,200. Her salary at Birmingham-Southern College was $200. Katherine Price Garmon, interview with author, September 8, 1990, Birmingham, Ala., tape and transcript in possession of author.

40. Garmon interview, photocopy of the Popenoe pamphlet in possession of author, original in the possession of Mrs. Garmon; John D'Emilio and Estelle B. Friedman, *Intimate Matters: A History of Sexuality in America* (New York: Harper and Row, 1988), 241–42.

41. Of twenty-eight female physicians included in *Notable American Women: The Modern Period: Biographical Directory,* ed. Barbara Sucherman and Carol Hurd Green (Cambridge: Harvard University Press, 1980), only two are called surgeons (esp. see Allan M. Brandt, "Virginia Kneeland Frantz," 247–48); Branscomb, interviews with author, December 13 and 14, 1986, November 18, 1989.

42. Branscomb, interview with author, November 18, 1989.

43. Ibid.

44. Ibid., transcript, 30; Branscomb, interview with author, August 23, 1985, September 2, 1985. On hen medics, see "Pauline Stitt: Public Health Advocate," in Regina Markell Morantz, Cynthia Stodola Pomerleau, and Carol Hansen Fenichel, eds., *In Her Own Words: Oral Histories of Women Physicians* (Westport, Conn.: Greenwood, 1982), 110.

45. Branscomb, interview with author, November 18, 1989, transcript, 9–12.

46. Branscomb, interviews with author, August 23, 1985, September 2, 1985. Dr. Mason's picture and a summary of his career are found in Holley, *History of Medicine in Alabama,* 161–62; Louise H. Branscomb, "Primary Dysmenorrhea," *The Journal of the Medical Association of the State of Alabama* 12 (1942–43): 81–85.

47. Branscomb, interviews with author, August 23, 1985, September 2, 1985, November 18, 1989.

48. Carter interview

49. Branscomb, interview with author, November 18, 1989, transcript, 21–22.

50. Carter interview; Branscomb, interviews with author, August 23, 1985, September 2, 1985, November 18, 1989, transcript, 25. In the latter interview, Branscomb said that in her medical practice she had "about 95% or better results with just the diaphragm before the pill."

51. Branscomb, interview with author, November 18, 1989, transcript, 16–17; Charles F. Zukoski, Jr., interview with author, September 4, 1990, Birmingham, Ala., notes in possession of author; Scrap Book, 1932–1954, Maternal Welfare Association of Birmingham, Alabama, League for Planned Parenthood and Planned Parenthood League of Alabama, Planned Parenthood Headquarters Archives, Birmingham, Ala. Zukoski and his late wife, Bernadine, were among the leaders of the early child-spacing movement in Birmingham during the 1930s. See Mitch Mendelson, "'Button Gwinnett' is still trying to improve world," *Birmingham Post-Herald,* September 5, 1990. Button Gwinnett, the name of a signer of the Declaration of Independence from Georgia, is Zukoski's pen name.

52. Branscomb, interviews with author, August 23, 1985, September 2, 1985, November 18, 1989, transcript 17, 20–21; Scrap Book, Maternal Welfare Association.

53. D'Emilio and Friedman, *Intimate Matters,* 244.

54. Branscomb, interview with author, November 18, 1989, transcript, 18–19, 26–28; Branscomb to author, March 15, 1990, Birmingham Ala., hand-written letter, signed; Zukoski interview; Scrap Book, Maternal Welfare Association.

55. Branscomb, interviews with author, August 23, 1985, September 2, 1985, November 18, 1989. In the Annual Report of the Maternal Welfare Association of Jefferson County, 1935–36, it was noted that the Junior League of Birmingham had pledged $50 a month for a year to help pay the salary of the birth control clinic nurse, Miss Hunter (Scrap Book, Maternal Welfare Association).

56. Branscomb, UNRRA application.

57. Branscomb, interview with author, November 18, 1989, transcript 17–20. Even well-established male doctors who participated in the early birth control movement drew criticism. For example, according to his granddaughter, Mrs. Charles L. (Frances) Robinson, Dr. Lee F. Turlington, an obstetrician and gynecologist who was one of the leaders in the movement in Birmingham, "upset a lot of people" (quotation in Judy Haise, "Solar house is memorial to Turlington," *Birmingham News,* undated article in file of Reynolds Medical Library, Hill Sciences Library, University of Alabama at Birmingham). However, Turlington, who was later elected president of the Southern Medical Association, had done his internship at St. Vincent's Hospital in Birmingham and had established his practice with another doctor before his involvement with the birth control movement began in 1930. He was twelve years older than Branscomb ("Lee F. Turlington, M.D.: Southern Medical Association's Fifty-Sixth President," *Southern Medical Journal* 54 [February 1961]: 214–15, reprint in Reynolds Medical Library, University of Alabama at Birmingham).

58. Branscomb, interview with author, November 18, 1989, transcript, 2, 4–5, 43–44.

59. Ibid., 2.

60. Branscomb, interview with author, November 18, 1989; Weaver, "Louise as a Neighbor," 4.

61. Dr. Louise H. Branscomb, interview with Anne V. Mitchell, March 12, 1990, Birmingham, Ala., tape and transcript in possession of author, 4.

62. Atkins, *The Valley and the Hills,* 224.

63. Ibid., 144.

64. Branscomb, interviews with author, August 23, 1985, September 2, 1985; Branscomb, interview with Anne V. Mitchell, March 12, 1990, transcript, 4. Also see Branscomb, interview with Anne V. Mitchell, January 5, 1990, Birmingham, Ala., tape and transcript in possession of author, 52–53; Branscomb, UNRRA application; Zukoski interview; Branscomb, interview with author, November 18, 1989, December 19, 1990.

65. Morantz, Pomerleau, and Fenichel, eds., *In Her Own Words,* 125.

66. Branscomb, interview with author, July 31, 1987; Dorah Sterne, "Tribute to Louise Branscomb," speech presented at Birmingham Public Library Southern Women's Archives Distinguished Service Award Luncheon, September 15, 1979, typed document, photocopy, in possession of Anne V. Mitchell; Mitchell, "Swimming in the Mainstream," 60, 93–94; see also picture of fourteen women,

including Branscomb and Melson Barfield-Carter, of the Altrusa Club, 1934, in the Louise H. Branscomb Papers, 1909–1934, Manuscripts Department, Perkins Library, Duke University, Durham, N.C.

67. Morantz-Sanchez, "So Honored, So Loved?," 242; Sterne, "Tribute."

68. Mitchell, "Swimming in the Mainstream," 1, 60–99, 101. In 1986, Dr. Branscomb was recognized as one of one hundred leading Methodist women in mission by the Women's Division of the Board of Global Ministries, United Methodist Church. She was one of thirty-eight living honorees (see U.S. Congress, Senate, "Tribute to Dr. Louise Branscomb" by Senator Howell Heflin, 99th Cong., 2nd sess., *Congressional Record*, vol. 132 [April 28, 1986]). In 1989, the United Methodist Women of the North Alabama Conference established the annual "Louise Branscomb Barrier Breaker of the Year" award, honoring a Methodist "willing to take risks (in their Christian service) and to stand up for the rights of women and ethnic minority persons" (see *United Methodist Christian Advocate*, July 6, 1990, p. 11).

69. Louise H. Branscomb diary, September 1918–August 1920, photocopy in possession of Anne V. Mitchell, May 2, 1920, entry, 180–82.

8. Loula Dunn
Alabama Pioneer in Public Welfare Administration
SWAIN

The author is grateful for the financial support given her research by a Travel to Collections grant from the National Endowment for the Humanities and for the assistance of David Klaassen and the staff of the Social Welfare History Archives at the University of Minnesota.

1. Clarke A. Chambers, "Women in the Creation of the Profession of Social Work," *Social Science Review* 60, no. 1 (March 1986): 1–3, 6–7. Chambers describes the work of such legendary leaders as Jane Addams, Florence Kelley, and Edith and Grace Abbot.

2. Ibid., 22–24.

3. *Current Biography 1951* (New York: H. W. Wilson, 1952): 175–76; *Who's Who in America* 26 (New York: H. W. Wilson, 1950): 757.

4. Robert Horton Dunn, telephone interview with author, April 14, 1991. Grove Hill residents Harvey and Elizabeth Jackson possess the Clarke County High School yearbook, the *Klarkkountian*, for 1915 and 1916, which pictures the Dunn sisters. The 1917 volume provides news about the 1916 graduates. The Jacksons suggest that Loula likely helped finance Minnie's college attendance (telephone interview with author, April 6, 1991).

5. Martha H. Swain, "Loula Friend Dunn," in *Biographical Dictionary of Social Welfare in America*, ed. Walter I. Trattner (Westport, Conn.: Greenwood Press, 1986): 259–62. A sketch from the *Alabama Official and Statistical Register* (1943) is among the Survey Associates Records, box 135, Social Welfare History Archives (hereinafter SWHA), Walter Library, University of Minnesota, Minneapolis.

6. Elizabeth H. Davidson, *Child Labor Legislation in the Southern Textile States* (Chapel Hill: University of North Carolina Press, 1939): 18, 224, 235–37; Dewey W. Grantham, *Southern Progressivism: The Reconciliation of Progress and Tradition* (Knoxville: University of Tennessee Press, 1983), 185, 195; Loula Dunn, "Public Welfare in Alabama," speech to Marion (Ala.) American Association of University Women, May 11, 1940, in Loula Dunn Papers, box 1, folder 3, SWHA.

7. Mrs. L. B. Bush, "A Decade of Progress in Alabama," *Journal of Social Forces* 2, no. 4 (May 1924): 539–45.

8. James Leiby interview with Frank Bane, February 15, 1965: 91–92, Regional Oral History Office, University of California, Berkeley. Permission to quote courtesy of The Bancroft Library.

9. John A. Salmond, *A Southern Rebel: The Life and Times of Aubrey Willis Williams, 1890–1965* (Chapel Hill: University of North Carolina Press, 1983): 48–49.

10. William R. Brock, *Welfare, Democracy, and the New Deal* (Cambridge, England: Cambridge University Press, 1988), 233–35.

11. Salmond, *Southern Rebel*, 49. Dunn was close to Aubrey and Anita Williams, an association that is documented in her correspondence with Frank Bane after the Williamses returned to Montgomery when Williams assumed the editorship of the *Southern Farmer* (Frank Bane Papers, box 3, University of Virginia Library, Charlottesville).

12. Brock, *Welfare, Democracy, and the New Deal*, 235; Roger Biles, "The Urban South in the Great Depression," *Journal of Southern History* 66, no. 1 (February 1990): 84; Loula Dunn to Josephine Brown, September 24, 1934, Field Reports (1933–36), Harry Hopkins Papers, Franklin D. Roosevelt Library, Hyde Park, N.Y.

13. Salmond, *Southern Rebel*, 87. While the records are silent regarding her negative response to an appointment by the Social Security Board as a regional director of southern states in the late 1930s, it may well be that Dunn remembered the ardors of her prior travels with the FERA (see Frank Bane to John G. Winant, March 7, 1945, Bane Papers, box 3).

14. Loula Dunn memoir, Columbia Oral History Collection (hereinafter COHC), Texas Women's University Library, 14–15 (microfiche copy in Library, Texas Women's University, Denton).

15. Dunn memoir, 5. Graves is quoted in the APWA newsletter, the *Washington Report* 11, no. 7 (August 1976): 6.

16. Odum to Dunn, November 22, 1937, Dunn to Carstens, November 6, 1937, Dunn Papers, box 1, folder 2.

17. *Survey Midmonthly* 74, no. 2 (February 1938): 57; *Child Welfare League of America Bulletin* 20, no. 1 (January 1941): 8.

18. APWA minutes, June 29, 1938, December 17, 1939, APWA Papers, box 1, folder 5, SWHA.

19. Dunn to Kellogg, February 11 and 13, 1939, Lansdale to Kellogg, February 12, 1939, Paul U. Kellogg Papers, supplement to box 4, SWHA.

20. Springer to Dunn, February 27, 1940, May 8, 1941, Survey Associates Records, box 135, folder 1059.

21. Loula Dunn, "The Future of Public Welfare in Alabama," *Alabama Social Welfare* 4, no. 8 (August 1939): 7–8, 16.

22. Dunn to Springer, May 19, 1941, Survey Associates Records, box 135, folder 1059; Loula Dunn, "People, Politics, and Public Welfare," published as a bulletin of the APWA, June 1941, pp. 6–8, 11–12.

23. Dunn to Springer, January 8, 1941, Survey Associates Records, box 135, folder 1059; Loula Dunn, "Public Welfare Services to Children in Alabama," *Child Welfare League of America Bulletin* 21, no. 3 (March 1942): 5–6, 9; Loula Dunn, "Intensified Needs of Children in Times of Defense," speech to Child Welfare League of America, November 8, 1941, Dunn Papers, box 1, folder 3.

24. Mary Martha Thomas, *Riveting and Rationing in Dixie: Alabama Women and the Second World War* (Tuscaloosa: University of Alabama Press, 1987), 68–72; Dunn to Close, May 18, 1942, Survey Associates Records, box 135, folder 1059.

25. Dunn to Close, May 15, 1943, June 4, 1943, Survey Associates Records, box 135, folder 1059. See Kathryn Close, "Day Care Up to Now," *Survey Midmonthly* 79, no. 7 (July 1943): 194–97.

26. "The Work of the Tolan Committee," *Proceedings of the National Conference of Social Work 1942* (New York: Columbia University Press, 1942), 183; Loula Dunn, "Powder Mill Town," *Journal of Educational Sociology* 15, no. 8 (April 1942): 460–71; Thomas, *Riveting and Rationing*, 15–16.

27. "War and the Disadvantaged," *Survey Midmonthly* 79, no. 2 (February 1943): 55; Loula Dunn, "Public Welfare's Responsibilities in Time of War," *Tennessee Public Welfare Record* 7, no. 5 (May 1944): 5–11.

28. War Services Committee agenda, August 26–27, 1942, APWA Papers, box 1, folder 6; Dunn to Kathryn Close, February 21, 1942, Survey Associates Records, box 135, folder 1059; Emma Lou Mason, "Volunteers and the Civilian Defense Program," *Alabama Social Welfare* 7, no. 8 (August 1942): 6–8.

29. Fred K. Hoehler to Governor Frank Dixon, July 5, 1941, unidentified Canadian newspaper clipping, July 1941, Dunn Papers, box 1, folder 2.

30. Dorothy Crook (OWI) to Dunn, July 28, 1944, Dunn Papers, box 1, folder 6; Fred Hoehler to Dunn, August 15, 1944, Dunn to Hoehler, August 31, 1944, Fred Hoehler Papers, box 1, folder 8, SWHA.

31. Dorothy Crook to Dunn, January 17, 1945, OWI press release, February 28, 1945, OWI, "Program for Miss Loula Dunn," Dunn Papers, box 1, folder 6; Dorothy Crook, "Representing American Women," *Independent Woman* 25, no. 2 (February 1946): 38.

32. (Montgomery) *Alabama Journal*, May 2, 1945; Loula Dunn, "Impressions of Great Britain," *Public Welfare* 3, no. 6 (June 1945): 122–24, 144.

33. Informal notes of Social Security Board minutes, April 26, 1945, record group 47, National Archives, Suitland, Md.; Dunn, "Impressions of Great Britain," 124.

34. WAAC, Report of the Corps Interviewing Board, June 22, 1942, Dunn to Oveta Culp Hobby, July 15, 1942, Dunn Papers, box 1, folder 7; Loula Dunn, "The Wartime Graduate: Her Obligations and Opportunities Today," Dunn Papers, box 1, folder 2; "Look Applauds," *Look* 14, no. 19 (September 12, 1950): 21.

35. Speech list, Dunn Papers, box 1, folder 5; Dunn to Hoehler, April 13,

1944, Hoehler Papers, box 1, folder 8; Dunn to Bane, December 13, 1945, Bane Papers, box 3.

36. Loula Dunn, "Your Alabama Public Welfare Service," August 17, 1948, Dunn Papers, box 1, folder 4.

37. Ibid.

38. Loula Dunn, "Public Welfare in 1945," *Public Welfare* 3, no. 1 (January 1945): 1.

39. Dunn's testimony on August 25, 1945, appeared as "Full Employment and Public Welfare," *Public Welfare* 3, no. 10 (October 1945): 218–21, 240.

40. Loula Dunn, "Full Employment and Child Welfare," *Child Welfare League of America Bulletin* 25, no. 2 (February 1946): 1–3. Dunn at the time was vice president of the league.

41. Dunn to Close, July 27, 1948, Survey Associates Records, box 135, folder 1059; Loula Dunn, "Social Welfare's Contribution to Social Problem Prevention," *Public Welfare News* (North Carolina State Board of Public Welfare) 9, no. 4 (December 1946): 15–16; Loula Dunn, "Public Welfare Belongs to the People," *Public Welfare* 6, no. 11 (November 1948): 217.

42. Loula Dunn, "Statement on Pending Federal Social Security Legislation," House Ways and Means Committee (April 1949), copy in APWA Papers, box 44, folder 8.

43. Robert F. Wagner to Aubrey W. Williams (then editor of *Southern Farmer*), October 13, 1945, copy in Dunn Papers, box 1, folder 1. The post went to Watson B. Miller, who had been the assistant administrator of the Federal Security Agency.

44. John T. Caldwell to John Steelman, June 28, 1949 (copy), Dunn to Jonathan Daniels, June 29, 1949, Dunn Papers, box 1, folder 2; "A Woman in Mr. Truman's Cabinet—Well, Why Not Make It Loula Dunn," *Mobile Press Register*, June 23, 1949. Copies of the letters written by the congressional delegation are also in box 1, folder 2, Dunn Papers. Alabama representative Carl Elliott inserted the editorial in the *Congressional Record*, 81st Cong., 1st sess., A4205, June 30, 1949.

45. Dunn to Hoehler, July 19 and 23, 1946, August 1, 1946, Hoehler to Dunn, July 23, 1946, Hoehler Papers, box 2, folders 21–22, 27–28.

46. Raymond R. Paty to Dunn, October 28, 1946, Dunn Papers, box 1, folder 2; Dunn to Hoehler, November 14, 1946, December 18, 1946, Hoehler Papers, box 2, folders 27–28.

47. Register to APWA Papers, 3–4; Peter Romanofsky and Clarke A. Chambers, eds., *Social Service Organizations* (Westport, Conn.: Greenwood Press, 1978), 1:131–38. The fullest account of the APWA's history is Narayan Viswanathan, "The Role of the American Public Welfare Association, 1930–1960" (Ph.D. dissertation, Columbia School of Social Work, 1961).

48. As the honorific president of the APWA from 1944 to 1946, Dunn was aware of the problems but had no authority to deal with them. Correspondence between Elizabeth Wickenden, director of the Washington office, and Fred Hoehler is especially revealing (see Hoehler to Wickenden, January 25, 1949, Hoehler Papers, box 4, folder 52; Wickenden to Hoehler, January 31, 1949, Hoehler Papers, box 35, folder 348).

The selection committee was composed of Raymond M. Hilliard (chair), New

York state commissioner of welfare; Ellen Winston, commissioner of welfare in North Carolina; and J. Milton Patterson, Maryland's director of public welfare.

49. Hilliard to Hoehler, May 16, 1949, Hoehler to Hilliard, May 20, 1949, Hoehler Papers, box 35, folder 348; Dunn to Springer, June 2, 1949, Dunn Papers, box 1, folder 8; Dunn to Bane, March 15, 1949, Bane Papers, box 3.

50. Dunn to Bane, Louis Brownlow, and Charles Merriam, all June 2, 1949, Dunn Papers, box 1, folder 2.

51. Hoehler to Dunn, June 20, 1949, Hoehler Papers, box 35, folder 348; Wickenden to Dunn, June 21, 1949, Dunn Papers, box 1, folder 2.

52. Brownlow to Dunn, June 22, 1949, Emmerich to Dunn, June 23, 1949, J. T. D. O'Leary to Dunn, July 2, 1949, Springer to Dunn, July 14, 1949, Dunn Papers, box 1, folder 2; Dunn to Bane, June 20, 1949, Bane Papers, box 3.

53. Springer to Dunn, April 18, 1949, Bane to Survey Associates Award, April 21, 1949, Bane Papers, box 3.

54. Dunn to Springer, June 30, 1949, Dunn Papers, box 1, folder 3; Dunn to Herbert Emmerich (copy), July 5, 1949, Dunn to Hoehler, July 5, 1949, Hoehler Papers, box 35, folder 348.

55. APWA board minutes, July 8, 1949, Joseph Baldwin (president, APWA) to Dunn, July 8, 1949, Dunn to Baldwin, July 11, 1949, APWA Records, box 1, folder 8.

56. Dunn to Folsom, July 18, 1949, Dunn to state Board of Public Welfare, July 18, 1949, Dunn Papers, box 1, folder 2; "Loula Dunn," *Alabama Social Welfare* 14, no. 9 (September 1949): 2.

57. Press release, Dunn Papers, box 1, folder 2. Austin, a native of Selma, Alabama, and a graduate of Alabama College and Peabody College, had also attended the New York School of Social Work and Tulane University. She had been associated with aspects of public welfare in Alabama since 1932 and had been Dunn's assistant since 1948.

58. *Montgomery Advertiser,* July 19, 1949; *Mobile Press Register,* July 22, 1949; *Alabama Journal,* July 19, 1949; *Alabama Magazine,* quoted in *Montgomery Examiner,* July 28, 1949. Congressman Carl Elliott inserted the *Press Register* editorial, "What Others Think of Loula Dunn," in the *Congressional Record,* 81st Cong., 2nd sess., A4752, July 25, 1949.

59. Bane to Dunn, July 23, 1949, Katharine Lenroot to Dunn, August 1, 1949, Dunn Papers, box 1, folder 8. Folder 8 contains dozens of congratulatory letters from state commissioners of public welfare and APWA regional leaders.

60. Dunn to Mary Underwood, August 8, 1949, Dunn to Springer, August 9, 1949, Dunn to Arthur J. Altmeyer, August 17, 1949, Dunn to Emma Lundberg, August 24, 1949, Dunn Papers, folders 8–9, SWHA.

61. "Comings and Goings at the APWA," *Survey* 85, no. 9 (September 1949): 490; "Rankin File," *Montgomery Journal,* July 18, 1949.

62. "Loula Dunn Honored at Washington Reception," *Washington Report* 11, no. 7 (August 1976): 6.

63. Eveline Burns memoir, COHC, 164; Charles I. Schottland memoir, COHC, 26; "APWA Mourns Death of Loula Dunn," *Washington Report* 12, no. 7 (August 1977): 3.

64. *Washington Post,* June 30, 1977.

65. Wilbur Cohen, interview with author, March 2, 1984, Austin, Tex., tape in possession of author.

66. Maurine Mulliner memoir, COHC, 298; Schottland memoir, COHC, 60–61; *New York Times,* June 26, 1950.

67. Maybelle M. Turner (secretary to Dunn) to Mrs. Hildreth Nichols, November 23, 1957, Dunn Papers, box 1, folder 1.

68. *Public Welfare* 24, no. 1 (January 1966): 27–28; "Loula Dunn Honored at Washington Reception," 6; *Montgomery Advertiser,* June 30, 1977.

69. *Washington Post,* June 30, 1977; Gertrude Springer, "My Friend, Miss Loula," *Alabama Social Welfare* 14, no. 9 (September 1949): 16; Robert H. Dunn, telephone interview with author, April 14, 1991.

70. *Congressional Record,* 95th Cong., 1st sess., 22442, July 12, 1977.

71. "Two Women To Be Inducted into State Hall of Fame," *Mobile Press,* June 1, 1982. The author is grateful to Ellen Faurot, librarian, Bowling Library, Judson College, Marion, Alabama, for providing a copy of the Loula Dunn file in the records of the Alabama Women's Hall of Fame. Terry Foster, Dunn's greatnephew, who resides in Grove Hill, provided a file of newspaper notices on the Judson Award and on Dunn's death.

9. Stepping Out of the Shadows into Politics
Women in the Alabama Legislature, 1922–1990
HAWKS

1. Alabama House of Representatives, *House Journal* (1919), 1:846–47, quoted in Lee N. Allen, "The Woman Suffrage Movement in Alabama, 1910–1920," *Alabama Review* 11 (April 1958): 97.

2. *Alabama Official and Statistical Register* (Montgomery, 1923), 135.

3. "Beautiful Reception Honoring Mrs. Wilkins," unidentified newspaper clipping, vertical file, Alabama State Department of Archives and History, Montgomery (hereinafter cited as ASDAH).

4. Ibid.

5. Statistics provided by the Center for the American Woman and Politics, National Information Bank on Women in Public Office, Eagleton Institute of Politics, Rutgers University, 1989. Although one woman has entered the legislature since the compilation of the report, one has resigned, so that the numbers and percentages remain the same.

6. *Montgomery Advertiser,* February 19, 1922.

7. *Alabama Official and Statistical Register,* 135.

8. "Beautiful Reception."

9. See *Journal of the House of Representatives . . . 1923,* 2 vols. (Montgomery, 1923); *Journal of the House of Representatives . . . 1926–27,* 2 vols. (Montgomery, 1927).

10. *Birmingham News,* October 27, 1938.

11. Unidentified newspaper clipping, November 1, 1973, vertical file, ASDAH. She was appointed secretary of state upon the resignation of Howell Turner in 1944 and elected to a full term in 1946. In 1950, she was elected state

treasurer. In 1954, she began her first of four terms on the Public Service Commission.

12. *Birmingham News,* July 28, 1936; *Montgomery Advertiser,* August 5, 1936; unidentified newspaper clipping, (Demopolis, July 28, [1936]); clipping from *Alabama* magazine, June 11, 1943, vertical file, ASDAH.

13. *Birmingham News,* October 27, 1938, May 30, 1943.

14. *Montgomery Advertiser,* September 14, 1952, December 4, 1952, January 15, 1953.

15. Ibid., November 2, 1973.

16. "Clara Stone Fields," *Mr. County Commissioner,* May 1963, p. 3; *Montgomery Advertiser,* June 30, 1963.

17. *Mobile Register,* December 25, 1963; *Montgomery Advertiser,* March 28, 1965.

18. *Montgomery Advertiser,* August 15, 1965.

19. Ibid., February 14, 1965.

20. *Mobile Register,* December 25, 1963; *Montgomery Advertiser,* March 28, 1965.

21. *South: News Magazine of Dixie,* January 21, 1963, January 1967.

22. *Mobile Register,* December 25, 1963; *Montgomery Advertiser,* August 13, 1967.

23. *Mobile Register,* February 27, 1964; (Montgomery) *Alabama Journal,* May 8, 1970.

24. Questionnaire completed by Kylie T. Berryman, August 15, 1983, in possession of author.

25. *Alabama Journal,* May 12, 1977; Berryman questionnaire.

26. *Birmingham News,* May 10, 1970.

27. Questionnaire completed by Retha Deal Wynot, January 24, 1983, in possession of author.

28. *Alabama Journal,* September 6, 1971.

29. Ibid.

30. *Montgomery Advertiser,* April 18, 1972.

31. *Mobile Press Register,* February 10, 1973.

32. Ibid.

33. Ibid.

34. *Montgomery Advertiser,* March 4, 1973.

35. *Alabama Journal,* September 6, 1971.

36. *Montgomery Advertiser,* December 31, 1974.

37. Ibid., January 22, 1978.

38. Questionnaire completed by Marilyn Quarles, August 1, 1983, in possession of author.

39. *Montgomery Advertiser,* January 22, 1978.

40. Ibid.

41. Quarles questionnaire.

42. *Montgomery Advertiser,* July 4, 1978.

43. Ibid.

44. Quarles questionnaire.

45. Ibid.

46. Ibid.

47. Ibid.

48. See, for example, *Montgomery Advertiser,* August 18, 1976, January 22, 1978.

49. *Alabama Journal,* May 12, 1977. Ward replaced G. J. Higginbotham, who had become a senator.

50. Questionnaire completed by Shelby Dean Ward, January 12, 1983, in possession of author.

51. Ibid.

52. Ibid.; *Alabama Journal,* May 12, 1977.

53. *Alabama Journal,* April 27, 1977. Thomas succeeded John Porter, who was appointed to the state Pardons and Parole Board.

54. *Alabama Journal,* July 6, 1977.

55. Ibid.

56. Ibid.

57. *Montgomery Advertiser,* June 27, 1978.

58. Questionnaire completed by Louphenia Thomas, August 5, 1983, in possession of author.

59. *Alabama Journal,* September 27, 1978.

60. *Birmingham News,* July 10, 1977.

61. Legislature biographical sheet completed by Martha Jo Smith; copy in Smith file at *Montgomery Advertiser* library.

62. *Montgomery Advertiser,* October 2, 1981.

63. Data sheet on Mary S. Zoghby, representative, House District 97, completed in 1983, copy in possession of author.

64. *Mobile Register,* May 6, 1981.

65. Mary S. Zoghby, interview with author, Mobile, August 8, 1983, taped copy in possession of author.

66. *Tuscaloosa News,* April 29, 1981.

67. *Montgomery Advertiser,* February 7, 1989.

68. *Birmingham News,* February 20, 1983.

69. Ann Bedsole, interview with author, Mobile, August 8, 1983, taped copy in possession of author.

70. *Alabama Journal,* January 3, 1983.

71. Ibid.

72. Ibid.

73. Bedsole interview; *Birmingham News,* November 7, 1982; *Vanguard USA,* October 28, 1982; *Alabama Journal,* March 30, 1989.

74. Yvonne Kennedy, interview with author, Mobile, August 9, 1983, taped copy in possession of author.

75. *Montgomery Advertiser,* September 20, 1981; *Birmingham News,* February 20, 1983. Kennedy was elected to fill the unexpired term of Gary Cooper, who had become commissioner of pensions and security.

76. *Montgomery Advertiser,* September 20, 1981.

77. Kennedy interview.

78. *Montgomery Advertiser,* September 20, 1981.

79. Ibid., February 22, 1987; Kennedy interview.

80. Kennedy interview; *Montgomery Advertiser,* April 13, 1989.

81. *Montgomery Advertiser,* February 8, 1987; Kennedy interview.

82. Kennedy interview.

83. *Birmingham Times,* January 29, 1981. Escott replaced Earl Hilliard, who had moved to the Senate to fill the seat of U. W. Clemons, appointed by President Jimmy Carter to a federal judgeship.

84. Sundra Escott, interview with author, Birmingham, August 4, 1983, taped copy in possession of author; questionnaire completed by Sundra E. Escott, January 17, 1982, in possession of author.

85. *Birmingham Times,* January 29, 1981.

86. Escott interview and questionnaire.

87. Ibid.

88. Data sheet of Jarushia (Jeri) Thornton, [1982], copy in possession of author.

89. Jarushia Thornton, interview with author, Birmingham, August 4, 1983, taped copy in possession of author; *Birmingham World,* July 31, 1982; Thornton data sheet.

90. *Birmingham News,* September 13, 1983.

91. Ibid., September 27, 1983.

92. Ibid.

93. Ibid., February 20, 1983.

94. Ibid.

95. Ibid., October 27, 1983.

96. Ibid., March 16, 1983.

97. *Montgomery Advertiser,* September 10, 1987.

98. Ibid., March 18, 1987, May 5, 1987, November 18, 1987; *Alabama Journal,* May 13, 1987, July 26, 1989.

99. *Alabama Journal,* July 26, 1989.

100. *Montgomery Advertiser,* August 14, 1989, October 17, 1989.

101. *Alabama Journal,* December 7, 1989.

102. *Montgomery Advertiser,* December 12, 1989, February 2, 1990. The two men indicted with her, Jim Wright and John W. Rogers, were acquitted.

103. Ibid., February 2, 1990.

104. *Alabama Journal,* February 2, 1990.

105. *Montgomery Advertiser,* February 5, 1990.

106. *Alabama Journal,* May 15, 1989.

107. Ibid., February 13, 1988, April 13, 1988.

108. *Montgomery Advertiser,* November 16 and 18, 1989.

109. Ibid., November 18, 1989; *Alabama Journal,* May 17, 1989.

110. *Alabama Journal,* November 21, 1989.

111. Questionnaire completed by Frances "Sister" Webb Strong, March 15, 1989, in possession of author; *Montgomery Advertiser,* November 10, 1983, June 2, 1986, June 5, 1986.

112. Strong questionnaire.

113. *Montgomery Advertiser,* January 21, 1985.

114. *Alabama Journal,* January 30, 1985.

115. *Montgomery Advertiser,* February 10, 1986.

116. Ibid.
117. Ibid.
118. *Alabama Journal,* June 10, 1986.
119. *Montgomery Advertiser,* June 2, 1986.
120. Ibid.
121. Ibid., June 5, 1986.
122. Strong questionnaire.
123. Questionnaire completed by June Bugg, July 10, 1984, in possession of author; *Alabama Journal,* May 7, 1985, March 20, 1987; *Montgomery Advertiser,* March 20, 1987.
124. *Montgomery Advertiser,* September 29, 1988; *Alabama Journal,* September 29, 1988.
125. Questionnaire completed by Beth Marietta, November 12, 1984, in possession of author.
126. *Montgomery Advertiser,* November 8, 1986, January 28, 1987; *Alabama Journal,* March 18, 1987.
127. *Montgomery Advertiser,* November 11, 1988, March 1, 1989; *Alabama Journal,* January 25, 1989, February 24, 1989.
128. *Alabama Journal,* February 14, 1985, April 6, 1988, February 9, 1989; *Montgomery Advertiser,* January 24, 1986, February 2, 1986, July 18, 1987, April 8, 1988, January 18 and 26, 1990.
129. *Montgomery Advertiser,* February 27 and 28, 1989.
130. Ibid., November 9, 1989. She replaced Charles Adams, whom Governor Hunt had appointed Russell County revenue commissioner.
131. Steve Prince, "White Males Dominate Offices," *Montgomery Advertiser,* March 11, 1990.
132. *Birmingham News,* July 28, 1936; unidentified newspaper clipping, Demopolis, June 28, [1936], vertical file, ASDAH.
133. *Montgomery Advertiser,* June 30, 1963.
134. Ibid., August 18, 1988.
135. Quoted in Prince, "White Males."
136. *Montgomery Advertiser,* March 18, 1987. Floor leaders were Bedsole, Davis, and Marietta. Committee chairs were Zoghby (banking), Marietta (oil and gas and local legislation No. 3), and Bedsole (agriculture, conservation, and forestry). Vice chairs were McDowell (local legislation No. 2) and Escott (small business).
137. CAWP statistics, 1989.
138. Kennedy interview.
139. *Montgomery Advertiser,* March 9, 1990.
140. *Alabama Journal,* February 22, 1990.
141. Ibid.
142. *Montgomery Advertiser,* February 6, 1990.
143. Ibid.
144. Ibid.
145. Ibid., February 15, 1990.
146. Ibid., February 6, 1990.
147. Ibid.

148. Joanne Varner Hawks, "A Select Few: Alabama's Women Legislators, 1922–1983," *Alabama Review* 38 (July 1985): 199.

10. *"Alive to the Cause of Justice"*
Juliette Hampton Morgan and the
Montgomery Bus Boycott
SUMME

1. Margaret L. McClurkin and Dixie Lou Fisher, "Miss Juliette Morgan," *Alabama Librarian* 5 (1957): 91.

2. Grover Hall, Sr., letter to Frank P. Morgan, July 28, 1938, Frank P. Morgan Papers, Alabama Department of Archives and History, Montgomery.

3. Virginia Foster Durr, telephone interview with author, February 19, 1981.

4. Lila Bess Morgan scrapbooks 4–5, Alabama Department of Archives and History, Montgomery; Durr interview.

5. Morgan scrapbook 4, newspaper clipping entitled "A Happy Childhood."

6. Studs Terkel, foreword to Virginia Foster Durr, *Outside the Magic Circle: The Autobiography of Virginia Foster Durr*, ed. Hollinger F. Barnard (Tuscaloosa: University of Alabama Press, 1985), xi. Durr summarizes the importance of marriage for the southern woman by saying, "The consequences of not being loved were plain: you didn't get married. You got to be an old maid and that was the worst fate that could befall you."

7. Morgan scrapbook 4.

8. Durr interview; Morgan scrapbook 4.

9. Morgan scrapbook 4; Carl Carmer, *Stars Fell on Alabama* (Tuscaloosa: University of Alabama Press, 1985), 13–14.

10. Morgan scrapbook 4.

11. Ibid.

12. Ibid.

13. Juliette Morgan, "The College Woman—1932," letter to *Montgomery Advertiser*, May 11, 1932.

14. Juliette Morgan, "In Reply to a Birmingham 'Yankee,'" letter to *Montgomery Advertiser*, July 1, 1938.

15. Morgan scrapbooks 4–5.

16. Juliette Morgan, letters to *Montgomery Advertiser*, "Chance to Lose," January 7, 1943, "Tragic Era," March 11, 1943, "Lend-Lease," March 26, 1943, "Trade Agreements," April 24, 1943.

17. Juliette Morgan, "Speaks Out," letter to *Montgomery Advertiser*, October 26, 1946.

18. Juliette Morgan, "Wilkinson Victory," letter to *Montgomery Advertiser*, May 20, 1948. The Dixiecrats chose South Carolina governor Strom Thurmond as their presidential candidate.

19. Morgan, "Wilkinson Victory."

20. Morgan scrapbook 5.

21. Juliette Morgan, letter to Grover Hall, Jr., June 3, 1952, Lila Bess Morgan Papers, Alabama Department of Archives and History, Montgomery.

22. "Miss Juliette Morgan," *Birmingham World,* June 26, 1952.

23. Juliette Morgan, letter to editor of *Birmingham World,* June 26, 1952, Lila Bess Morgan Papers.

24. Juliette Morgan, letter to *Montgomery Advertiser,* November 19, 1946.

25. Morgan scrapbook 5. For examples of letters written to publicize Humane Society interests, see Juliette Morgan, letters to *Montgomery Advertiser,* "Unto the Least of These," May 8, 1956, "Bill Requiring Humane Slaughter," March 21, 1957.

26. Interview with Truman Hobbs, February 19, 1981. In this interview, Judge Hobbs offered his personal reflection on the situation at that time, stressing the combustive effects of the 1954 Supreme Court decision in the Montgomery community.

27. J. Mills Thornton, "The Montgomery Bus Boycott," 1955–56, *Alabama Review* 33 (1980): 167, 171–72.

28. Ibid.

29. Juliette Morgan, letter to William A. Gayle, July 13, 1955, Lila Bess Morgan Papers.

30. Thornton, "Montgomery Bus Boycott," 201–3. For the definitive analysis of the emerging boycott goals, see Taylor Branch, *Parting the Waters: America in the King Years 1954–1963* (New York: Simon and Schuster, 1988).

31. Juliette Morgan, "Lesson from Gandhi," letter to *Montgomery Advertiser,* December 12, 1955. Taylor Branch in *Parting the Waters* (p. 144) commented on how this quote from Morgan must have been received by her fellow white citizens, saying, "These last words confirmed her status as something of a ninny, even among those white people who admired the grandeur of her learning. Who of sound mind could write that a shift by Negro maids in their common mode of transportation was more important than all the past glories of Montgomery? . . . Only the rarest and oddest of people saw historical possibilities in the bus boycott."

32. Martin Luther King, Jr., *Stride toward Freedom* (New York: Harper and Row, 1958), 199; Stephen B. Oates, *Let the Trumpet Sound: The Life of Martin Luther King, Jr.* (New York: Harper and Row, 1982), 76.

33. Morgan, "Lesson from Gandhi."

34. Branch, *Parting the Waters,* 150.

35. This pattern is evident in most detailed discussions of the boycott. For specific comments on white harassment of dissenters, see Durr, 241–88.

36. Virginia Foster Durr, quoted in Juan Williams, *Eyes on the Prize: America's Civil Rights Years, 1954–1965* (New York: Viking Penguin, 1987), 82–83.

37. For examples, see David J. Garrow, *Bearing the Cross: Martin Luther King, Jr. and the Southern Christian Leadership Conference* (New York: William Morrow, 1986), 28; Branch, *Parting the Waters,* 144; and Oates, *Let the Trumpet Sound,* 77.

38. Branch, *Parting the Waters,* 144.

39. Garrow, *Bearing the Cross,* 28.

40. Durr, *Outside the Magic Circle,* 245.

41. Ibid., 28. See also Branch, *Parting the Waters,* 154.

42. Clifford J. Durr, letter to Carey McWilliams, November 16, 1956, Clif-

ford J. Durr Papers, Alabama Department of Archives and History, Montgomery; Juliette Morgan, "Stand Overdue," letter to *Tuscaloosa News*, January 14, 1957.

43. Thomas R. Thrasher, "Alabama's Bus Boycott," *Reporter*, March 8, 1956, 13–16.

44. Morgan, "Stand Overdue."

45. Durr, *Outside the Magic Circle*, 277.

46. "Judge: The Law and Frank Johnson," Bill Moyers interview with Frank M. Johnson, "Bill Moyers Journal," PBS, July 24, 1980.

47. Ibid.

48. Ibid.

49. Joe Azbell, telephone interview with author, February 21, 1981.

50. Morgan, "Stand Overdue."

51. Hobbs interview.

52. Durr interview.

53. Branch, *Parting the Waters*, 144.

54. "Juliette Morgan Stays at Library," *States' Rights Advocate*, March 1957, 2–3.

55. Durr interview.

56. Juliette Morgan, letter to Lila Bess Morgan, May 15, 1957, Lila Bess Morgan Papers.

57. King, *Stride toward Freedom*, 199.

58. Durr interview.

59. Morgan scrapbook 5.

60. Branch, *Parting the Waters*, 139.

61. Mary Y. Dobbins, letter to *Montgomery Advertiser*, July 25, 1957.

Contributors

ADELE LOGAN ALEXANDER lectures and writes about African-American and women's history. She is a doctoral candidate at Howard University and teaches at the University of Maryland. She is the author of *Ambiguous Lives: Free Women of Color in Rural Georgia, 1789–1879* (1991).

ANN WILLIAMS BOUCHER received her doctorate from the University of Connecticut. She is Director of the Honors Program at the University of Alabama in Huntsville and the author of *Alabama Women: Roles and Rebels* (1978).

HARRIET E. AMOS DOSS is Associate Professor of history at the University of Alabama in Birmingham. She did her graduate work at Emory University and is the author of *Cotton City: Urban Development in Antebellum Mobile* (1985).

ELIZABETH FOX-GENOVESE teaches history at Emory University, where she is the Eleonore Raoul Professor of the Humanities. Her most recent books include *Within the Plantation Household: Black and White Women of the Old South* (1988) and *Feminism without Illusions: A Critique of Individualism* (1991).

JOANNE VARNER HAWKS is Director of the Sarah Isom Center for Women's Studies at the University of Mississippi. She has conducted research on women in southern legislatures and women in Mississippi. She is the coeditor with Shelia L. Skemp of *Sex, Race and the Role of Women in the South* (1983).

NORMA TAYLOR MITCHELL is Professor of history at Troy State University. She did her graduate work at Duke University and is a specialist in the history of women and religion.

SHERYL SPRADLING SUMME is a graduate of Troy State University and has a master's degree from Vanderbilt University. She has taught secondary-level and junior college history and currently is teaching at the Advent Episcopal School in Birmingham.

MARTHA H. SWAIN is Professor of history at Texas Woman's University. She is the author of *Pat Harrison, the New Deal Years* (1978) and the forthcoming *Ellen Woodward: Southern Gentlewoman and New Deal Official.*

MARY MARTHA THOMAS was Professor of history at Jacksonville State University until her retirement in 1992. She is the author of *Riveting and Rationing in Dixie: Alabama Women and the Second World War* (1987) and *The New Woman in Alabama: Social Reform and Suffrage, 1890–1920* (1992).

SARAH WOOLFOLK WIGGINS is Professor of history at the University of Alabama in Tuscaloosa and has edited the *Alabama Review* since 1976. She is the author of *The Scalawag in Alabama Politics, 1865–1881.*

Index